*About the Editor*

Marie Korpe is the executive director of Freemuse (Freedom of Musical Expression), and is a Swedish journalist with many years of varied international experience.

*About this book*

Banning music strangles the very soul of a culture. *Shoot the Singer!* surveys contemporary cases of music censorship world-wide for the first time. It also examines the causes, methods and logic behind contemporary attempts to prevent people from hearing certain kinds of music by governments, commercial corporations and religious lobby groups and authorities.

In this volume, cases come from a surprisingly wide range of countries, including Palestine, Turkey, North Korea, Mexico, France, Israel, South Africa, Afghanistan, Burma, Cuba and the United States. It is particularly striking how different authorities, in diverse societies, worry enormously about music, and use a broad range of techniques to repress it.

As well as presenting particular cases, this volume also explores the logic behind these concerns (including two instances where censors themselves explain what they were doing). Contributions are from scholars, journalists and the testimonies of musicians themselves.

*About Freemuse*

Freemuse is the only international organization dedicated to documenting present-day cases of global music censorship – affecting both performers and composers and their audiences – and to developing a global network in support of them, to publicize cases and to describe the mechanisms of censorship.

Freemuse – the World Forum on Music and Censorship – was founded in 1999 and opened its secretariat in 2000: <www.freemuse.org>. Freemuse receives core funding from the Royal Danish Ministry of Foreign Affairs and Swedish International Development Cooperation Agency (Sida).

MARIE KORPE | editor

# Shoot the singer!

Music censorship today

Zed Books

LONDON | NEW YORK

*Shoot the singer! Music censorship today* was first published by
Zed Books Ltd, 7 Cynthia Street, London N1 9JF, UK and Room 400,
175 Fifth Avenue, New York, NY 10010, USA in 2004 in association
with Freemuse, Wilders Plads 8H, DK-1403 Copenhagen K.

www.zedbooks.co.uk

Editorial copyright © Freemuse, 2004
Individual chapters © individual contributors, 2004

This book was published with financial support from

EUROPEAN
CULTURAL
FOUNDATION

Cover designed by Andrew Corbett
Set in FF Arnhem and Futura Bold by Ewan Smith, London
Index: ed.emery@britishlibrary.net
Printed and bound in Malta by Gutenberg Press Ltd

Distributed in the USA exclusively by Palgrave Macmillan, a division of
St Martin's Press, LLC, 175 Fifth Avenue, New York, NY 10010.

A catalogue record for this book is available from the British Library.
US CIP data are available from the Library of Congress.

ISBN 1 84277 504 9 cased
ISBN 1 84277 505 7 limp

# Contents

# Illustrations

# Acknowledgements

First of all I want to express my gratitude to the musicians who have been willing to share their personal stories of censorship with Freemuse. I'm also grateful to those who have contributed material presented to the 2nd World Conference on Music and Censorship in Copenhagen in 2002. The book came about due to the firm support of the Freemuse executive committee, which inspired me to seek an international publisher. I would also like to say thanks to the writers who have contributed stories from parts of the world Freemuse have not yet been able to include. Your contributions enrich the book and give it a larger geographical scope.

Special thanks to former Director at the Royal Danish Ministry of Foreign Affairs, Danida, Ambassador Ellen Margrethe Løj, who initially believed in the setting up of an organization advocating musicians' and composers' right to freedom of expression. Without her support Freemuse would never have come into being.

Without the financial support from the Royal Danish Ministry of Foreign Affairs and from the Swedish International Development Cooperation Agency, Freemuse could not have existed.

I'm most grateful too, for the support of Vanessa Reed of the European Cultural Foundation, which has made this book possible through its financial help. Many thanks to the collaborators at Zed Books for being patient and supportive throughout the production of this book.

Finally I'm very grateful to my husband and co-founder of Freemuse, Ole Reitov, who has been my sparring partner and supporter during the work with the book, and last but not least to my two colleagues at Freemuse, Jim Q. Holm for coordinating the CD insert and for providing most essential assistance, and Johannes Skjelbo for related IT-assistance in the long processing of the book.

*Marie Korpe, executive director*

# Preface

For thousands of years, music has been one of humanity's most essential cultural expressions. And when music is banned, the very soul of a culture is being strangled.

Censorship of music has existed ever since the time of ancient Greece. Plato wrote on music – good music and bad music – suggesting that bad music had to be controlled or banned as it had the potential to divert people away from the Good Life. Furthermore he decried musical excess as the ruin of the state, saying that the effect of bad music is like the effect of bad company.

Plato recognized the power of music and deemed it potentially dangerous to people and society. Since ancient Greece this philosophy of good and bad music has been repeated throughout the history of musical censorship. Jewish, Christian and Muslim scholars have at times described music as a source of sin and vice, and other things secular. The Swedish fiddle, the Inuit drum in Greenland and African drums have been deemed instruments of the Devil by religious authorities or colonial powers.

A representative of American Protestantism in the 1920s characterized jazz as 'the accompaniment of the voodoo dancer, stimulating the half-crazed barbarian, to the vilest deeds' (D'Entremont 1998: 34). Music censorship under the Third Reich hit a number of musical styles – Jewish, Roma and modernist. In Soviet Russia, the major targets were modernist composers such as Shostakovich and Prokofiev, whose music was considered to be alien to the Soviet people.

When, in the 1950s, rock 'n' roll music came on the scene, medical doctors and parental groups advised that children should not listen to it, claiming it was harmful to young people.

These historical examples show that music at all times has been recognized as powerful, and censorship today is practised according to the same ideas. Why is music censored? 'Censorship is based on fear,' according to musician Johnny Clegg, describing personal experiences of censorship under the apartheid government in South Africa.

In this volume, cases come from a wide diversity of countries, including Israel, Turkey, North Korea, Mexico, France, South Africa, Afghanistan, Burma/ Myanmar, Cuba and the United States. Contributions are from scholars, journalists and musicians themselves, most of them participants at the 2nd World

Conference on Music and Censorship, arranged by Freemuse in Copenhagen in September 2002.

In addition to presenting a large number of specific instances, this volume also explores the logic behind censorship concerns, including two instances where censors themselves explain what they were doing.

It has been my intention to make this book accessible and interesting reading for people involved in the music field: artists, students, scholars, music producers and music lovers.

*Marie Korpe*

*References*
D'Entremont, Jim (1998) 'The Devil's Disciples', *Index on Censorship*, 27(6): 32–9.

*On Censorship*

Censorship does not work
without the tacit cooperation
of the censored.

In fact, it, inadvertently,
gives the power of survival
to what it is censoring.

What is not relevant will disappear
on its own without the help of censorship.
And what is relevant will stay regardless.

One can never censor the power of truth.
It is beyond the control and manipulation
of bureaucratic clerks.

yoko ono 2004

ONE | **Introduction**

# 1 | What is music censorship? Towards a better understanding of the term

MARTIN CLOONAN

How can we determine when a piece of music is being censored? This simple question has occupied my mind for some time. At one level the answer seems obvious. If some person or body prevents a musician or group of musicians from performing a musical work, then clearly that appears to be a case of censorship. But what if a body refuses to publish a musician's work because they feel it is of no commercial value, or if a radio station decides not to play a record which it believes its audience won't like? Is that censorship? If so, in the latter case are country music stations guilty of censoring rap and metal?

In short, it soon becomes apparent that what constitutes censorship of music is a more complex matter than might immediately be thought. There will inevitably be some grey areas. It may not even be possible to come up with a definition of musical censorship which is suitable for every time and place. There may be grounds for some cultural relativism. Here I do not intend to come up with a definition of censorship, but to problematize the issue. I want to suggest that it is important to think through the terms we use and to develop some criteria by which to judge actions. In short, there is a need to try to determine what is meant by censorship before any investigation of cases of musical censorship can begin. This is particularly important for an organization such as Freemuse, which is dedicated to fighting musical censorship.

As an academic, I tend to look to the academic world for reference points. One welcome development here has been the spread of popular music studies, so that popular music is now taught and researched in departments of music, anthropology, sociology, adult education, film studies and in many other places. This burgeoning study has brought forth a whole new literature, including works on the regulation and censorship of music. But most popular music academics who have written about censorship have not defined the term. Thus there is a need to look farther afield.

The *Shorter Oxford Dictionary* refers readers to the office of censor for its definition of censorship (although it also allows for subconscious self-censorship). Five types of censors are then identified: (i) those who occupied such positions in ancient Rome; (ii) 'a person who exercises supervision over the conduct or morals of others'; (iii) 'an adverse critic'; (iv) officials with the power to suppress media (especially in wartime); and (v) a psychological power to limit thought.

This is quite a menu from which to choose and, with the possible exception of ancient Rome, it is probable that music has been subject to all these forms of censorship. But it is important to note the common elements in these definitions. The first four involve people or organizations doing something to other people and/or to an art form, whereas the final one involves a form of self-censorship. So censorship seems to be something which can be imposed from outside a person or organization or from inside. But this raises the question of whether censorship has to be *deliberate* or not. Does censorship have to involve someone saying this is absolutely not allowed, or can it involve simple omission? (a particularly important question in an age of globalization).

More broadly, it is clear that censorship can be multi-faceted. It can range from the restriction of certain materials (often pornography) to outright banning (again frequently with pornography, but also including 'subversive' political literature or literature that promotes such things as drug usage or euthanasia). Music often gets caught up in censorship that has been designed for other media. For example, the UK's Obscene Publications Act (1959) was designed to combat obscene literature, but has been used against popular music.

For many commentators censorship has to be *systematic*. It has to be part of a deliberate process, often at the behest of government or its agencies. However, the demarcation between censorship as the prerogative of government and censorship via the workings of the market has become blurred in recent years as the mass media have developed and media ownership has become ever more concentrated. It appears to be harder and harder for dissident voices to be heard in mainstream media. Public-sector broadcasting has declined at the same time as other media have proliferated. But more radio and television stations have not brought more choice. On the contrary, the rise of companies such as Clear Channel has led to less diversity, more formatting and a decline in regional variation. This narrowing of public space can be seen as a form of market censorship in which musicians face more and more obstacles in reaching an audience. The fact that this been accompanied by major record companies signing fewer new artists and sacking many existing ones exacerbates the problem. Here censorship is not via deliberate acts of outlawing free expression, but by limiting public space.

For many commentators an alternative form of distributing music and of overcoming all sorts of censorship lies in the Internet. However, this possible form of salvation has yet to produce a promotional tool which can match the might of the major corporations' advertising budgets. In general, the issue of the relationship between free-market capitalism and freedom of expression is a complicated one, but it is one which has implications for musicians.

Another way of thinking through what constitutes censorship is to see it as a process of restricting or forbidding which can take place on three levels. The first is prior restraint or the silencing of free expression prior to publication. In music this may take the form of a record company refusing to release a track because of its lyrical content. The next level is restriction. Hence CDs may be sold in some places to restricted audiences or some tracks or pop videos may be played at certain times of the day when an adult audience is listening (and children generally not). The third level is that of suppression. In music this might mean making distribution of a published record illegal. It may also involve forbidding performances by certain acts. So once an act of censorship has been detected, it is then necessary to determine what *sort* of censorship is taking place.

To repeat, my argument is that before a claim of musical censorship is made it is important to think about what is meant by censorship. In essence the question that arises is the extent to which it is felt that the free market can ensure the dissemination of the widest possible range of music.

In terms of more formal acts of censorship, it is clear to me that the notion of levels of censorship is a useful way of conceptualizing matters. Thus when one hears about a case of musical censorship it is important to consider whether it actually is a case of censorship and, if so, what sort of censorship it is. Consideration should also be given to what the agency of censorship is (government, private company, pressure group, etc.). For Freemuse such issues are not merely theoretical, they are immensely practical. Until we know what we are fighting against, we may not know what we are fighting for. Thus thinking through what constitutes censorship is part of the process of fighting against it.

# 2 | Music as a parallel power structure

ALENKA BARBER-KERSOVAN

*The political potential of music*

As numerous cases show, the freedom to produce, perform and distribute music can be severely restricted.[1] To a greater or smaller extent this applies to all historical epochs as well as to the modern era, to different cultures and different societies. But where is the logic behind it? Why is music a subject of censorship? Why are musicians a subject of repression? What makes music so important that it is often considered in political terms?

In order to answer these questions we have to remember that the ancient Chinese ascribed high political value to their music. Music was also a political matter for the ancient Greeks, and Plato advised in his *Politea* that town administrators should avoid the introduction of new musical genres, because a change in the basis of music always implies a change in the basic social order.[2] This belief in the political power of music has persisted to the present day, and some scholars, for instance Jacques Attali in his *The Political Economy of Music* (1989), or authors celebrating the 'Rock 'n' Roll Revolution', still argue along very similar lines. As different as their explanations might be in detail, they are based on the same assumption, namely that the political potential of music is a variable of the music itself, of its internal aesthetic structure.

It cannot be denied that certain musical patterns do have a certain effect on the listener – compare, for example, dance music with a lullaby – and that there is a certain amount of intersubjectivity in the judgement of musical pieces.[3] But this fact on its own does not make music political. A chord or a scale is neither left nor right, and that's why a particular piece of music cannot automatically be assigned a certain political orientation.[4] Theodor Adorno pointed out that in Nazi Germany and in the Soviet Union the same musical pieces were forbidden, but for totally different reasons. For him the fact that the Soviets denounced the music that the Nazis called 'cultural bolshevism' as 'bourgeois decadence' was an indication that the stigma that political structures impose on musical structures mostly has nothing to do with the music and its content.[5]

*Social aspects of music*

Lacking a fixed meaning, a piece of music is open to different projections, interpretations and identifications. Furthermore, a piece of music can have a different meaning for different groups of consumers or in different historical, geographical and social contexts. The same individual can perceive a piece of music differently under different circumstances. This leads us to the following conclusions:

1. If musical structures do not have a fixed meaning and thus cannot be political on their own, the reasons why music is subject to censorship and why musicians are subject to repression must be sought elsewhere. In this respect a possible point of departure could be the observation that musicians hardly ever play music for themselves. Music-making is a social occasion and it implies complex relationships within a music group itself, between the musicians and other participants in a musical event, for example the public, between different musical formations and institutions, with other parts of the society, with the musical representations of different nations or ethnic groups.

2. Since musical reality is a social one, specific forms of music-making and singing may be subject to change and dependent on various historical, cultural and technological variables. But they also possess a number of common traits and qualities. The most important among these is the integrative and disintegrative force of music. Music provides a communal basis for social relationships, and at the same time it also draws demarcation lines between different social agglomerations, whereby 'we' are mostly connotated in a positive sense and 'the others' in a negative sense.[6]

Therefore, if we talk about musical subcultures such as hippies, punks and hip-hop fans, we talk about music-centred social groups. These socio-aesthetic coalitions include individuals with the same, and exclude those with different, musical preferences. They appropriate certain locations and other musical infrastructures and protect what they consider to be their 'musical territory' by all available means, sometimes even through verbal and physical violence. Further, we find expressions such as 'Woodstock nation', 'rave nation' or 'MTV nation', which imply semantic connotations that are very close to political issues. Terms such as 'Neverland', 'Graceland' and 'Madonnaland' even suggest a kind of miniature state within a state.

*Music as a sensual instrument of power*

The integrative force of music is based on values and normative orientations. In most cases these orientations are implicit and yet able to fulfil their social function even if the protagonists involved are not aware of them. This mechanism is especially effective in live music rituals, including Western-style

7

classical concerts or spectacular pop music shows. As much as they may differ in form and structure, their function is the same: they unite people and stimulate the feeling of belonging to a certain community.

Owing to these properties, i.e. being able to manipulate people and/or to transmit values and stabilize social systems, music can be considered as a 'sensual instrument of power'.[7] This also explains why politicians have a rather ambivalent relationship with music.[8] On the one hand they foster what they consider to be conforming musical bodies and institutions in order to strengthen their own system of social control. Besides institutions such as the European state opera houses, which by virtue of their names alone reveal their close relationship to political authorities, we should mention musical events marking political occasions and the military music of national anthems. These are icons of a shared collective history of nations demanding respect, so that, for example, Jimi Hendrix's deconstruction of 'The Star-Spangled Banner' or the reggae version of the 'Marseillaise' by Serge Gainsbourg were considered as humiliations of these resounding symbols of state power.

On the other hand, state and other secular and/or religious authorities try to suppress unwanted forms of musical expression. In general, all participants in the process of musical communication, i.e. musical institutions, music lovers, the media and production and distribution agencies, can become subjects of repression. However, in most cases repressive measures, such as censorship, are applied against musicians. There is a very good reason for this, because in a musical ritual two groups of individuals are essential: the 'musicians' and the 'public' – i.e. the 'stars' and the 'fans' respectively. Their relationship, which has been simplified here for the sake of better understanding, is very similar to the political structures of power, implying the complex interaction between domination and subordination.

This mechanism is especially strong in the European music tradition. One should recall the romantic cult of the genius, whereby biographies of Ludwig van Beethoven[9] or Richard Wagner transported these composers into the realm of immortality. Also many great conductors and virtuosi were anything but modest. The pianist Vladimir Horowitz remarked: 'I feel that on the stage I am a King and a master of the situation' and 'I am a general. The keys are my soldiers and I have to command them.'[10] The conductor Herbert von Karajan declared: 'I am going to be a dictator', and in practice he was extremely successful in imperializing a large proportion of the classical musical environment.[11]

*Musical ritual as a love affair*

But contrary to those who are in control, musicians do not stake a leadership claim on birth or tradition, nor do they acquire leadership through any kind of usurpation: their position results from the possession of certain skills and capacities that the average member of a social group does not have. Furthermore, in contrast to other kinds of leadership that may use quasi-legal measures including brutal forms of subordination such as military, police or other means of state repression, the relationship between musicians and public is what the conductor Kurt Furtwängler called a 'love affair, based on mutuality'.[12] 'Power is a very strong aphrodisiac,' confirmed Madonna in one of her numerous interviews, 'and I am a very powerful person.'[13] In another interview she stated: 'I will not be happy before I am as famous as God'.[14]

Not all musicians exercise their charismatic leadership as a Horowitz, a Karajan or a Madonna do. But in all musical rituals conducted as a love affair – and this applies to a large extent also to music transmitted through the mass media[15] – the psychological mechanisms regulating the relationship between the 'stars' and the 'fans' are very much the same. The public identifies with the musicians. It idealizes them and adores those skills, capacities and personality traits that the listeners themselves would like to possess. The musicians play the role of an ideal ego, the imaginary person that the listeners would like to be. For them, musicians are role models and opinion-formers from whom not only musical likes and dislikes but also norms, values and – if articulated at all – political opinions will be sought.

In a musical ritual conducted as a love affair norms and values are commonly transmitted at a symbolic, highly emotionally charged level. But since, according to Antonio Gramsci, norms and values, including political norms and values, can be determined at the levels of 'feeling', 'knowledge' and 'understanding', and since the relationship between 'feeling', 'knowledge' and 'understanding' is fluid,[16] a residual musical message can also become imprinted on the rational and cognitive level. And to a large extent this is the point where the authorities start to get nervous. As a rule, the more repressive a political regime is, the more attention it will pay to the musical scene and the harder the repression it will bring to bear against musicians who are not willing to conform.

### References

1 M. Korpe (ed.) (2001) *Speeches from the 1st World Conference on Music and Censorship*, Copenhagen: Freemuse.

2 *Platons sämtliche Werke in zwei Bändern* (1925), Vienna.

3  H. Bruhn, R. Oerter and H. Rösing (eds) (1993) *Musikpsychologie. Ein Handbuch*, Hamburg.

4  H. Rösing (2000) 'Kann Musik politisch sein? Zur Rolle der Musik in Stanley Kubricks Film Full Metal Jacket', in C. Floros, F. Geiger and T. Schäfer (eds), *Komposition als Kommunikation. Zur Musik des 20 Jahrhunderts*, Frankfurt, Berlin, Berne, New York, Paris.

5  T. W. Adorno (1972) *Dissonanzen. Musik in der verwalteten Welt*, Göttingen, p. 67. See also S. Eisel (1990) *Politik und Musik. Musik zwischen Zensur und politischem Miß-brauch*, Munich, Bonn.

6  K. H. Delhees (1994) *Soziale Kommunikation. Psychologische Grundlagen für das Miteinander in der modernen Gesellschaft*, Opladen, and G. Bierbrauer (1996) *Sozial-psychologie*, Stuttgart, Berlin, Cologne.

7  F. K. Prieberg (1991) *Musik und Macht*, Frankfurt, p. 188.

8  Ibid.

9  T. DeNora (1995) *Beethoven and the Construction of Musical Genius. Politics in Vienna, 1792–1803*, London.

10  Cited in H. Epstein (1988) *Der musikalische Funke. Von Musik, Musikern und vom Musizieren. Begegnungen und Gespräche mit berühmten Interpreten*, Berne, Munich, Vienna, pp. 2, 29.

11  Cited in N. Lebrecht (1992) *Der Mythos vom Maestro*, Zurich, St Gallen, p. 129.

12  Cited in H. Epstein, op. cit.

13  Cited in D. Diederichsen, C. Dormagen, B. Penth and N. Wörner (1993) *Das Madonna Phänomen*, Hamburg, p. 24.

14  Cited in M. St Michael (1990) *Madonna. Selbstbekenntnisse*, Munich, p. 84.

15  A. Hepp and R. Winter (eds) (1999) *Kultur – Medien – Macht*, Opladen, Wiesbaden.

16  A. Gramsci (1983) *Marxismus und Literatur: Ideologie, Alltag, Literatur. Aus den Jugendschriften. 1913–1922. Aus den Gefängnisschriften. 1929–1935*, Hamburg.

# 3 | Music as a useless activity: conservative interpretations of music in Islam

JONAS OTTERBECK

In many religions, music in different forms is a topic of dispute. This chapter deals with conservative interpretations of Islam hostile to music, but also some slightly more moderate views. But first let me state, so that there will be no misunderstanding, that what I am about to say does not apply to all interpretations of Islam, all regions or historical periods. There are other much more liberal interpretations. Why should I be focusing on interpretations that could be considered as giving a negative image of Islam? There are several reasons. One is that these interpretations have had and continue to have some influence from time to time on laws, social practices, the social position and reputation of musicians, etc. Another is that the interpretations are also fairly well known among more liberal Muslims. A third is that there is a preconception among many that Islam as a religion is proscriptive when it comes to music. A fourth is that there are very few Islamic scholars who would say that all forms of music are acceptable. Thus my aim is to demonstrate that Islam can embrace different interpretations and understandings of music by showing that there is more to the conservative interpretations than a close reading of the major sources of Islam and Islamic theology. Behind the interpretation lies the perception of the interpreter.

## A short summary of Islamic theology

In classical Islamic theology there are rules on how to establish whether a practice or a view is *halal* (permitted) or *haram* (forbidden). First you consult the Koran. If there is a clear view in the holy book this has primacy over other sources. You further investigate the Hadith literature, the stories about Muhammad and *al-Sahâba* (the companions of Muhammad) and *at-Tâbi-ûn* (the generation after *al-Sahâba*), sometimes referred to as the *as-Salaf* (the forefathers). The Hadiths are considered by religious experts in Islam to be the Prophet Muhammad's guidance to coming generations, and is thus seen not as divine speech, as is the Koran, but as a prophet's guidance founded on his insights into – his gnosis of – Islam. The study of the Hadiths is a complicated matter and much time is devoted to it when training to be an Islamic scholar.

If a Hadith supports the Koran everything is fine; if there is a conflict the interpreter must try to understand whether there are other possible ways to understand the Koranic verses or the Hadith in question. If nothing is said on the matter in these sources, comparable situations are looked for. Finally, if the interpreter cannot establish a view based on his reading, there is always the possibility of expressing a qualified view based on a general understanding of the religion. Another major source is the historical traditions of the scholars of the Islamic law schools.

We need two other tools to understand the foundations of this kind of Islamic theology. You can classify a deed or a view as *halal* or *haram*, but you can also, at least according most theologians, divide the *halal* category into four different sub-categories: obligatory, recommended, neutral, and disliked deeds and views. The second tool is the principle that you may not forbid what Allah has permitted, and you may not permit what Allah has forbidden. These tools have to be understood in relation to each other.

We will immediately practise this knowledge with the help of a model constructed by the late Muslim art historian Lois Lamya al-Faruqi. In a couple of articles, al-Faruqi discusses different interpretations and tries to reach a middle-way interpretation.

First, al-Faruqi distinguishes between two forms of what she calls 'artistic engineering of sound' (*Handasah al-Sawt*): *mûsîqâ* and *non-mûsîqâ*, both being tonal expressions but culturally understood as different for theological reasons (al-Faruqi 1989).[1] Since everyone, even the most liberal of theologians in Islam, must admit that *mûsîqâ* can be considered a problem, a division separating the Koranic chant, the call to prayer, the Pilgrimage Chants and other categories closely related to religious rituals, etc., must be made in order to be able to consider these as unproblematic (see Figure 1). Some Hadiths can be interpreted as permissive towards certain kinds of music, or perhaps rather towards music played on certain kinds of occasions, for example family and celebration music, occupational music and military band music. Al-Faruqi makes allowance for them in her model, which is not to the liking of hardliners. I will return to them below.

Classical Arab music and folk music, both categories that could be said to have a pre-Islamic or non-Islamic origin, have been other much-discussed categories. Classical music developed after the codification of the Koran and after the events the Hadiths speak about, so nothing is said on this matter. If folk music is dealt with or not in the Hadiths is a matter of dispute. Generally, Islamic scholars have not held these musical categories in high esteem. But still, since there is no explicit text on these, many scholars regard them as neutral. The hardliners see matters differently.

The final category, almost always disregarded, is sensuous music. In Alexandria in September 2002 I got the opportunity to talk to Amna Mohamed Nossier, professor of Islamic studies at the al-Azhar University of Alexandria. When talking about music, her general attitude was that music is not a problem; in itself it is always *halal*. When I continued to press her on this matter, she brought up the issue of the content of lyrics and the place and social situation in which music is played. This is a classical, well-founded, liberal-minded attitude that can be found throughout Islamic history and which is also, according to my understanding, the prevailing attitude among scholars in public positions in Egypt. Let us now turn to the hardliners.

According to the real hardliners almost no kind of *mûsîqâ* is acceptable, the sole exception being that women are allowed to play a minor hand-drum called the *daveh* (like a tambourine without any rattles) in the company of other women. No men are to be present. Men are not allowed to play the *daveh*. The next step is allowing young girls to sing songs at *'id* (religious feasts), and women to sing for other women at celebrations (but only 'decent' songs). This is looked upon as either *makruh* (discouraged) or *haram*. The hardliners try to construct their argument in a classical way. I will not go into their arguments explicitly, but I will mention that a more moderate scholar, the famous Yusuf al-Qaradawi, writes that he differs with them although 'such opinions remain in tune with the views of a number of early and contemporary *'ulamâ'* (al-Qaradawi 1995: 32). He further argues that one should not denounce the extremists' position as non-Islamic, but rather respect it, arguing that there are better, more moderate positions in tune with Islamic truth. Thus, al-Qaradawi admits their interpretation as a possible position, even if he thinks it an interpretation that needs to be reworked.

## Music as a useless activity

On the hardline Internet site Islam Questions & Answers (<www.islam-qa.com>) there are several articles on music. The central article, sometimes referred to in other shorter ones, is number 5,000, entitled 'Ruling on music, singing and dancing'. In my print version it totals thirteen pages, filled with arguments against any practice of music, singing and dancing. One of the major modern sources used is the late Sheikh Muhammad Nasir ad-Din al-Al-bânî (*d.* 1999), who lived in Jordan. In 1994 he published a book called *Tahrîm âlâta t-tarab* (The prohibition of musical instruments).

In the text it is argued that music is to be understood as 'idle talk', quoting the Koran surat Luqman 31: 6. In the early exegesis of the Koran this phrase is connected with any activity considered morally questionable such as slander or lying, but also sometimes with singing and the playing of instruments. This kind of talk is further connected to the voice of Satan misleading the believers. Instead of giving praise to Allah and learning about Islam, musicians engage in useless and sometimes harmful activities. This is in fact one of the central arguments against music. Music is useless. Nothing is produced; nothing is achieved. For this reason amateurs, rather than professional musicians, are praised for their musicality by some moderate hardliners. Professionals have to spend too much time practising, time they should use remembering Allah. The fact that some hardliners tolerate military and occupational songs is often backed by arguments about their increasing motivation and productivity (al-Ghazali [d. 1111], cited in Shiloah 1995). In the modern age the cost of buying music is contrasted with the use that money could be put to as *sadâqa* (alms).

### Music and passion

One of the more thorough studies of Islam and music is Amnon Shiloah's *Music in the World of Islam*. In chapter 4, called 'Islam and Music', he reviews classical Islamic sources. He writes that: 'one finds repeated belief in the over-whelming power of music, which exerts an irresistibly strong influence on the listener's soul' (Shiloah 1995: 34). In the same spirit, Abu Hanîfa (d. 767) wrote: 'Musical instruments are the wine of the soul, and what it does to the soul is worse than what intoxicating drinks do' (cited on <www.islam-qa.com>). Music causes believers to stray from the devotional life, and it should be treated as other prohibited activities such as gambling and drinking, according to the ninth-century theologian and jurist Abî 'l-Dunyâ (d. 894) in his book *Dhamm al-malâhî* (The book of the censure of Instruments of Diversion) (Shiloah 1995 34). The crucial issue here is the presumed and acknowledged power of music. Music is seen as a rival for the passion of humans. Passion should be devoted to Allah. Instead this passion is wasted on something useless but powerful that might become an obsession. It can also spread in society, causing a general decline in decency and morals.

### Music and sinful living

The above leads to a discussion on the sinful living connected to listening to or performing music. Just as a footnote, it might be mentioned that the hardliners tend to separate listening from hearing; the latter is not forbidden but should be avoided. Intention is one of the most important concepts in Islamic morals, ritual and jurisprudence. If the intention is to listen and enjoy, then it is sinful, but if someone by accident hears but is not set on enjoying, then it is no sin.

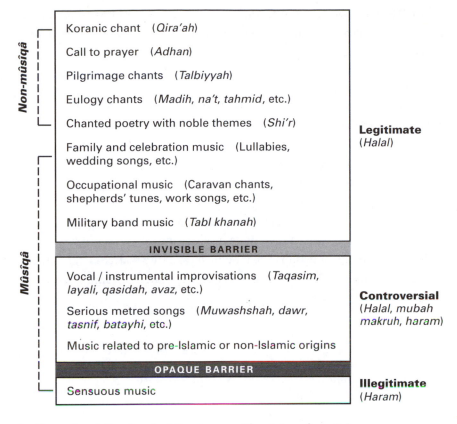

**Non-mûsîqâ**
- Koranic chant (*Qira'ah*)
- Call to prayer (*Adhan*)
- Pilgrimage chants (*Talbiyyah*)
- Eulogy chants (*Madih, na't, tahmid*, etc.)
- Chanted poetry with noble themes (*Shi'r*)

- Family and celebration music (Lullabies, wedding songs, etc.)
- Occupational music (Caravan chants, shepherds' tunes, work songs, etc.)
- Military band music (*Tabl khanah*)

**Mûsîqâ**

INVISIBLE BARRIER

- Vocal / instrumental improvisations (*Taqasim, layali, qasidah, avaz*, etc.)
- Serious metred songs (*Muwashshah, dawr, tasnif, batayhi*, etc.)
- Music related to pre-Islamic or non-Islamic origins

OPAQUE BARRIER

- Sensuous music

**Legitimate**
(*Halal*)

**Controversial**
(*Halal, mubah makruh, haram*)

**Illegitimate**
(*Haram*)

**1 Hierarchy of *Handasah al-Sawt* genres (the status of music in the Islamic world) (al-Faruqi 1989)**

More liberal minds tend to claim that there is no harm inherent in music as such; more important is the company in which music is listened to or played. In other words, it is where, when and with whom you perform or listen to music that is crucial. If music is associated with forbidden pleasures such as drinking alcohol, taking drugs, flirting or having sex, etc., then that music is regarded as forbidden because it contributes to the sins. Real hardliners would say that music in itself incites sins.

### Music and cultural imperialism

A final and equally important reason for a proscriptive attitude among the hardliners is the fact that much music is influenced by non-Islamic, Western musical traditions, or is produced in the Western world. Music can be seen as part of a Western, and sometimes specifically North American, cultural imperialism. This competes with and draws attention from Allah and Islam, and this is considered a violation of the rights Allah has over man. Incorporating this

15

kind of Western-style music is furthermore seen as a deterioration of Muslim culture. This reaction can be seen as part of the counter-power strategies relating to globalization and Western hegemony.

## Summary

The modern hardliners have identified music as a serious rival to Islam. They find a possible interpretation in Islamic tradition leading to a proscriptive attitude to music. They use the Koranic phrase 'idle talk' to associate music with deeds and ideas inspired by Satan. They further emphasize the uselessness of music and its association with forbidden behaviour and sin. Finally, they claim that modern youth is preoccupied by non-Islamic, Western-style music.

To combat this, their strategy is to ban music and musicians if they have the power to do so, or at least attack them, verbally and at times physically. The logic behind this attitude is their fear of music as a rival source of passion and pleasure, but also their fear of losing a battle of cultural hegemony to global, Western-style consumerism.

## Note

1 There are other classifications. Imam Chelebi, a seventeenth-century scholar, distinguished between three categories of music: 'music coming from birds, from the human throat, and from instruments' (van Nieuwkerk 1996: 10).

## References

Abu-Lughud, Lila (ed.) (1998) *Remaking Women: Feminism and Modernity in the Middle East*, Princeton, NJ: Princeton University Press.

al-Albânî, Muhammad Nâsir ad-dîn (1994/2002) *Tahrîm âlâta t-tarab*, Beirut: Ma'ussasat ar-rayyât.

al-Faruqi, Lois Lamya' (1989) 'The Shari'ah on Music and Musicians', *al-'ilm*, 9 (January).

al-Qaradawi, Yusuf (1995) *Islamic Awakening between Rejection and Extremism*, Herndon: International Institute of Islamic Thought.

Armbrust, Walter (1996) *Mass Culture and Modernism in Egypt*, Cambridge: Cambridge University Press.

Khalaf, Rabî ' bin Ahmad (1991) *Kashful-ghitâ'i an hukm samâ' al-ghinâ'i li-ibn Qayyim al-Jawzi*, Cairo: Maktabatu as-sanati.

Shiloah, Amnon (1995) *Music in the World of Islam. A Socio-cultural Study*, Aldershot: Scholar Press.

Sidddîqî, Muhammad Zubayr (1993) *Hadîth Literature: Its Origin, Development and Special Features*, Cambridge: Islamic Text Society.

van Nieuwkerk, Karin (1996) *'A Trade Like Any Other': Female Singers and Dancers in Egypt*, Cairo: American University in Cairo Press.

## Internet resources

Islam Questions & Answers: <www.islam-qa.com>.

# TWO | Asia

# 4 | Music censorship in Afghanistan before and after the Taliban[1]

JOHN BAILY

The Taliban in Afghanistan imposed one of the most extreme examples of music censorship ever reported. Whereas censorship usually involves restrictions on the performance of certain kinds of music, or the gagging of particular individuals whose views are judged inimical by those in positions of control, the Taliban imposed a ban on all forms of what they considered to be 'music'. It is important to understand that the concept of music in Afghanistan is intimately bound up with musical instruments; the ban on music meant a ban on instruments and the sounds they produce. This included all forms of instrumental music and singing accompanied by instruments, irrespective of type. When the Taliban took control of Kabul in 1996 they published a number of decrees, including the following:

> To prevent music ... In shops, hotels, vehicles and rickshaws cassettes and music are prohibited ... If any music cassette found in a shop, the shopkeeper should be imprisoned and the shop locked. If five people guarantee the shop should be opened the criminal released later. If cassette found in the vehicle, the vehicle and the driver will be imprisoned. If five people guarantee the vehicle will be released and the criminal released later.
>
> To prevent music and dances in wedding parties. In the case of violation the head of the family will be arrested and punished.
>
> To prevent the playing of music drum. The prohibition of this should be announced. If anybody does this then the religious elders can decide about it. (Rashid 2000: 218–19)

The disembodied audio-cassette, tape waving in the breeze, became the icon of Taliban rule. Musical instruments were destroyed; they were hung from trees in mock execution or burned in public in sports stadia, where public executions, amputations and floggings were also carried out. For example, the local Herati newspaper, *Itafaq-e Islam*, announced on 10 December 1998 that Herat's Office for the Propagation of Virtue and Prevention of Vice had seized a number of unlawful instruments and goods, which were set on fire and destroyed in Herat's stadium. The newspaper cited the following Hadith to justify this action: 'Those who listen to music and songs in this world, will on the Day of Judgement have molten lead poured into their ears.'[2] The list of destroyed goods was reported as follows: fourteen truckloads of hashish plants; seven twelve-by-twenty-four-inch colour TVs; ten VCRs; four small and large cassette players; 3,500 video cassettes; 5,500 unworthy photos; ninety-five statues (toy figurines); fifty plastic dolls; ten musical instruments and accessories (such as instrument cases).

The one musical instrument that was exempted from this ban was the frame drum (*daireh*), which anyway is not regarded as a musical instrument in the full sense of the word (Baily 1996). It is mainly played by women to accompany their domestic singing and dancing and has important religious significance, its use having been sanctioned on one occasion by Prophet Muhammad (Roy Choudhury 1957: 66–7, cited in Baily 1988: 148). The frame drum continued to be sold in the bazaar in Kabul, although the extent to which it was used in its traditional role was highly circumscribed. The many musical instruments kept at Radio Afghanistan were destroyed, though curiously the grand piano in one of the studios survived. Perhaps the Taliban, with their very limited experience of cultural diversity, did not recognize this huge object as a musical instrument. The Chishti *khanaqah* in Kabul's Shor Bazar, an important place for Sufi musical gatherings, much patronized by Kabul's musicians, also had its instruments destroyed.

During the Taliban period (1996–2001) no music was broadcast by the radio station in Kabul. The station was renamed Radio Sharia, and its output was mainly news and religious programmes. Women had no role as broadcasters. The large tape archive, including five thousand hours of music, survived. In the early days of Taliban rule a number of tapes of Indian film music and Iranian popular music were offered by the archive's staff as constituting the music archive, and these recordings were destroyed. The main body of the archive remained on its shelves, the sign saying 'Archive' was removed from the doors and local staff colluded in the deception that there was no archive. The Taliban established their own collection of recordings of speeches, sermons and chants. The TV station's video archive also survived, though in this case the Taliban made no use of the visual medium, considering representations of animate beings sinful. Nevertheless, they did not destroy the television equipment in the studios, possibly thinking that it might have its use one day, or at least have some retail value.

Many of Afghanistan's professional musicians had already gone into exile before the arrival of the Taliban. Poorly educated hereditary musicians from cities such as Kabul, Mazar, Herat, Kandahar and Jalalabad generally went to neighbouring countries like Pakistan, Uzbekistan and Iran, while some from a more educated background made their way to the West. Many of Kabul's musicians from the Kucheh Kharabat (the musicians' quarter in the old city) set up business premises in Khalil House, an apartment block in University Road, Peshawar. Something like twenty-five music groups were located in one building. It was a hothouse of musical activity, with a lot of teaching and practice going on, and informal music sessions where young musicians competed to show off their virtuosity and technical skills. As usual, the main source of musicians' income came from playing at wedding celebrations.

In *Breaking the Silence* the *delruba* (a bowed lute) player Amruddin describes movingly how he tried to take his instrument with him to Peshawar.

> When the Taliban took Mazar-e Sharif I had a shop with instruments from both East and West. When the Taliban came we buried some and burned some, we got rid of them all. I kept just one *delruba*. It belonged to my father and was very dear to me. I wanted to keep it till I died. But on the way to Herat there were many checkpoints. At first no one noticed my *delruba*. I had removed the strings and stripped it to the bare wood. But in Herat a local boy recognized what it was. He smashed it to pieces against the car. I don't mind the other things but that *delruba* meant a lot to me. (Broughton 2002: 25–10)

Those musicians left in Afghanistan had to find other ways to make a living. Ahmad Rashid Mashinai,[3] a *sarinda* (another bowed lute) player, became a butcher. 'They stopped the music and destroyed my instruments. I needed another job so I had to become a butcher. I've been working here for five years. I had to feed my family' (ibid.: 2–22). Some had to rely on begging. John Simpson's film *Islam's Year Zero* (BBC2, 7 December 1996) showed the pathetic situation of a prematurely aged Kabuli tabla player who had buried his drums. 'I can't pay rent. The owner has thrown me out. I can only afford one meal a day. The other two I have to forgo. My children are all hungry. They say to me, "Father, what should we do?" I tell them there's nothing I can do. I was young, now I'm old. You see these hands [that once played the drums], now they stretch out asking for help. I feel this is all very shameful and degrading.'

While the Taliban banned all forms of what they perceived to be 'music', they allowed the performance of various types of unaccompanied religious singing, and they created a new genre, the Taliban *tarana* (song), a word usually translated in English as 'chant'. The texts were usually in Pashto, but sometimes in other Afghanistani languages too, such as Dari and Uzbek. The texts made frequent reference to the Taliban, their commitment to Islam, their readiness to sacrifice themselves for their country, and their *shahids* (martyrs), who died for the cause. Recorded *tarana*s made substantial use of electronic

21

effects such as delay and reverberation, much favoured in the secular music of this part of the world. *Tarana*s in Pashto used the melodic modes of Pashtun regional music (such as *Pari* and *Kesturi*) and were strongly rhythmic, with frequent use of the two-part song structure that is typical of the region. In other words, it was like Pashtun folk music but with new texts and no musical instruments, and therefore 'not music'.

Some musicians who remained in Kabul were forced to sing them. Aziz Ghaznawi, a well-known singer of popular songs, and today in charge of musicians at the radio station, described his experience:

> After two years a big-shot Taliban minister sent for me. He said, 'Why don't you sing? Don't you like our regime?' 'That's not true,' I protested, afraid they would kill me. 'No one invited me to sing,' I said. 'What if I ask you now?' he replied. 'Of course I will sing,' I said. He handed me the text:
>
>> 'When the conquering sun rises
>> It brings light to the darkness.'
>
> I went home and showed it to my wife. 'If I sing, I betray my principles. If not, I must flee the country.' I have a family of fifteen. My mother had just died, and I had no money to flee. My wife said, 'You've no choice. You've got to sing.' (Broughton 2002: 32–24)

And so he did:

> The evil night has gone
> The morning sun has risen
> Thanks to you fighters peace has come
> The river will kiss your feet a hundred times.

However, some singers were more willing to record for the Taliban. In Peshawar in 2000 I met a Kabuli musician who had recently returned from Kabul, where he had gone to record some unaccompanied *na't*s (songs in praise of the Prophet Muhammad) for Radio Sharia.

Punishments for playing music or being caught with cassettes seem to have varied greatly, from confiscation of the goods and a warning to severe beatings and imprisonment. Despite these measures there was, of course, a lot of secret music activity. Western journalists loved to report how their drivers would play music in their vehicles, then put on a Taliban *tarana* when they came to a checkpoint. In Herat, BBC correspondent Kate Clark was surprised to find that taxi drivers drove about the city playing music cassettes freely. There was undoubtedly a great deal of secret music-making and listening to music. As one man put it: 'Whenever there is a marriage party we have to have music, to

**2** During their rule in Afghanistan, the Taliban arranged bonfires of 'evil' music (tapes, records, videos and CDs) (at the time of going to press all efforts have been made to locate the copyright owner of this photograph).

dance, to enjoy ourselves. But we were not allowed to have such instruments, to play it, but secretly we did' (ibid.: 5–50). Instruments were hidden behind false walls or buried in the ground. Many houses in the cities have a basement area which is used in the summer as a refuge from the heat. Such rooms lent themselves readily to underground music sessions. Although the frame drum was the one instrument not proscribed, women were very careful about their traditional music sessions. Shugla said: 'Kabul and the whole country was like a prison for women. It was not a happy place. Every family knew the Taliban were watching. We would only risk playing if we were a hundred per cent sure it was safe. Lookouts were posted to watch for Taliban coming. Then we'd silence our music and hide our tambourines [*dairehs*]' (ibid.: 31–46).

Even the broadcast *tarana* could have another meaning. Nairaz, another radio singer who stayed in Kabul under the Taliban, explained: 'I was put in charge of "songs without music". They wanted to hear me sing, so I chose one that went: "Remember the poor are protected by God/One day He will answer their cries/And their oppressors will be punished." The Taliban liked the song but didn't understand its deeper meaning. They were proud Pashto speakers, but I sang in Farsi and the song was a big hit' (ibid.: 34–24).

The best example of resistance to the Taliban comes not from the field of music but from the film *Titanic*. In November 2000 the BBC's Kate Clark came up with the extraordinary story that while cinema, TV and video were all banned in Afghanistan, this film was undergoing an incredible surge of popularity. Everybody in Kabul seemed, somehow, to have seen it, in some cases many times. Even the Taliban seem to know all about it. According to a joke current at the time, a mullah was giving his Friday sermon to a crowded audience and warned them that they were committing many sins, that they were sinful people. He told them, 'I know you are listening to music, you're hiring video players, you're watching films. You should be careful. You're all going to be damned, and drown just like the people in the *Titanic* film!' Leonardo DiCaprio's haircut in the film became very popular in Kabul as the '*Titanic* haircut', and many barbers were punished for styling it. Clothes, rice, motor oil, all were sold with a *Titanic* logo, such as 'TITANIC. Best Quality'. Expensive wedding cakes were baked in the shape of the *Titanic*, and the most expensive added the iceberg as a supplement. The bazaar that had recently appeared in the bed of the dried-up Kabul river was dubbed Titanic Bazar. Various reasons could be suggested for the popularity of the film, but it is surely relevant that the love story is in the classic Leyla and Majnun or Yusuf and Zurlaika mould.[4]

During the war that led to the defeat of the Taliban spontaneous outbursts of music greeted the liberation of the towns and cities. Music in Afghanistan has always been associated with joyous occasions, such as wedding festivities and the country fairs held over a period of forty days in spring. For most people the end of Taliban control over their area was occasion for rejoicing and for music-making, whether through playing cassettes loudly in the streets or even playing musical instruments. The very sound of music became a symbol, even a signal, of freedom. Once you heard music coming from your local radio station you knew the Taliban had lost control. The sound of music signalled a return to (comparative) normality; a lack of music is symptomatic of a dysfunctional society.

However, the Taliban did not start all this censorship of music. Self-imposed censorship of music certainly existed in the time of the king (1933–73), though perhaps more in the sense of an awareness of what was and what was not appropriate for particular occasions. The kind of censorship associated with the Taliban started during the jihad, when musicians were caught in the cross-fire between communists and the mujahidin. The celebrated Pashtun woman singer Naghma described her experience:

> During the communist times I was singing on television. I was in danger from people who objected to me singing. They were the mujahidin of Islam. They

wanted me to sing for them and not appear in public. On one side the communists wanted me to sing for them, and the mujahidin wanted me on their side.
Several times people tried to shoot me when I performed. Many times I was told
to stop singing for the communists. My husband and I had threats and our lives
were in danger. But I continued to perform and one night when I was out they
killed my sister in error because she looked like me. (ibid.: 16–37)

A number of singers left Afghanistan, not wanting to compromise themselves or find themselves caught between opposing factions. And several
million Afghans went into exile, mostly in Pakistan and Iran. In Iran strict
music censorship was already in place, initiated soon after Khomeini's revolution in 1979, and lasting until the end of the war between Iran and Iraq in
1988. In Pakistan things were more complicated. Pakistan has a great diversity
of regional music. It has a film music industry, and shares the classical traditions of northern India. Most of the Afghan refugees in Pakistan lived in camps
under the control of one or other of the seven mujahidin parties. There was a
strong fundamentalist ethos, with music banned – not only live performances
and listening to audio cassettes, but even listening to music on the radio. One
reason given was that most of the people living in these miserable conditions
had lost family members in the war and were in a state of mourning, which
made the playing of music inappropriate.

Paradoxically, there was a brisk business in mujahidin tapes recorded by
refugee musicians. A new style of tabla playing, imitating the sound of gun-
fire, was developed. On some tapes the sounds of real battle were mixed into
the music. Naqib, a mujahid, states: 'When the Russians invaded Afghanistan
we mujahidin had to fight a jihad. Although it was a holy war we still listened
to music. We were not narrow-minded, music was our entertainment. There
was the sound of weapons firing. These tapes calmed us down when we were
fighting. When we sat with our friends this was our entertainment' (ibid.:
14–30).

After the fall of the communists in 1992 when the Rabbani coalition government came to power, censorship was heavy. The situation in Herat is best
documented (Baily 2001). The Herat region was controlled by Ismail Khan,
a Rabbani supporter and a highly successful mujahidin commander during
the jihad. Herat under Ismail Khan was deeply austere, with senior religious
figures in positions of power and influence. The Office for the Propagation
of Virtue and the Prevention of Vice had been established, and this clamped
down on many activities that were later to become targets of Taliban censure.
The hobby of pigeon-flying was proscribed, on the grounds that it could lead to

men spying on the courtyards of their neighbours' houses. For similar reasons, flying kites from the rooftops was banned.

There was also heavy censorship of music, but a certain amount of musical activity was allowed. Professional musicians had to hold a licence, which specified the kinds of songs they could perform, namely songs in praise of the mujahidin and songs with texts drawn from the mystical Sufi poetry of the region. The licences also stipulated that musicians must play without amplification. Music could be performed by male musicians at private parties indoors. Technically, it could also be played at wedding parties, and spring country fairs, but experience had shown that at such events the religious police often arrived to stop the performance. They would confiscate the instruments, which were usually returned to the musicians some days later when a fine or bribe had been paid. Herat's professional women musicians were forbidden to perform and several were imprisoned.

There was very little music on local radio or television. If a song was broadcast on television one did not see the performers on screen, but rather a vase of flowers. Names of performers were not announced on radio or television. An instrument maker had reopened his business in one of the main streets, keeping an eye open for the religious police. The audio-cassette business continued, with a number of shops in the bazaars of Herat selling music cassettes.

The censorship of music in Kabul at this time was less severe than in Herat; President Rabbani tried to set up an Office for the Propagation of Virtue and the Prevention of Vice, but certain members of the government, such as Ahmad Shah Masud, did not support such strong measures for controlling the populace. In the dying days of the Rabbani era, before the fall of Kabul to the Taliban, Gulbuddin Hekmatyar was appointed prime minister in a new coalition government. He was the leader of one of the most extreme mujahidin parties and he lost no time in closing Kabul's cinemas and banning music on radio and television.

The situation in Afghanistan today is in many ways a reversion to the immediate pre-Taliban period, with the Northern Alliance the successors to the Rabbani coalition, and Hekmatyar in alliance with remnants of the Taliban and other extreme fundamentalists. Strong censorship of music continues. Within Kabul itself there is a complete ban on women singing on radio and television, and on the stage or concert platform.[5] Women can announce, read the news, recite poetry, act in plays, but they cannot sing. This ban has been the subject of intense argument within radio and television organizations, which are under the control of the Ministry for Information and Culture. The justification for the ban on women singing is that to do otherwise would give the government's fundamentalist enemies an easy way to stir up trouble. In the case of television, a further reason is given, namely that there are no competent women singers in Kabul today, and the tapes in the video archive (dating mainly from the communist period) show women wearing clothes that these days would be considered too revealing. This justification obviously does not apply to women singing on radio. A third reason, that it would place the women in danger of attack, cannot be accepted either, because most of the music broadcast is from the archive. This was the reason offered to explain why women were not allowed to sing at the BBC World Service's concert celebrating its seventieth anniversary in December 2002. Ironically, the one city where women seem able to perform on local radio and television is Kandahar, formerly a Taliban stronghold. On 13 January 2004, Reuters reported that Kabul Television had shown old footage of the Afghan woman singer Parasto performing without a headscarf. However, this new freedom was short-lived after it was denounced by a prominent Supreme Court judge.

If there is some censorship of music within Kabul, protected and patrolled by International Security Assistance Force (ISAF) teams, outside the city much stricter censorship is imposed by local fundamentalist commanders. Two incidents near Kabul were reported during my stay in October 2002. In one, musicians from Kabul city were invited to play at a wedding in a village in Kabul province, towards the Shomali Plain. During the wedding local police arrived to stop the festivities, and the host and two musicians were arrested and taken to the local police station. There they were severely beaten at the order of the local police chief. The next day elders from the village came to ask for their release. They were freed and warned never to return.

In another incident two musicians were killed when hand grenades were thrown at a wedding party in Paghman, near Kabul. In this case it is not certain that the attack was provoked by the presence of musicians, or whether it was due to some other kind of dispute. Musicians from Kabul have become very wary about where they will go to play and for whom; they have to feel adequately protected. Less well-documented reports from other parts of the country show that musicians are by no means free to follow their profession. Music, as ever, remains a sensitive indicator of trends in the broader sociocultural context. Freemuse will continue to monitor the situation.

## Notes

1  This chapter is based on the Freemuse report 'Can you stop the birds singing?', first published in May 2001. In updating it I have drawn extensively on Simon

Broughton's film *Breaking the Silence*, which was shot in Kabul and Peshawar in January 2002, shortly after the departure of the Taliban from most parts of Afghanistan. The film, for which I acted as consultant, includes some very useful interview material which I present here as transcriptions. I refer to this film as Broughton 2002, with timings of relevant excerpts given in minutes and seconds (e.g. 25–10 means 25 minutes and 10 seconds in from the start of the film). I have included further information from other journalistic sources, as well as my own observations made during visits to Kabul in October 2002 and 2003.

2  This Hadith is found in the writings of the sixteenth-century jurist Ibn Hajar Haytami of Egypt (*d.* 1567 c.e.). I am grateful to Kathie Brown for this information. The Hadith seems to have had common currency in Pakistan.

3  He's called 'The Machine' not because he plays like one but because of his ability to learn very quickly by ear, like a tape machine (tape recorder).

4  Perhaps at a deeper level the ship was a symbol of an Afghanistan foundering on the iceberg of civil war. Or perhaps we see the *Titanic* as a symbol of the Taliban themselves, seemingly impregnable but in the event unsound.

5  Kabul's grand theatre, the Kabul Nanderi, stood in ruins. However, there was some theatrical life, and plays could be staged in the city's cinemas. In addition, there were several auditoria where concerts could be held, for example at Radio Afghanistan, Kabul University and Lycée Esteqlal.

## References

Baily, John (1988) *Music of Afghanistan: Professional Musicians in the City of Herat*, Cambridge: Cambridge University Press. With accompanying audio cassette.

— (1996) 'Using Tests of Sound Perception in Fieldwork', *Yearbook for Traditional Music*, 28: 147–73.

— (2001) *'Can you stop the birds singing?' The censorship of music in Afghanistan*, Copenhagen: Freemuse. With accompanying CD.

— (2003) *Ethno-musicological fieldwork in Kabul to assess the situation of music in the post-Taliban era*, unpublished report to the British Academy's Committee for Central and Inner Asia.

Broughton, Simon (2002) *Breaking the Silence. Music in Afghanistan*, documentary film (58 mins), screened BBC4, 11 March 2002, London: Songlines Films.

Rashid, Ahmad (2000) *Taliban. Islam, Oil and the New Great Game in Central Asia*, London: I.B. Tauris.

Roy Choudhury, M. L. (1957) 'Music in Islam', *Journal of the Asiatic Society, Letters*, 23(2): 43–102.

# 5 | Music for the great leader: policy and practice in North Korea

KEITH HOWARD

A recalcitrant Stalinist anachronism? This is the common perception of the Democratic People's Republic of Korea (North Korea) beyond its fortified and carefully sealed borders. North Korea considers the bad image it has abroad as proof of a capitalist attempt to destroy it, and tends to restrict access further still whenever it encounters hostile press reports. Pak Dong Tchoun, North Korea's representative at UNESCO in Paris, reminded us in July 1995 how 'extremely reluctant' his country would remain to open its doors to journalists who 'write horrible calumnies about our regime the minute they leave the country. We want journalists who show good will and want to promote friendship between peoples, not subvert our regime and sovereignty. The [Western] mass media must not write articles that are not encouraging.' Negative press, or TV serializations of 'untruths' – and occasionally interviews with defectors – published in its southern cousin, the Republic of Korea (South Korea), generally induce bellicose threats, as North Korea shouts it will kill the responsible reporters and bomb newspaper buildings.

Typing 'North Korea + Censorship' offers a fruitful search on the Internet. North Korea, with Afghanistan, we read, is the only country in the world where people have neither the right nor the technical means to access the Internet; countering this, North Korea established a national intranet, the Kwang Myong Net, in 2001. International telephone calls are forbidden, except to high party functionaries and foreign diplomats; television and radio sets are preset before distribution to receive only North Korean media; the import of videotapes, CDs and foreign publications is prohibited. The press is routinely censored, we are told, because its function is 'to explain, disseminate, advocate and help accomplish Kim Il Sung's instructions and Kim Jong Il's policies, and to further strengthen the Proletariat dictatorship as well as to strengthen politico-ideological unity and solidarity among the people' (*Encyclopaedia* VI 1983). There is no freedom of expression in print; all publications must reflect the unitary policy (*yuil sasang*) fostered by the fact that the leadership and the people are said to be in complete accord. We read that the mission of the press is to glorify the leadership, to advocate party policy, to generate popular agitation, and so on. Article 46 of the Penal Code does indeed dictate harsh measures, from confiscation of property to the death penalty, for 'reactionary propaganda and agitation', presumably the publication of materials criticizing state or leadership. And some reports claim as many as 250,000 North Koreans are imprisoned as 'criminals' guilty of 'ideological transgressions' among those held in an extensive gulag.

Other reports tell of hagiography surrounding the autocratic and monolithic leadership, seen best in the virtual deification of Kim Il Sung (1912–94), in life the Great Wise President-for-life Dearly Beloved and Sagacious Leader, and in death the Eternal President. Kim's son, Kim Jong Il (b. 1942), is now de facto leader, as head of the Korean Workers' Party. Kim Senior, we hear, effectively expelled the Japanese colonial power from the Korean peninsula in the 1940s and defeated the Americans in the Korean War; he single-handedly built the socialist paradise, overseeing industrial and agricultural reforms (based most notably on 'models' he developed at the Kangson steel mill and during fifteen days spent with the farming community of Changsan-ri). Histories are doctored to prove his paramount role. Inscriptions praising Kim cut into the bark of trees in the mountains on the border between North Korea and China are claimed to be the writings of 1930s guerrillas, and are meticulously preserved under glass; photographs are altered, removing those later found to be 'enemies of the state' and moving Kim to the centre; more recently, all photographs of Kim himself have been subject to a judicious use of an air brush to remove the unsightly growth on his neck that was present for the last two decades of his life. And visitors arriving in Pyongyang are today routinely presented with flowers. But these are not a gift, for the first port of call for all us visitors is a massive 20-metre-tall bronze statue of Kim where, in front of TV cameras, we must place the flowers, showing to all and sundry that we have come to pay our respects. North Korean promotion of Kim Il Sung and Kim Jong Il, surely, feeds the cynicism of international observers.

North Korea, though, maintains that the reality is different. North Korea signed the International Covenant on Civil and Political Rights in 1981, submitting its first report in 1984 and the second in 2001, some seventeen years later (and twelve years overdue: the covenant prescribes the submission of reports every five years). The 2001 report admitted to thirty cases in which publication was prohibited, twenty-seven concerning encyclopaedias, maps and magazines, and three dealing with military matters. It reported two or three annual demonstrations, but contrasted these with 600 public rallies held in support of the state and its leadership. This suggests that little censorship needs to be practised. And the North Korean ambassador to the United Nations, addressing the Human Rights Committee in July 2001, brushed aside all criticism with the comment that 'The Democratic People's Republic of Korea has developed a Korean style of human rights which reflects the desires of the people.'

Where, then, is the truth? In artistic policy and practice, the problem and the solution are all bound up in ideology. Ideology shifts over time, and in the history of North Korea can be divided into four distinct periods. Ideology is a matter of control, asserted from the centre, but arguing that this, within a 'revolutionary' spirit, reflects the wishes and desires of the people. The centre controls access to training and work; there is no space for dissent. In this account of music, it is useful to start with quotations from Kim Il Sung and Kim Jong Il, as is compulsory in North Korean publications. Here, though, I offer annotations that would be missing in North Korea.

'We are making a revolution, and we should inspire the people to the revolutionary struggle by means of songs' (Kim Jong Il, *For the Further Development of Our Juche Art*, a speech originally given in 1975, published in English translation in 1992). Here is our cue, taken from socialist realism, to a Korean ideological policy influenced not just by Maxim Gorky and Andrei Zhdanov, but also by Mao Zedong's 'Talks at the Yan'an Forum on Literature and Art' from 1942. A problem soon emerged for North Korea, though, as the artists-turned-ideologues who were part of the Korean communist faction at Yan'an, most prominently the established literary scholar Kim Yubong, represented a challenge to the autocratic rule of one leader, Kim Il Sung. They were purged during the Korean War. As Kim built his base power moved towards those who had been active on North Korean territory through the last years of Japanese rule, who, according to Chong-Sik Lee and Marshall Pihl, were 'made up preponderantly of the illiterate and the indigent' (Lee 1963: 9; Pihl 1993: 94). This was an unfortunate beginning for North Korean art, literature and music.

Revolution required something new: 'It is unthinkable that songs which the aristocrats of old days used to sing while drinking could also suit the emotions of our youth who are building socialism' (Kim Il Sung, cited in Bunge 1981: 94). Musical genres associated with any elites of the past had to go. Instruments associated with the literati, notably the six-stringed long zither, the *kômun'go*, despite its historical importance as the only distinctly Korean instrument developed on territory now belonging to North Korea, must be abandoned. But artistic production, by its very nature, and because of the requirement for high levels of skill, is elitist. This extends to art genres with roots among the common folk. Even *p'ansori*, the celebrated one-person vocal form mixing song (*sori*), narrative (*aniri*) and dramatic action (*pallim*), quickly suffered, because it is: ' ... ridiculous to imagine soldiers rushing to battle inspired by *p'ansori*' (Kim Il Sung, ibid.: 94).

Music must serve the revolution, but this had a number of unavoidable implications. First, artists must suffer. They had trained in elitist institutions, often in Japan or elsewhere abroad, and their families would have had money, either because they were aristocrats or landowners of some standing in Korea's historical consciousness or since they had worked for the hated Japanese colonialists who had ruled Korea until 1945. Filtering socialist realism through Mao, Kim Il Sung in 1951 gave his 'Talks with Writers and Artists' (published in *Selected Works* 1, 1971: 305–12). Artists, he said, were 'engineers of the human soul', whose works should serve the people as a 'powerful weapon and great inspiration'. They had, though, 'lost touch with life' and lagged 'behind our rapidly advancing reality' (this closely echoes Mao, for which see *Selected Works* 3, 1965: 81). Artists must 'learn from the lofty spirit of ordinary people', since they 'should know that the genuine creator of great art is always the people'. Purges began.

The politics of many artists are left of centre, so not surprisingly many had moved from Seoul to Pyongyang in the years following the 1945 division into a capitalist-leaning South Korea sponsored by America and a communist-leaning North Korea sponsored by the Soviet Union. Among those we know who moved were the following musicians: Kim Sunnam, An Kiyong and Ri Konu (composers), Yun Naksun, Pak Unyong and Chon Chonggil (all composers), Pak Yonggun and Chon Hakchu (music critics), Kang Kangil, Kwon Wonhan, Ko Chongik, Kim Hyongno, Shin Mak, Ri Kyongp'al, Ri Kyunam, Ri Pomjun, Chong Tokyong, Chong Yongjae, Cho Kyong, Ch'oe Pongjin, Ch'oe Huinam, Shin Yongt'ae, Ch'oe Ch'angun and Kim Yongt'ae (singers), Pak Hyonsuk and Yi Inhyong (pianists), and Kim T'aeyon, Mun Hakchun, An Songgyo, Ri Kangyol, Ri Kyesong, Ri Yongch'ol and U Talhyong (all string instrumentalists). What awaited them? Kim Sunnam (1917–86) illustrates. He had an impressive past, writing nationalist music and setting up left-wing associations for musicians, and in the North he started well, being appointed as head of composition at the Pyongyang National Music School in 1948. But in 1952 he was purged, forbidden to compose, and sent to Shinp'o, an isolated port on the east coast in South Hamgyong province. He was rehabilitated in late 1964, and for three years some of his works were heard and published in the capital. By 1970, he had again been sent to Shinp'o; little is known about the last period of his life. The most prominent Korean dancer, Ch'oe Sunghui (1911–?), known internationally under her Japanese name of Sai Shoki, also settled in Pyongyang. She set up a school and was given a number of official posts, and until 1964 she appeared in occasional lists of dancers. Then she abruptly disappeared. It appears that her husband fell out of favour, and both were executed together with their daughter. Too little information exists to show what happened to each and every artist, but few of those who moved northward after 1945 managed to adjust.

A new proletarian artist was required without links to the old world; in music this is exemplified by Kim Won'gyun (*b.* 1917), today's most celebrated composer, but until 1947 a farmer who just happened to write a song: '*Kim Ilsong changgun ui norae*' (Song of General Kim Il Sung).

By 1960, Kim Il Sung's ideologues were telling the people that all artistic production belonged to the masses, the *inmin*, who 'could write rather better works than the professional writers who are confined to their offices' ('Talks with Writers, Composers, and Film Workers', a speech given on 27 November 1960 and published in *Selected Works* 2: 594–5). This was not just a broadside aimed at 'high' art, but also reflected a shift in policy. It was interpreted within a mass movement, the *Ch'ollima undong* announced in late 1957, normally glossed the 'Galloping Horse Movement'. *Ch'ollima* is a mythical horse of great strength said to be capable of taking its rider 1,000 *li* – about 100 miles – in a day. The movement resonates with Mao's '100 Flowers' speech, given a year before in 1956. The latter reflected emerging rivalries between Khrushchev and Mao, the former as the reformist of politics, economics and artistic production after the death of Stalin. Pyongyang would instinctively want to side with Mao, promoting himself as the true leader of communism. But by 1957 they were aware of the downside of his policy, the popular criticism that emerged once indigenous forms of art were once more allowed, a criticism that could only be controlled through official sanctions against the 'poisonous snake' that dared to challenge the regime. North Korea shifted from the new revolutionary forms of artistic production to encompass Korean indigenous forms, and sought a marriage between the two while simultaneously strengthening control from the centre. Now Kim Il Sung alone gave detailed instructions to his people. In the arts, he was responsible for rationing themes and materials, ensuring that correct political content replaced notions of style or personal creation. The resulting ideology led to monochromatic cultural performances.

However, and as emerged in China, the vernacular was now considered the repository of the proper Korean spirit. So, folk songs must be allowable. Scholars were sent to the provinces to find those who remembered the old forms. But local traditions from the past needed to serve the revolution in the present, so: 'It is our duty to recover and enrich all excellent folk art during our party's era in which cultural art is blossoming and advancing' (Kim Il Sung, cited in translation by Kim Yol Kyu 1992: 88). For 'enrichment' read 'correct political content'. Artists were instructed to avoid 'nihilism', a concept equated with 'the denial of the brilliant heritage left to us by our ancestors'. Presentation must avoid 'resurrectionism' and the 'desire to resuscitate indiscriminately everything belonging to the past'. Lyrics were revised and approved, diatonic melodies replaced Korean modes, and vocal production was standardized to match the *yuhaengga* (Japanese *enka*) popular songs inherited from the early twentieth century and the bel canto of Soviet models. Out went the nasal resonance typical of folk songs in the north-west; out went the emotional intensity of sorrowful folk songs. Out went 'immoral' subjects, and in came sentiments of bountiful harvests, national rebuilding and peace and happiness. Creativity has little place here.

In song composition, profundity is supposedly guaranteed because ideology is placed above mature individual talent. Yet artistic integrity, the mainstay of European artistic creation, must always be subservient to the leadership, since the leader is the sole arbiter. To Kim Jong Il, in his *For the Further Development of Juche Art*:

> Before good songs can be produced prettily-worded texts are necessary. The words should be poetic. But many [lyrics] are turned into prose ... [so] no good songs can be produced ... Our creators of music do not accept Party policy with sensitivity. I gave them the task of composing powerful songs capable of inspiring the masses ... but as yet they have failed to produce a good song about grand construction. We not only need lyrical songs, but also many militant songs.

Kim Jong Il's criticism allowed no room for disagreement. Yet composers faced something of a dilemma, for he continued: 'As I have constantly emphasised, creation should never be repetitive. In creation similarity and repetition mean death. We cannot call that which plagiarises melodies from other songs and assembles them creative work.' And: 'Because our composers produce songs without doing any foundation work for creating melodies with specific features, there appear only complicated songs, and no masterpieces.'

The Galloping Horse Movement marks the time when the unitary policy, *yuil sasang*, began to be promoted. Cue mass dances, song festivals and games, based on the mass youth events taken from northern Europe in the early twentieth century in Hitler's Germany and Stalin's Soviet Union, but which continue to this day in Pyongyang. Elsewhere, I have written about the annual celebration by youth workers of Kim Il Sung's birthday; in April 2000, this involved some 50,000 dancers on Kim Il Sung Square (formerly Stalin Square) dancing in perfect synchronization. In 2002, this was subsumed into the Arirang Festival, a two-month spring festival that at its height, and as reported by the BBC, involved 150,000 dancers. And press reports also tell us that the Pyongyang Hall of Culture holds a weekly dance event attended by some 600 people, each paying a small entry fee of five won. As a shift in ideology, *yuil sasang* matured as *juche*. This latter is the North Korean policy of self-reliance, although it is somewhat mischievously transliterated by some commentators as 'bloody-mindedness'. The politics of *juche* are complex and chimerical. *Juche* is said to be new, emancipating and scientific; in reality it is monolithic, anti-internationalist and anti-hegemonic, ascribing revolutionary responsibility to Kim Il Sung:

> The beloved leader ... discovered the truth of the Juche idea ... and proclaimed it to the whole world ... after verifying its correctness through practical struggle ... The leader saw through the mistakes of the communists and nationalists ... and took a road different from theirs ... Drawing on serious lessons derived from such flunkeyism and dogmatism, the leader clarified the truth that a revolution should be carried out ... in an independent and creative way. (Kim Chang Ha 1984: 17–18, quoting Kim Jong Il).

In *juche*, the ideology is adjusted once more, squaring all circles so that artists reflect the leader who reflects the people. To ensure this, and with one eye to the Cultural Revolution taking place across the border, two control filters were introduced. *Chongjaron* (seed theory) held that the creative seed is both unique to a given artist and consistent with party orientation; *chipch'e yesul* or *chipch'e ch'angjak* (collective art or collective creation) echoed the collectivizations of agriculture and industry beloved in socialist states by removing the individual and imposing collectives of composers, performers, and so on. The result was a complete subordination of all musical activity into state bodies, which continues to this day. Specialist instrumental and vocal teaching is given at *haksaeng sonyon kungjong* (children's palaces), one per province and two in Pyongyang, including the flagship facility built in 1989 near the birthplace of Kim Il Sung, the Man'gyongdae Children's Palace. A single music academy, the Pyongyang Music and Dance College, trains musicians and dancers to professional levels. In 1992, 1,500 students were enrolled in its departments for Western music, vocal music, Korean music, composition and education. Institutes conduct specific research: the Minjok akki kaeryang saopkwa (People's Instrument Improvement Collective) has since the 1960s been responsible for modifying and updating traditional instruments; the P'yongyang muyong p'yogibop yon'gushil (Pyongyang Dance Notation Study Institute) promotes a dance notation system; and the Minjok umak yon'gushil (People's Music Study

35

Institute) and Yun Isang umak yon'guso (Isang Yun Music Study Institute) conduct musicological research. Instrumentalists, vocalists and composers are employed in the orchestras and chorus attached to the National Theatre, the P'i pada kaguk tan (Sea of Blood opera company), the P'yongyang minjok umaktan (Pyongyang People's Music Ensemble), the film companies, and in Maoist-style propaganda squads deployed throughout the countryside to encourage 'workers to greater successes through artistic agitation' in their ever-present 'speed battles'. The two Pyongyang circuses have orchestras, as do some military/police organizations. And there are three ensembles for popular music (the restriction in number is based on Soviet practice): Mansudae yesultan (Mansudae Art Troupe), Wangjaesan kyong umaktan (Wangjaesan Light Music Band), and Poch'onbo kyong umaktan (normally glossed in English as 'Pochonbo Electronic Orchestra'). In 2000, when I last visited Pyongyang, Wangjaesan had issued forty-five albums, and Pochonbo eighty-five.

*Juche* has much to answer for. In terms of music, the 1970s saw the emergence of 'revolutionary operas' within a collectivized, *juche*-ized genre known after the first as the *P'i pada* (Sea of Blood) style. These told of supposedly 'immortal' and 'revolutionary' exploits. By the 1980s, they had been joined by 'people's operas' (*minjok kaguk*), based on folk tales, and again written by a collective of composers. Songs and themes from these were spun off to create symphonies (the first, again without any named composer on the score, was *P'i pada* in 1975) and instrumental pieces. Instruments were revamped, traditional instruments 'improved' (*kyeryang* is the Korean term used) so that they could play Western diatonic melodies; the claim is that the instruments now take the best from the Western orchestra and the best from Korea, although there is evidence of rethinks and several reworkings in relation to the *ongnyugum* (a table zither with connections to the orchestral harp but using bridges based on an old design from the Korean *kayagum*) and the *haegum* (originally a two-stringed spiked fiddle, but now four four-stringed instruments tuned to match orchestral violins, violas, cellos and basses). Film music began to be ascribed to committees. For example, the film *Yun Sangmin*, one part of the multi-film series *Minjok kwa unmyong* (Nation and Destiny), tells of the composer Isang Yun (1917–95), his abduction and imprisonment by South Korean agents, and his composition of a symphony. Appearing in 1992, the film lists five composers in the credits: Ri Chongo, Song Tongch'un, Chon Ch'angil, Ko Suyong and Kim Yongson. Isang Yun, because he wrote in an avant-garde, serialist manner, and despite his role as titular head of the study institute bearing his name, could not be considered populist, and therefore had no music to offer the film company.

Observing from outside, it is difficult to find the gaps. Ideology seems to maintain strict control, and there is no musical production possible at the professional level outside state institutions. Local production is carefully monitored and manipulated, through the slow-drip release of new songs by the three popular music ensembles, through state-controlled media, and through mass dancing to these same songs choreographed by state artistic agitators in each factory work cell, each farming village and each university class. No foreigner visiting North Korea has successfully broken through the rhetoric to discover what artists, writers and musicians truly feel about their situation. And, in a country where Article 46 of the Penal Code dictates harsh penalties for 'reactionary propaganda and agitation', it is doubtful we will ever be allowed to know while the current regime is in place.

## References

NB: Speeches and other publications authored by Kim Il Sung, Kim Jong Il and other ideologues in the DPRK are or were published in Pyongyang by the Foreign Languages Publishing House. They are, as is the regime's custom, republished frequently in many different collections; details are therefore omitted here.

Academy of Sciences (eds) (1988) *Choson ui minsok nori*, Seoul: P'urunsup (originally published in Pyongyang by the Institute of Archaeology, Academy of Sciences).

Bunge, Frederica M (ed.) (1981) *North Korea: A Country Study*, Washington, DC: Foreign Area Studies, American University.

Buzo, Adrian (1999) *The Guerilla Dynasty: Politics and Leadership in North Korea*, London: I.B. Tauris.

Foster-Carter, Aidan (1992) *Korea's Coming Unification: Another East Asian Superpower?*, London: Economist Intelligence Unit.

— (1994) *North Korea after Kim Il Sung*, London: Economist Intelligence Unit.

Han Chungmo and Chong Songmu (1983) *Chuch'e ui munye riron yon'gu*, Pyongyang: Sahoe kwahak ch'ulp'ansa.

Howard, Keith (1993), 'Where did the old music go?', *Minjok umakhak* (Journal of the Asian Music Research Institute, Seoul), 15: 122–51.

Kim Chang Ha (1984) *The Immortal Juche Idea*, Pyongyang: Foreign Languages Publishing House.

Kim Ch'oewon (1991a/b) 'P'i pada'-shik hyongmyong kaguk 1 and 2. *Chuch'e umak ch'ongso* 4 and 5, Pyongyang: Munye ch'ulp'ansa.

Kim Yol Kyu (1992) 'A study on the present status of folklore and folk arts in North Korea', *Korea Journal*, 32(2): 75–91.

Kim Yongsuk (ed.) (1987) *Choson umak chonjip*, Pyongyang: Munye ch'ulp'ansa.

Lee Byong Won (1993) 'Contemporary Korean musical cultures', in Donald N. Clark (ed.), *Korea Briefing 1993*, Boulder, CO: Westview, pp. 121–38.

Lee Chong-Sik (1963), 'Politics in North Korea: pre-Korean War Stage', in Robert A. Scalapino (ed.), *North Korea Today*, New York: Praeger, p. 9.

McDougall, Bonnie (1980) *Mao Zedong's Talks at the Yan'an Conference on Literature and Art*, Ann Arbor: University of Michigan Press.

No Tongun (1989) *Han'guk minjok umak hyondan'gye*, Seoul: Segwang umak ch'ulp'ansa.

Perris, Arnold (1985) *Music as Propaganda: Art to Persuade, Art to Control*, Westport, CT: Greenwood Publishing.

Pihl, Marshall R. (1993) 'Contemporary literature in a divided land', in Donald N. Clark (ed.), *Korea Briefing 1993*, Boulder, CO: Westview, pp. 79–98.

Ro Ikhwa (ed.) (1989) *Ri Myonsang chakkok chip*, Pyongyang: Munye ch'ulp'ansa.

Suh Dae Sook (1988) *Kim Il Sung: The North Korean Leader*, New York: Columbia University Press.

U Chang Sop (1988) *The Chamo System of Dance Notation*, Pyongyang: Foreign Languages Publishing House.

Umak toso p'yonjippu (eds) (1994) *Choson Kayo 2000 Kokchip*, Pyongyang: Munhak yesul chonghap ch'ulp'ansa.

Zhdanov, Andrei (1950) *Essays on Literature, Philosophy and Music*, New York: International Publishers.

# 6 | Burma: music under siege

AUNG ZAW

Music has provided a rallying point for the masses during political upheavals in Burma, just as it has elsewhere in South-East Asia. It has served as a potent response to the rapid political and social displacements brought on by neo-colonialism, industrialization and dictatorship.

Yet simultaneously, music has been appropriated to serve the Establishment by strengthening national cohesion, promoting entrenched power structures and spreading selected values and information to the multitudes.

Thanks to governments tolerant of criticism and Western musical styles, many musicians now enjoy freedom in their own countries. But musicians in the many Asian countries controlled by dictatorships have been silent for decades. Burma is one such country, where musicians and songwriters face severe censorship.

In Burma, the anti-British independence movement coalesced around songs such as 'Nagani' (Red Dragon), which promoted national pride, prosperity and education. 'Nagani' remains popular with the opposition movement today. The traditional and modern music that criticized repressive rule and political in-justices empowered South-East Asia's political movements, so it is no surprise that the region's authoritarian rulers frowned upon such melodious sounds.

Nevertheless, South-East Asia's dictators understood music's power. From Indonesia's Suharto to Burma's General Ne Win, they appropriated tunes and musicians to defuse political tensions while serving their own political agendas.

In the early 1970s, a tempestuous Ne Win stormed the Inya Lake Hotel near his lakeside residence. Infuriated by the caterwauling of Burma's only rock band, which was playing in a banquet hall at the time, the strongman kicked over the drums and screamed at a bewildered audience for revelling in the ear-splitting music.

Although serious political limitations remain, much of South-East Asia now enjoys greater freedom of expression in the media and in art. But over the past forty years, the attitudes of the Burmese regime have barely changed. The military junta maintains a close watch on musicians, artists and journalists through the draconian Press Scrutiny Board (PSB).

The PSB was inaugurated by Burma's late dictator General Ne Win in the early 1970s. Comprised of a group of Burmese intellectuals and prominent writers, its original purpose was to correct Burmese spellings. But it was later transformed into an agency charged with censoring all media content, including lyrics and songs. What is worse, the Ne Win regime later appointed retired army officers to head the agency. That the officers also happened to be writers made little difference. The agency expanded, more staff were appointed; and the government's intolerance towards criticism became visible in magazines, journals and cartoons.

The days of Ne Win are gone. But the new regime, now known as the State Peace and Development Council (SPDC), has only increased political repression and heavy-handed censorship. Led by generals, this council has been governing the country illegitimately for more than a decade. Under the rule of the SPDC, Burma was named an enemy of the press by international media watchdog groups. Its freedom of expression practically evaporated as the PSB developed even more structures to censor news as well as lyrics.

But it must be remembered that, once upon a time, Burma did enjoy press freedom and free expression.

*Press laws and regulations*

Burma's original 1947 constitution stipulated that citizens had the right 'to express freely their convictions and opinions'. The musicians, artists and journalists of Burma exercised this right to such a degree that, following the country's independence from the British, its press was regarded as one of the freest in Asia. Newspapers could report and comment on the country's affairs with little fear of reprisal. Musicians also faced little harassment or restrictions on content.

But when General Ne Win or 'Sun of Glory' seized power in 1962, this freedom began to wither. He established a Revolutionary Council (RC) comprised of army leaders to oversee the country's affairs. A confirmed xenophobe, the general banned Western music and dancing in an effort to preserve Burmese culture.

In his article 'Straight Outta Rangoon', Thailand-based journalist Shawn L. Nance writes:

> After seizing power in 1962, the military quickly moved to ban clubs featuring Western-style music – along with beauty contests and dance competitions – in order 'to preserve the Burmeseness of the culture'.
>
> The ban was only partially successful, as the emergence of rock music in

the late 1960s sparked an irrevocable trend that brought new socio-cultural tensions to the surface, and created rifts, not only between artists and authorities, but also between different generations of music fans. Burma's newest musical phenomena similarly reflect resentments against imposed discipline and reveal aspirations for cultural freedom. They also possess similar abilities to offend the ears and sensibilities of many, especially the older generation. (Nance 2002)

In 1962, the RC introduced a Printers and Publishers Registration Act, which led to the prosecution and imprisonment of many journalists and writers. Some newspapers and magazines were closed or nationalized, while foreign journalists and news agencies were kicked out of the country. This marked the beginning of the dark ages for information in Burma.

As nationalization took effect, the music industry in Burma also suffered a setback as the regime prohibited all export and import licences pertaining to music. Speaking on condition of anonymity, a Rangoon-based music producer says, 'Since we could not import musical instruments, recording equipment, long-play discs or even music magazines, the Burmese music industry suffered economically as well as technologically' (Zin 2002).

By then head of the Burmese Socialist Programme Party (BSPP), Ne Win drew up a new constitution in 1974. The constitution granted nominal freedom of expression, but all forms of public expression were subjected to the PSB to ensure that this expression took place only 'within the accepted limits of the "Burmese Way to Socialism"'. Article 157 of the 1974 constitution declares: 'Every citizen shall have the freedom of speech, expression and publication to the extent that such freedom is not contrary to the interest of the working people and socialism.' Thus the 'Burmese Way to Socialism' has simply been a pretext for the Burmese Way to Silence.

Under the State Protection Law, the Burmese government can declare a state of emergency in part or all of Burma 'with a view to protecting state sovereignty and security and public law and order from danger'. And in doing so it may also restrict any fundamental rights of citizens.

In the early 1970s, young Burmese began to appreciate pop music. But they could not hear it on Burma's state-run radio station. Myanmar Radio was on the air as early as 1936, while the British still ruled. This led to the formation of the Burma Broadcasting Service (BBS) in 1946, just before Burma regained its independence. A television system was introduced to Burmese audiences in the late 1980s. By then BBS was known as Myanmar Television and Radio. In 1997 it was renamed Myanmar Radio and Television (MRTV) under the Minis-

41

try of Information (ibid.). Despite the ban on Western music, it was gaining in popularity among young urban Burmese, including the sons and daughters of the reigning generals. But the audience was limited to those who could afford cassette players. Meanwhile, the state-run radio station had to operate under government supervision. The board of MRTV established certain criteria – including vocal quality and lyrics – for the selection of songs. And in most cases the board rejected Western-style compositions.

In his book *State of Fear*, Burma observer Martin Smith writes that when 'Ne Win banned all western music as "decadent", a popular underground culture known as "stereo" music sprang up to compete with the stylized "mono" music played on State radio'. Shawn Nance comments: 'Despite attempts by the conservative ruling class to nip Burmese pop music in the bud, however, technological changes worked in favour of the progressive forces. The new sound systems that music producers adopted in the 1970s contributed to a better audio quality. When the censor board refused to play their cover songs on the state-owned radio station, young musicians recorded those songs in private studios and distributed them through music production shops' (Nance 2002). Eventually these 'stereo' songs became very popular among young Burmese.

Unfortunately, as Ne Win and his authorities continued to crack down on dissent and press freedom, musicians also felt the heat. In the 1970s, the government went so far as to persecute musicians for wearing their hair long. In some cases, army soldiers forced university students to reduce their manes to crew cuts. They too were victims of Ne Win's campaign against 'Western culture' and 'stereo' music.

Nevertheless, the Burmese immediately embraced the music that was being privately produced and distributed.

Maung Thit Minn, a famous songwriter who began his career in the 1970s, said there was little pressure from PSB authorities at first. 'We had freedom to write and record as we liked,' says the composer from Rangoon. But later all materials, lyrics and covers had to be submitted to the government before recording could proceed.

The Central Registration Board asked publishers to heed the following regulations. They also applied to novels, journals and magazines, and would later apply even to songs. Officially barred is:

anything detrimental to the Burmese socialist programme;
anything detrimental to the ideology of the state;

anything detrimental to the socialist economy;

anything which might be harmful to national unity and solidarity;

anything which might be harmful to security, the rule of law, peace and public order;

any incorrect ideas and opinions which do not accord with the times;

any descriptions which, though factually correct, are unsuitable because of the time or the circumstances of their writing;

any obscene (pornographic) writing;

any writing which would encourage crimes and unnatural cruelty and violence;

any non-constructive criticism of the work of government departments;

any libel or slander of any individual.

## Pop music under the socialist regime

Despite the PSB regulations and a xenophobic leadership, 'stereo' songs became popular among city dwellers and would later spread to provincial towns. Burmese radio continued to refuse to play Western-style music, but not for long.

Although the Burmese-language service of the BBS continued to reject Western-style cover songs, many of the 'stereo-song' pioneers were able to reach a wider audience using the half–hour 'Local Talent' programme, aired by the BBS English service every Saturday night. By singing on the programme in English, artists such as Tony Hundley, Joyce Win, Marie Conway and Jimmy Jack would later become famous 'stereo' singers under the names Bo Bo Han, Nwe Yin Win, Tin Moe Khaing and Lasho Thein Aung (Zin 2002).

Unfortunately they were not singing original compositions. Instead they sang compositions from Western countries or neighbouring countries such as India, China and Japan.

A number of bands also emerged at about the same time. They were known as Electronic Machine, Playboy, The ELF, and The King. At long last, pop music had invaded Burma. Sensing this rising tide of popularity, authorities exploited pop music in their political campaigns.

Shawn Nance writes:

Interestingly, Burma's socialist dictators suddenly changed their tune and started using pop music for propaganda purposes. When the socialist regime planned to hold a referendum in 1973, they used stereo-style songs to mobilize mass support for their political agenda. One famous stereo singer, Aung Ko Latt, sang a song titled 'Let's Go to the Polling Booth', which was highly promoted by the government. Since the government did not have any intention to support the development of pop music except to use it for propaganda, Burmese pop music remained unable to enter into the mainstream state-owned media. (Nance 2002)

Thus the BSPP had given its unofficial approval of 'stereo' music. Only then did this underground phenomenon become popular and generally accepted.

In 1973, a band named Thabawa Yinthwenge (The Wild Ones) became well known among Burmese. One of its members was an ethnic Shan from Shan state, Sai Htee Saing. Singing Burmese songs with a distinct accent, he soon became a household name.

While he and his close friend Sai Kham Lait – also an ethnic Shan – were studying at Mandalay University, Htee Saing began singing at concerts and functions in the former capital. He was later persuaded to come down to Rangoon to record. It was the start of a new life for him.

Played day and night, Htee Saing's songs became popular not only among Shan but also among lowland Burmese. Many believe that those of Htee Saing's songs composed by Sai Kham Lait contained some discreet social message; nevertheless they became countrywide hits. The modest lyrics were often about love mixed with ruminations on life and struggle.

In the early days, some of Kham Lait's songs were about civil war and the struggles of life in his homeland. But as the PSB began to flex its muscles, Kham Lait had to avoid words such as 'smoke', 'guns' and 'peace'. And although the PSB carefully scrutinized his songs, his lyrics often contained

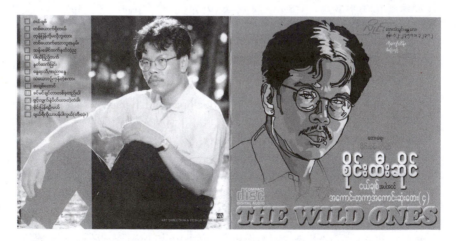

3  **The pop singer Sai Htee Saing's first album released in August 1982 (courtesy of Inya).**

political messages conveyed through hidden meanings. In this way he eluded the censors.

Despite this government straitjacket, Htee Saing was a very important phenomenon. He had helped pave the way for other ethnic singers, who have since become established figures in Burma's music industry. And, more importantly, his songs were original.

This led to the flourishing of so-called 'own tunes' bands and songs, which took their place alongside cover versions in the hearts of the Burmese. This explosion of music accorded well with Burma's popular tea culture, in which mostly male Burmese sit for hours in tea shops while chatting about everything, because in addition to selling tea, shop owners can play 'stereo' songs to attract more customers. Many tea shops in downtown Rangoon and its suburbs ply customers with 'stereo' songs. Customers even bring their favourite tapes to play. Owners able to afford the installation of powerful speakers can blast out the latest album, thereby guaranteeing that they will draw more customers than their competitors.

Khine Htoo, Khin Maung Toe and Khin One were among the first to sing original pop songs that became hits among young Burmese. Also emerging were many songwriters and musicians, such as Maung Thit Minn, Thukhamain Hlaing, Ko Ne Win, Ko Maung Maung and Ko Lay Lwin.

Indeed, the early 1970s were a time of relative freedom for musicians, singers and composers to produce their work without interference from the authorities. But this period was short lived. According to Maung Thit Minn, by the late 1970s producers were required to submit lyrics to PSB officials before recording.

Authorities began noticing some hidden or political meaning in the songs, said Maung Thit Minn. For instance, 'War and Peace', the signature song of the 1980s sensation Khine Htoo, never made it to the record store shelves because of its strong political bent. But it became one of his most requested songs in concert until the authorities banned him from performing it live. 'The authorities don't want the Burmese to be reminded of civil war and political struggle by the ethnic nationalities,' says Mun Awng, another famous singer of the late 1980s.

As Ne Win and his cronies continued to exercise dictatorial rule while finding few solutions for the deteriorating economy, it is understandable that they should funnel their helplessness into wrath against musicians and songwriters. Some famous composers of the 1970s complained that the government barred them from recording their songs.

Consider 'Scarecrow', a popular song among Burmese guitarists and singers. Because it describes soldiers fighting in the civil war, no one dares to sing it in public:

Dead or alive

Sacrificing my life for my country
Gold and silver, silver stars on my shoulder
Oh my friend, what honour and rewards I would get
My heart is crying
While my mouth was muzzled from telling the truth
A pierce through my eyes which have seen the truth
Oh my friend, I am a scarecrow in human form
Though I am alive, I am no longer living.

Also well known among musicians is the song 'Battle for Peace' by famous composer Ko Ne Win. But PSB officials rejected it and asked the producer to rewrite it. The PSB cited as inappropriate the song's use of the words 'blood', 'march' and 'enemy'. Here are the original lyrics:

Emerald lake flowing with cool and calm green water
Sing a song in soft melody
In a sleepless silent night
The red blood in brave step has marched on

In return for the lives sacrificed
A compelling chance has come to hand
To reap what we have sown
Time is ripe – don't lose it – we march to take the debt

No fear
Struggle will be on the path ahead
For our true cause and peace
The red blood in bravery
Has marched towards the enemy.

Mun Awng, a well-known singer of the late 1980s, is all too familiar with this protracted process. To get songs such as 'Demon's Rule/Man's Rule' by the censorship board, Mun Awng's producer would treat PSB officials to expensive dinners and a few thousand kyats. PSB officials, he says, 'have always been corrupt'.

But it is believed that nowadays the 'tea money' is much more substantial.

The celebrated movie star Kyaw Hein began singing cover versions in the 1970s and by the late 1980s was very popular. His songwriter was Maung Thit Minn. The songs were philosophical, religious and preoccupied with death. According to musicians, some of his songs were not approved. But his album was released because of tea money and his connection with high-ranking officials.

For example, Maung Thit Minn said that he did not know why the PSB passed the song 'Serious Discussion with Mom', which was fairly political. Popular among young and old Burmese alike, the song is about a conversation between a son and his mother. The son asks his mother to allow him to open a door because he wants to help the world and its people. The lyrics definitely inspired many young Burmese fed up with Ne Win's regime and the deteriorating economy. Ironically, they were written not by Maung Thit Minn; they are from the song 'Mama' by the band Genesis:

> I am your son – I am not a selfish person you know, Mom
> Oh please let me go Mom for the sake of world and people
> Please open the door, please do not stop me …
> I won't give up.

Maung Thit Minn says, 'I wrote [songs] because I felt like I was choking. I wanted the authorities to open the door for the people.'

The song 'Truth from Cemetery' is full of the meaning of life. Though it is gaudy, it appealed even to elderly Burmese. The melody was based on 'Money for Nothing' by Dire Straits:

> You can see people are pretending to cry while flapping fans
> Wonder when my turn is due who will come and cry like this
> I am a guest in the world
> What about you? What are you going to do?
> Be courageous
> Many will come and praise you after you die
> Now it is futile between cemetery and
> Greed, anger and human being.

Unable to sing some songs banned on stage or on cassette, Mun Awng, Khine Htoo and other singers found alternative venues in which to reach audiences. Women's dormitories at Rangoon University became a popular platform on which to express creative ideas, especially for unknown singers and musicians.

Marathon serenade sessions became customary. Groups of students would bring their guitars, banjos and violins to show off their abilities and hone their

musical skills, sometimes in the hope of impressing the dormitories' residents. It was common for the women to send complimentary food and snacks to
the troupes – via campus security guards – who would often continue singing
and playing until the small hours of the morning.

Singers are impelled to include a minimum of four 'constructive songs' on
their albums, and Mun Awng says that this weighs heavily on the conscience
of artists and audience alike: 'Whether we like it or not, we were forced to
write these songs.' In songbooks, producers were ordered to print some songs
praising the 'Burmese Way to Socialism' or the Tatmadaw 'Armed Forces'.
Authorities were jittery of any criticism as the country continued to face economic problems.

In 1987 the United Nations deemed Burma a Least Developed Country (LDC).
The 'Burmese Way to Socialism' was a total failure. As the country faced crisis,
writers and composers became critical of the government.

Meanwhile the government carefully scrutinized songs, lyrics, poems,
articles and novels that depicted the bleak economic and social problems in
Burma. This policy became increasingly heavy-handed until Burma faced a

4   **Mun Awng today lives in exile in Oslo, Norway, where he is engaged in the
movement for democracy in Burma (courtesy of *Irrawaddy* magazine).**

nationwide uprising in 1988. Ironically, the spark of the uprising was 'stereo' music being played at a tea shop near the Rangoon Institute of Technology (RIT).

In March 1988, RIT students sitting in a tea shop asked its owner to play a Sai Htee Saing tape. At another table were some local residents. They had requested a song by notable singer Kai Zar, and this was now playing. But the students insisted on Sai Htee Saing. Angered, the locals began to call Sai Htee Saing 'intellectual bullshit'.

A brawl broke out in which one student was injured, but the conflict did not end there. Students asked the police to take action against the locals, one of whom happened to be the son of a township chairman who was a member of the BSPP. His release angered students. Another fight broke out but this time it was political. Students at the forefront of Burma's political uprisings directed their ire against the incompetent government.

Riot police were deployed and students began chanting anti-government slogans. The BSPP government applied brutal force to break up the protests, the like of which they had not seen for many years.

When some students were killed, wider protests erupted in some universities and colleges in Rangoon. Thus began the nationwide 1988 democracy uprising that ushered in the demise of the Ne Win government.

## Censorship after the 1988 democracy uprising

The Burmese had enjoyed a brief spell of press freedom when millions of demonstrators marched down the streets in 1988. The country was in turmoil. Many local journals and newspapers began to cover so-called 'democracy news' without interference from the PSB. Musicians also joined the movement and sang 'democracy' songs. Interestingly, student union songs re-emerged. These songs had been banned since Ne Win demolished the Union Building with dynamite shortly after he came to power in 1962.

Musicians recorded and released pro-movement songs without consulting the PSB. Sadly their freedom was temporary. The military assumed power in September 1988. Many demonstrators were killed as troops dispersed the street protests in Rangoon and other major cities. With the rise of the SPDC, rule by iron fist had returned.

Under the SPDC, artists are asked to adhere to the government's national cause and four political objectives:

*National cause:*
1. Non-disintegration of the union.
2. Non-disintegration of national solidarity.

3. Consolidation of national sovereignty.

*Four political objectives:*

1. Stability of the state, community peace and tranquillity, prevalence of law and order.
2. National reconsolidation.
3. Emergence of a new guiding State Constitution.
4. Building of a new modern developed nation in accord with the new State Constitution.

Appointed by the new regime, PSB authorities paraded their skill at applying completely unclear guidelines to censor songs, poems, cartoons and articles. 'We cannot sing words like "human rights" or "democracy" in our songs. We cannot even sing "dark" or "tiny room",' says a songwriter in Rangoon.

The PSB formulated new regulations in addition to those already in place since the 1970s. Applying to VDOs (videos) and songs, the regulations addressed the following ten topics: politics, religion, ethnic minorities, the preservation of national culture, the preservation of morality, crime, violence, sex, obscenity and children.

Producers, but not singers, have to sign an agreement before recording and shooting VDOs. The agreement stipulates: 'If we do not follow these rules, it is our responsibility.' Maung Thit Minn says that love songs cannot use the word 'paradise' because it is not appropriate. Accordingly, he continues, songwriters prefer to write ambiguous lyrics, even when they are not political in nature. 'We don't write plainly. Therefore audiences can find meaning in the songs from different perspectives.'

SPDC authorities no longer require singers to sing 'constructive songs'; instead they bribe well-known singers to achieve their political objectives. Zaw Win Htut, one of Burma's most popular rock singers, was one of the victims of this policy.

Always performing before a packed house of admiring fans, Zaw Win Htut has become one of the country's wealthiest performers. In a recent interview he said that although he could afford to drive a luxury car like a BMW or Mercedes-Benz, he was aware that his fans must pinch pennies to buy his music. So he has endeared himself to the public by getting around town using his 1963 Chevy Impala.

The government decided to cash in on his fame by convincing him to croon propaganda tunes written by the military officer Mya Than San. Zaw Win Htut's release of *Maha*, an album chronicling the achievements of pagan dynasty kings, made him popular with the authorities but earned scorn from his fans. His popularity plummeted, and Zaw Win Htut's friends say that he won't dare repeat this mistake.

But his is not an isolated case. By employing 'divide and conquer' tactics on the musical battlefield, the regime has shown that it has a good ear for co-opting musicians and songwriters.

Sai Htee Saing would also succumb to the temptations of promoting government ideology. Like other musicians who have made the conscious decision to curry favour with the junta, he soon gained special privileges. Photos of the singer standing arm in arm with the generals were published in the state-run press. He sang songs written by Mya Than San, and as head of Burma's musicians' union he neglected the interests of the country's artists. So his audience quickly abandoned him.

'I bought his latest album out of curiosity,' admits one of his former fans. 'But I never listen to it.'

Tin Than Oo, now a high-ranking army officer, has been writing songs for the regime which implore listeners to maintain national unity and preserve the union spirit, to crush destructive elements and to promote the honourable role of the Tatmadaw.

Lay Phyu, the noted heavy-metal singer from Inle in Shan state, also landed himself in hot water – not with his fans, but with the authorities. In 1995 he released an album entitled *Power 54*, a thinly veiled reference to the University Avenue home address of opposition leader and Nobel laureate Aung San Suu Kyi. The authorities asked him to change the title, and the album was rereleased simply as *Power*.

A few years ago, Burma's esteemed pop singer Htoo Ein Thin released an album containing the song 'History's Bride', also known as 'Irrawaddy'. Once the song gained wide popularity the authorities realized it carried a political message. This discovery came too late to ban the album but Htoo Ein Thin has since been forbidden from performing this song in his concerts. The PSB learned a valuable lesson from this oversight and now exercises greater caution. It may take up to several months for the board to approve lyrics.

Since then officials have banned any songs about courageous women. They are afraid that the Burmese will be reminded of Aung San Suu Kyi. 'But you still can write about a woman, love and her beauty,' says Maung Thit Minn.

The movie star Kyaw Hein also fell out of the PSB's favour. Now in his fifties, in 1996/7 Kyaw Hein submitted songs written by Maung Thit Minn. Without giving any reason, the PSB did not approve them.

The word 'beggar' cannot appear in lyrics because, as one songwriter in Rangoon put it, the 'government doesn't believe that the country has beggars

51

but we have plenty of them [on the streets]'. Songwriters are also barred from writing about commodity prices or economic hardship. Words such as 'mother', 'dark', 'truth', 'blood' and 'rose' are prohibited without explanation. Songwriters and bands who tested the waters found that the government had zero tolerance.

Win Maw launched his music career in 1984 when he was a student at Rangoon University. But he soon found himself neglecting his studies. Instead he devoted his time to refining his craft as the lead guitarist for the amateur rock band Computer Control.

Eventually, Win Maw decided to leave school altogether to dedicate all his creative energies to the band, which included his only brother, Win Zaw, on bass. Although they never achieved great fame and fortune, Computer Control were talented enough to earn a nightly spot on the state-run Myanmar TV in 1994. As the use of the English language on Burmese television is strongly discouraged, Computer Control soon became known as Shwe Tan Zin, or Golden Melody. But the forced adoption of a new name elicited no complaints from the band, as the television spot afforded them the opportunity to reach a wider audience and keep their rock 'n' roll dreams alive.

But the pair's musical dreams turned into a nightmare in November 1996 when Burma's Military Intelligence Services (MIS) arrested the two brothers and Win Tin, the band's drummer. They were charged with singing anti-regime lyrics in remakes of Pink Floyd's 'Another Brick in the Wall' and Led Zeppelin's 'Stairway to Heaven'. Their music was subsequently banned from the airwaves, and in January 1997 the trio was sentenced to seven years' hard labour in prison.

Later that year, a group of musicians petitioned the SPDC for their release but their pleas were ignored. Win Tin served five years of his sentence at Tharawaddy Prison and was released on 16 August 2003. Win Zaw is currently serving out his sentence in Thayet Prison while his older brother Win Maw is being detained at Taungoo Prison

According to songwriters and producers in Rangoon, new singers prefer singing love songs to courting such severe punishments. 'No one wants to fight with the authorities. Producers are scared to death,' says a prominent songwriter who asked that his name be withheld.

Maung Thit Minn agrees that although many songwriters would like to write realistic and thoughtful songs, singers ask them to write love songs instead. 'We practise self-censorship, knowing which lyrics will be approved by the censor board,' he says.

He adds that the youth in Burma today like to listen to love songs. Singers also like to sing these repetitive songs about love triangles. Fearing reprisals from the censor board, young singers shun philosophical songs of the kind that Kyaw Hein and Khine Htoo sang in the past.

Singers and composers say that although many young people still prefer to listen to pop music, they are increasingly interested in hip-hop or alternative/modern rock. Sophisticated Rangoon residents tend to prefer modern rock and hip-hop, while suburban and rural people prefer songs with simple melodies. 'They are easy to mimic,' says Maung Thit Minn. But he adds that appreciation of music among the Burmese has not yet matured. 'Many Burmese prefer a mixed variety of songs – pop, country, rock and blues.' Many young performers still favour cover versions. 'Sleeping Child' by the band Michael Learns to Rock, for example, is sung with modified lyrics by five different Burmese bands.

Listeners also remain divided in their preference for covers or original songs. Shawn Nance writes: 'Some original composers have complained about music fans' preference for cover songs. They also accuse singers and cover songwriters of being complacent, putting moneymaking ahead of creativity' (Nance 2002).

'Singing cover songs is certainly the easiest way to achieve popularity and make money. But it's shameful. You could never sell rendition albums in the international market,' says an angry 'own tunes' composer who asked to remain anonymous.

Thukhamein Hlaing, Burma's best-known cover songwriter, offers a more forgiving view: 'You can't blame cover songs for the underdevelopment of Burmese original music. Cover songs have played a very important role in helping to improve Burmese fans' musical sensibilities.'

### Burma's powerful music council

Today the regime is more sophisticated in its dealings with musicians, who are already cowed into submission in any case. In the early 1990s, it established a 'music council' – known as Myanmar Music Asiayon (MMA) – whose members are prominent Burmese artists and singers. Ne Win's BSPP also established a music council but its SPDC incarnation is different.

The MMA is headed by SPDC cronies and sympathizers, and has been under the control of the military intelligence unit. The dreaded intelligence chief and 'Secretary One' General Khin Nyunt, who is chairman of social, educational and health organizations, often comes to 'observe' MMA functions and ceremonies and to give 'necessary instructions'. He is also a patron of the Leading Committee to Organize the Myanmar Traditional Cultural Performing Arts Competitions.

On 23 January 2003, Khin Nyunt attended a course in international music and the opening ceremony of the MMA, as reported in the official news organ *New Light of Myanmar*.

Then Secretary One told the crowd:

> Nowadays, artists and artistes including those of the new generation and the entire people are energetically protecting, preserving and promoting the traditions and culture, arts, literature, traditional mode of dress, and customs with patriotism under the leadership of the State.
>
> The conducting of the courses like these serves as a bridge between the Myanmar music and international music. This can be regarded as a good precedent. Thus, the Myanmar Music Asiayon should continue to conduct the courses. Based on patriotism, the new generation is required to preserve and promote the traditions and culture, arts, literature, Myanmar mode of dress and customs. The new generation and the doyen artists and artistes will have to harmoniously relay and promote the cultural heritage. The Myanmar Music Asiayon is required to preserve the cultural heritage and promote it till reaching the international level.

The head of the MMA is 'Accordion' Ohn Kyaw, a well-known singer in his sixties and a regime sympathizer. Two more powerful members of the MMA's ruling council are the singers and musicians Gantgawtaw Myo Aung and Hanzada Myint Wai.

Having these three figures in the council is very useful for the regime, as they serve as the eyes and ears of its censorship board. The council is powerful because all lyrics must now go through it before getting approval from PSB officials. Now the PSB need not strain to decode the meanings of 'suspicious' songs or lyrics; instead pro-government musicians do the lion's share of the work for them. Without the blessing of Ohn Kyaw and his partners, lyrics and songs won't be approved by the PSB.

A few years ago, some artists revolted against Ohn Kyaw's chairmanship and consequently found themselves in hot water. Disgusted by his attitude and alleged corruption, they sent General Khin Nyunt a petition letter seeking his removal before the council's annual election. The rebellion was led by the composer Win Min Htwe and the rock singer Lay Phyu, as well as by Min Chit Thu and Ko Myint Moe.

In addition to sending the letter, musicians attended a state-sponsored function where they donated hundreds of thousands of kyats to one of the renovation projects organized by the government. Officials exploited this unusual appearance, and the following day the state-run papers published a photo of the musicians and generals.

But the general who came to power through the barrel of a gun didn't much care for this rebellion in the MMA. In a blatant display of government favour, Ohn Kyaw, Myo Aung and Myint Wai were re-elected to the council in 2002. The council's annual election is always attended by the regime's information minister, who observes the whole election process and ensures that the government's agenda is followed.

As for the petitioners, Win Min Htwe, Min Chit Thu, Myint Moe and Lay Phyu, they were expelled from the council. After Ohn Kyaw was re-elected, they were also banned from singing or writing songs. Though they were issued with no written prohibition, it was understood that their expulsion from the council precluded the consideration of their songs by the PSB. This, according to Ohn Kyaw, was fit 'punishment' for the rebels. Nevertheless, Win Min Htwe can still write songs for movies and is allowed to publish poems and articles in magazines.

Meanwhile Ohn Kyaw and his hard-core council members continue to conduct business as usual, all in the service of their masters' objectives. Consider this news from a June 2000 issue of *New Light of Myanmar*. The headline reads 'Basic Music Course No. 1 Concludes, Course No. 2 Opens':

The conclusion of Basic Music Course No. 1 and the opening of Course No. 2 were held in Myananda Hall of the MMA in Dagon Myothit Seikkan Township on 4 June. The MMA sponsored courses in traditional performing arts and international music composition. Formed under the reign of the State Peace and Development Council, the MMA comprises all strata of the music world. Due to the government's assistance and MMA efforts, the latter [the hall] became the first of its kind in Myanmar: a place where musicians could enjoy recreation, discuss matters for the good of Myanmar's musical community, and practise music with the goal of propagating Myanmar's traditional music. Of particular significance is the construction of the Gita Beikman [Music Pavilion] building, where musicians and artistes can hold meetings and organize stage shows. The simultaneous emergence of two Gita Yeikmyouns [Buildings] for the very first time in Myanmar musical history is an effort of which musicians and artistes can be proud.

*You are what you wear*

Songs are not the only target of government censorship. Even stage and TV apparel is censored according to whether or not it 'preserves Burmeseness'. Musicians and singers who have chosen career survival over artistic integrity can expect invitations to perform at military fund-raising concerts, on the front lines to entertain soldiers, or on state-run Myanmar TV. But they have to be careful what they wear. Otherwise they may not be allowed to appear on stage or TV for some years.

In particular, female performers are barred from wearing earrings, skirts, fancy necklaces and bracelets. They are not allowed to dye their hair, and tattoos are taboo. Singers may not shake their bodies 'inappropriately' – as determined by the Myanmar TV censorship board.

Shawn L. Nance writes: 'Artists can expect to be forced to wear their hair short and uncoloured, restrict their dance movements to the casual and keep their earrings at home' (Nance 2002). But when performing live some liberties can be taken. As one popular rapper said, 'We can do and wear whatever we want.'

As if dress were not enough, authorities are even sensitive about colours. Singers appearing on Myanmar TV are not allowed to wear red because the censorship board unofficially deems it a 'political colour'. Yellow is also prohibited. Authorities say it represents the opposition and its leader Aung San Suu Kyi. Though Suu Kyi never announced that yellow was her favourite or her party's official colour, exiled activists once launched a campaign asking people in Burma to wear yellow to show their opposition.

Formality is important on Burmese TV too. Singers are not allowed to wear jeans, and if they appear in Western dress their bodies must be fully covered. Finally, the American flag may not be shown at all, nor can American T-shirts bearing certain numerals, e.g. 69 or 37.

One Burmese singer recalled that she had to leave a TV station after the censorship board decided that her dress was too Western. Having brought no extra clothes, she had to cancel her programme and return home in humiliation.

Military generals are undoubtedly the ones who run the show. Last year General Khin Nyunt made a speech at the presentation ceremony of the Seventh Performing Arts Competitions. He said that the Burmese should welcome the introduction of new styles into Myanmar traditional dance in accordance with the changing times. But the innovations should not be allowed to overwhelm original national characteristics. In other words, these characteristics must be left untouched. He continued: 'Even with the emergence of active, lively and vibrant innovative creations, it will be necessary to present more supple, pliant and graceful movements of our own national character of Myanmar dance.'

Three of the six objectives of the Myanmar Traditional Cultural Performing Arts Competitions are:

to perpetuate genuine Myanmar music, dance and traditional fine arts;
to preserve Myanmar national character;
to prevent the influence of alien culture.

The above-mentioned three objectives relate directly to the directive given by Secretary One. We should always pay serious attention to, profoundly observe and realize the three objectives. In other words, we should all uphold the objectives as the State's policy and the basic principle of the Competitions.

Khin Nyunt isn't alone. Senior General Than Shwe, who as chairman of the SPDC is Burma's most powerful leader, also encouraged the Burmese to preserve their culture and gave them guidance in that direction. At the concluding ceremony of Management Course No. 5 for Executives of the Union Solidarity and Development Association he remarked: 'You, the trainees, should preserve and safeguard the national culture. You must be modest, and all in all, you should stay away from immodest modes of living including wearing indecorous dresses. In other words, you should preserve and safeguard the national culture with national conviction.'

*New Light of Myanmar* elaborated on this as follows:

The guidance highlights the need to observe the law of modesty and to abstain from immodesty. We should observe modesty in our way of dressing and living and in our actions including the dance performance. There is an adage, which says 'Music adorns sound, sculpture adorns things, and dance adorns movements.' Thus, dance which is also an act of movement should not be immodest.

However, time and again, we are seeing threats against our genuine traditional dance and cultural traits. We should avoid doing things that may harm our genuine traditional dance and cultural traits. Especially, we must be careful that our traditional dance is not overwhelmed by the Indian dance, ballet, disco, tango and break dance. Indecent acts such as acting like a model girl and giving come-hither looks again and again will harm the national character. It is required for all the dance numbers to be free from immodest actions.

Artists are asked to attend some state-sponsored functions and cash donation ceremonies. For example, in March 2001 a ceremony was held at Tatmadaw Guest House, where Khin Nyunt received donations from artists' councils. The cash was for retired military veterans. The *New Light of Myanmar* said, 'There were lots of donors, including Myanmar Motion Picture, Music, Thabin [Festival] and Traditional Artists and Artisans Asiayons, social organizations, private donors and companies who came to give donations with much generosity.' In fact, many cash donation ceremonies were pre-arranged, with people being asked to donate set amounts of money.

## Burma's rap and hip-hop under the SPDC

In the late 1990s, rap and hip-hop music took off among the youth of Burma. Easily spotted in the streets of Rangoon are young and energetic Burmese wearing New York Yankees baseball caps turned backwards. But on VCDs and the local variation of MTV, this is not the case. Here the backward caps are banned.

Shawn L. Nance describes this scene in Rangoon:

> As show time nears, hundreds of Rangoon's hippest youngsters file into the amphitheatre jostling each other for a clear view of the stage. The carnival-like atmosphere is reinforced by scores of young women with dyed hair and mini-skirts that attract the attention of men donning denim jeans and t-shirts, some holding a can of Tiger Beer in one hand and a London cigarette in the other. Burmese *longyis* are conspicuously absent this evening. Occasionally the pungent odour of marijuana wafts by while some men are doubled over on the grass reeling in the effects of too much alcohol. Dozens of security guards stand watch. Everybody seems to know each other. (Nance 2002)

Burma's rap pioneer Myo Kyawt Myaing recites his lyrics:

> My name is Myo Kyawt Myaing
> I'm from Seven-Mile
> My father is U Kyawt Myaing and he is a pilot ...
> I have a lot of temporary girlfriends that I used to hang out with
> As everybody knows, as everybody knows, as everybody knows.

Some music observers say that Burma's rap and hip-hop are less political than they are elsewhere in the world. Again, this is due to censorship and the fear that songs critical of the country's situation will be rejected. 'They have practised self-censorship,' says Soe Thein, a veteran writer on music. However, some say that the rap and hip-hop songs accurately reflect the emotions of the younger generation.

Nance writes:

Burmese Rap and Hip-Hop music is in fact less about overt expressions of political and social discontent than it is an artistic stance. The fresh fashions may make cultural conservatives cringe but the content of the songs has yet to earn much contempt from government censors. Lyrics urge listeners to avoid playing the lottery, or heap scorn upon bad teachers, or confront the challenges of growing up. Writers admitted that they don't want to risk writing political lyrics but rather stick to love and life.

Like most Rap and Hip-Hop musicians in Burma, Myo Kyawt Myaing recites his lyrics, not to original tunes, but to remakes of famous American rappers such as Dr Dre, Eminem, Snoop Doggy Dogg, and, most surprisingly, NWA (Niggaz With Attitude) whose seminal 1988 single, 'F-Tha Police', is often credited for launching the sub-genre, Gangsta Rap. The controversial single's combination of profane bitterness towards racial inequality with anti-systemic gun-toting bravado elicited complaints from the FBI. (ibid.)

## The market and piracy

Rather than music schools run by the government, Burma has only private schools founded by guitarists and musicians. And even these schools are few and underdeveloped. Their students are energetic, but the lack of facilities and proficient trainers hampers their talents and enthusiasm. Serious and professional musicians are forced to order the latest songs and musical literature from friends who live abroad.

Musicians complain that opportunities are limited. And in part this is because the market for music in Burma is small. Burma has a population of 50 million; a best-selling musician might sell between 100,000 and 300,000 copies of a given tape. These days, cassettes sell for 600 kyats and CDs for 1,800. But since the 'stereo' songs became popular in 1970s, piracy has also boomed. Nance writes: 'Music pirates also cut deeply into the legal market. Zaw Paing, one of Burma's best selling artists of all time, sold over 300,000 copies of his hit album, *Myo Ah Win Nya* – a phenomenon that happens only once every five or six years. He also sold nearly 10,000 karaoke VCDs. But much to Zaw Paing's chagrin, buyers purchased nearly five times as many bootlegged copies of the album' (ibid.).

The government has a policy regarding VDO (video) piracy – a convicted pirate faces three years in prison – but none for audio. At Yuzana Plaza in downtown Rangoon, people are free to purchase pirated CDs and tapes. Musicians feel powerless to counter piracy.

And composers receiving small amounts of money for their work say that they have been treated unfairly. In 1971 a composer received 25 kyats per song; by 1980 this had risen to 100 kyats; by 1988 the figure was 500 kyats. Maung Thit Minn, who wrote a whole album for Kyaw Hein, received 300 kyats per song. At the time, a schoolteacher's salary was no more than 400 kyats per month.

After the 1988 political upheaval, the inflation rate rose and the pay for songs rose accordingly. Today, a songwriter receives 50,000 kyats per song and a singer 300,000 per song. But when Kyaw Hein attempted to buy the songs composed for him in 1996, he had to pay the current rate. As always, the producers turn a profit.

Burmese musicians cannot depend on copyright. Their musicians' union is riddled with government sympathizers and no longer represents the interests of the artists. So the musicians have little recourse when it comes to airing their grievances or claiming their due profits.

But a glimmer of hope has come in the form of a new FM radio station run by Rangoon's municipal government. The station went on the air in January 2002 and broadcasts from 7 a.m. to 7 p.m., playing Burmese pop music most of the time. 'It is an oasis in the desert,' says Thukhamein Hlaing. 'But since it is only for the Rangoon area, it is still just a drop in the bucket.' Currently the station is operated by Kyi Min Thein and Min Chit Thu.

## Music for the masses

Musicians in Burma are in a straitjacket. They understand the power of music but they are unable to display their skills and talents. The development of the music industry in Burma is hampered not only by a lack of resources but also by decades of political deadlock and military misrule.

Even attempts by musicians to address social issues such as HIV/AIDS are obstructed by conservative officials. Zaw Win Htut is a rock singer who recently performed at a concert sponsored by the United Nations Drug Control Programme the (UNDCP) at the Strand Hotel in Rangoon. Speaking to the BBC Burmese-language service during a recent visit to London, he said, 'I'll seek permission to hold outdoor concerts when I get back to Burma so that we musicians can join and work together for social betterment. I believe in the power of music.'

Meanwhile, many musicians in Burma complain that holding such outdoor concerts is becoming more difficult. Yet some still hope to organize a big open-air event to increase HIV/AIDS awareness and deliver an anti-drugs message to young people. 'Young people are now seeking an outlet for their frustrations. They need to be persuaded to channel their potential for betterment. We as singers have a responsibility,' says Zaw Win Htut.

But Mun Awng has preferred not to yield to government pressure. Instead he went into exile to sing his songs and wear his clothes without restriction and fear of censorship.

As musicians, Mun Awng and others both observed and participated in Burma's political upheaval. Throughout South-East Asia's history, music has been used to challenge corrupt, exploitative and unresponsive regimes. And so it has been in Burma. Songs such as 'Scarecrow', 'War and Peace' and 'History's Bride' helped the voiceless articulate strong resistance to military rule; and they served as a means of communication outside the anodyne state-run press and government-sponsored music. Music uniquely combines political realities with feelings and emotions. And though the military junta still toils to muzzle its critics, no doubt the music will play on long after the regime is silenced for ever.

## References

Nance, Shawn L. (2002) 'The Hard and Soft of It', *The Irrawaddy*, 10(7).

Zin, Min (2002) 'Burmese Pop Music: Identity in Transition', *The Irrawaddy*, 10(7).

# 7 | Uighuristan: politics and art

KURASH SULTAN AND MARIE KORPE

'Kurash' means 'fight'. Kurash Sultan, composer and musician, has been fighting for a separate state for the Uighurs, a Muslim minority group living in East Turkistan or Xinjian, a province in the north-western part of China. Xinjian was part of East Turkistan, which before 1884 and during 1933–34 and 1944–49 formed an independent state.

Kurash is one of the most popular artists in his home country, and his songs are known by almost every Uirghur. His fellow countrymen consider him a symbol of the fight for freedom. In 1993 he was sentenced to nine months' imprisonment because of his songs, which promoted an autonomous Uighuristan (East Turkistan).

During the 1980s Kurash made his breakthrough in his home country. At the age of twenty-nine he won a national song competition and became famous overnight. At the time he was a first-year student at the music conservatory in the capital, Urumchi. The following year he toured all over China, playing with his eighteen-man band. They performed over a thousand gigs and won awards in big music competitions, among them the prestigious Yellow Dragon Cup.

At this time he began to write new songs about his home country, Uighuristan, and this was the beginning of the end of his career and his popularity, at least in China. He had become more aware of politics, and the effects of the Chinese occupation of Uighuristan. During the Cultural Revolution in China the government attempted to dilute the Muslim population by settling masses of Han Chinese there, and replacing Muslim leaders. The area has good oil reserves and is today of great economic importance to China.

Kurash took a job at a cultural magazine in Urumchi and in his free time started to record his new material on cassette, distributing these himself. The songs soon became very popular, he says. Their lyrics sought freedom for Uighuristan from Chinese occupation. One of the songs, 'Do Not Sell Your Land', tells of the farmers who sold their land to the Chinese. 'The Chinese government moved many "robber" troupes to East Turkistan to control the area. They have bought large areas of land from poor farmers in East Turkistan during the past fifty to a hundred years. This is why I wrote my song "Do Not Sell Your Land",' Kurash says.

The song 'Guests' refers to a speech made by Mao when China annexed Uighuristan in 1949.

> Guests,
> Guests keep coming here,
> I give them my food,
> Then I have no food left
> Guests cannot give back.

'Mao insisted that we should see China as a guest in our country,' Kurash says. 'They said that after a time, when all was going well in Uighuristan, they would leave our country. We would again become an autonomous region. But in reality we became a colony. Mao's speech and promises are something all Uighurs remember.'

As the popularity of his songs grew, so he attracted increasing attention from the Chinese authorities. His music was banned and he was no longer allowed to appear in the media or perform his songs in public.

'The people who sold my cassettes were put in prison or had to pay a fine of thirty thousand yuan. People who listened to the cassettes had to pay a fine of three thousand yuan or go to prison for anything from three months up to three years. I was also living under strict surveillance. I lost my right to sing songs, perform and write poetry. That was very difficult for me. I started to produce soap to support myself and my family.'

In 1996, shortly after the Chinese authorities ordered a three-year house arrest, Kurash decided to flee the country with the help of friends. For a couple of years he moved between different countries in central Asia, finally settling in Kyrgyzstan. He continued to compose freedom songs with an even sharper edge than before. New titles such as 'Wake Up, Uighuristan' were brought out on audio cassette and large numbers were smuggled into his home country by people travelling across the borders.

But the powerful Chinese authorities reacted. After massive political lobbying from China, the Kyrgyz authorities arrested Kurash, who was put in jail. 'I published four cassettes in Kyrgyzstan but following a Chinese request I was jailed for nine months there. People have asked me if I could sing in the jail. No, I did not sing, but I howled under the beating and torture. It is a tragedy, happening in this supposed five-thousand-year "great civilization" called China.' According to Kurash, this happened 'because the Chinese are afraid of the independence movement for free East Turkistan'.

While in jail Kurash applied for political asylum, and through the UN he travelled to Sweden and was granted asylum in 1999. He continues to work in exile for the liberation of Uighuristan, and concludes: 'In my country Uighuristan the artists have worked for the party and art is only connected to the political party. For the Uighurs, not only daily activities but also feelings are controlled by the party through various tools.

'I love life and nature and that's why I love art. To me art is the most holy, most significant and most valuable thing in life. An artist's tragedy becomes art's tragedy, and art's tragedy destroys humanity. Today my art is not for the sake of art, but it is political art. My aim is to inspire people to justice, reality and freedom. What I'm trying to say is that in one of my hands I carry art, in the other politics. These are the two sides of me as a person. These evil things have come from the ferocious Chinese policy, and they will continue until we have justice.'

THREE | **Africa**

# 8 | Stopping the music: censorship in apartheid South Africa

ROGER LUCEY

When Marie Korpe asked us, as participants of the 2nd World Conference on Music and Censorship, to contribute articles for a book, I wished I had a hole in the floor to crawl into. I'd spent the best part of a week in the company of some of the finest and most honest academics I'd ever had the pleasure to meet. You see, I didn't even finish high school and I'd been invited to the conference purely on the basis of some incidents in my past that had become the subject of a documentary film. So I've written a very personal account of the process that led to me being invited in the first place. I'll leave the analysis and conclusions to you.

'Shit, my feet are killing me.'

My companion, Paul, is a heavy-set guy, in many ways typically South African with a healthy beer belly and a shock of thick grey hair.

'Would it be better if you took the boots off?' I ask.

'No, the bloody blisters are right on the soles of my feet,' he answers, his life-battered face clearly showing pain.

'Let's try and get to a café and we can sit and take it easy for a while.' I can't think of much else to suggest.

And so we carry on ambling down the banks of the Rhine on a beautiful autumn day in Frankfurt.

We finally arrive at a medieval square between the city centre and the river and take our places at a pavement café, wasting no time in getting ourselves a pair of bitterly cold beers. As the afternoon wears on, the headiness of several beers prompts us to tell stories about the past, and we sit and laugh out loud as we reminisce about the strange way in which our paths crossed – two slightly tubby middle-aged men enjoying a sunny European afternoon before returning to that land which is so strange and infuriating and painfully beautiful and compelling: South Africa. Nothing odd about that.

But Paul Erasmus is an ex-security policeman from the ranks of South Africa's much feared and loathed secret police force, who twenty years earlier had quietly and covertly changed the course of my life.

I had been a singer and songwriter plying my trade in the clubs and on the alternative stages of South Africa's very healthy music scene. But I was obsessed with the worsening political situation which was instilling fear in the hearts and souls of all South Africans. I started becoming known in the music scene around 1976, at about the time of the Soweto riots, and many of my songs reflected the social situation I found myself in. Add to this a big voice and a bigger attitude, especially with a couple of drinks in my belly before hitting the stage, and what you had was a loud-mouthed, long-haired kid raging against the government, the army, the police and any other fascist icon I came across. I knew I'd get into big shit sooner or later, but the way it happened was so weird, and even weirder was the fact that I only found out the truth of what happened fourteen years later, thanks to Paul Erasmus.

In July 1995, I was doing a show at the National Arts Festival in the Eastern Cape frontier town of Grahamstown. July in Grahamstown is when the winter bites hardest, and after the shows performers and festival-goers crowd the pubs and restaurants looking for warmth and company. It was a Friday night at the Cathcart Arms, and I met up with an old muso friend, the late, great James Phillips. James was already well oiled and the first thing he said to me was, 'Hey, you didn't need those cops to fuck up your music career, you were doing a great job of that yourself.' He was referring to a drug problem I'd developed in the early eighties.

'What are you talking about, you old drunk?' I asked.

He fished around in his bag and produced a copy of the South African alternative newspaper the *Mail and Guardian*.

Inside was a story about an ex-security policeman who was blowing the whistle on all the evil, secret things he had been doing and the high-up government officials who had ordered him to do it. Remember, 1994 was the year of SA's first democratic election, the Truth and Reconciliation Commission was in full flight and all sorts of stuff was coming out of the woodwork. The article included a chapter from a book Erasmus was writing in which he gave a detailed description of how he systematically went about shutting up the noisy, bothersome Roger Lucey – tapping my telephone, intercepting my mail, threatening club owners and record executives and conducting armed raids on my house. All this fourteen years after I finally accepted defeat and (apart from the odd performance) got into another line of work.

At the time I knew nothing of these shenanigans – or rather, I knew something was going on and that I was being targeted but I could never get any evidence. Obviously the raids on my house were pretty up front, but lots of 'lefties' got raided all the time, and because I'd been a bit of a dopehead I thought they could have been related to my bohemian ways rather than my political beliefs.

But none of the club owners or the record people ever admitted that they were getting leaned on by the cops. So in the end, with a broken marriage, a habit and my tail between my legs, I started trying to build a new life.

There was a certain comfort in reading the *Weekly Mail* article. In a way I felt exonerated and relieved that maybe my demise fourteen years earlier had not necessarily been because I was a crap musician. And so life carried on.

In 2001 I was working as the production manager (news) for a new national broadcaster based in Cape Town. I was on a deadline, and as with any new television station things would always go wrong just as the news was about to go on air. One particular evening my mobile phone rang, as it did every twenty seconds in the last thirty minutes before news hour. On the line was a voice that was vaguely familiar.

'Hello, Roger, it's Paul Erasmus here.'

I instantly thought it was one of my mates playing a joke on me. But my humour levels were not very high in the midst of trying to sort out all manner of chaos and get a news bulletin on air, so I let him have it with a high volume of choice Cape dialect insults, which included many references to his mother.

But he persisted. 'No, Roger, it really is me.'

I went silent for a few seconds. Now I recognized the voice. Erasmus had appeared often on TV newscasts over the previous years in connection with his submissions to the Truth and Reconciliation Commission. I knew his face and his voice well but had never met him in the flesh.

'Howzit, Paul, how ya doing?' I couldn't think of anything else to say. 'Um ... Hey, sorry about the insults, I thought it was a friend being silly.'

'No, that's all right. Listen, man, I just wanted to say that I'm really sorry about what happened back then. I know it probably doesn't mean much now but ... I just wanted to say sorry.'

He sounded awkward, and I was in a state of shock. The craziness of the newsroom receded into a kind of slow-motion disconnectedness.

'No, that's cool, Paul, I guess we all did what we thought was right and, um ... no, it's cool, really.'

I felt really stupid. Here was a person who had had a massively damaging effect on my life and all I could say was 'No, that's cool.'

'Listen, I wonder if you would do me a favour. My fifteen-year-old son lives with me, you know his mom divorced me when the shit hit the fan, and anyway he suffers from multiple sclerosis and he's a big fan of your music. Would you mind saying hello to him?'

'No problem, put him on.'

A quiet little voice came on the line, with that soft half-Afrikaans accent common to many kids who live in small South African towns.

'Hello, Uncle Roger, it's Dylan here. My dad said he was going to talk to you. I really like your songs, I've been listening to them since I was little.'

I had goose bumps all over my body. We carried on talking for a while then Paul got back on the line and we said goodbye.

Some time later, a sociologist from Rhodes University in Grahamstown by the name of Michael Drewett called me. I'd met him before; in fact he did his masters thesis on music and resistance in South Africa and he'd interviewed me. This time he was calling to say that he'd been researching the Roger Lucey/Paul Erasmus story and that he'd received a grant from a Danish organization called Freemuse to make a documentary about what had happened.

'Paul has agreed to participate and tell his side of the story. How would you feel about telling it from your side?'

The fact is that from my side the whole saga had been going round and round in my head and the whole affair felt like a huge chunk of unfinished business. So, after a short think, I thought it would probably be a good way to finally put the whole thing to bed for good. And I'd finally get to meet Paul.

When I did get to meet him it was an experience that filled me with a myriad of conflicting thoughts, ideas and feelings. Michael and the director, Doug Mitchell, arranged the meeting in a bar called the Devonshire that was frequented by cops and other undesirables during those dark years, and which was just around the corner from a little club called 'Mangles' where I first made my musical name. These joints are in the Johannesburg suburb of Braamfontein, near the University of Witwatersrand, and the place holds many powerful memories of my early years as a young muso.

As I drove into Braamfontein for the meeting, I was flooded with many of these memories, of the friends and colleagues who had died at the hands of the police, and my own rise and then sudden fall from grace. My hands were sweating wildly as I met Michael and Doug outside the Devonshire. They explained that Paul was already in the pub with the camera crew and I was to wait in the service passage and come into the pub when they called.

'OK, you can come!'

The two cameras were set up at the end of the long narrow bar room. Paul was sitting at the bar, leaning on one elbow.

I don't know what came over me, but as soon as I saw him I burst into laughter. Not of a derisive or cynical nature. Maybe it was laughter of relief.

'Howzit, Roger. Listen, man, I've already started on a whisky, I was so nervous, man, and I got a beer for you.'

I took a deep slug of the beer and we got chatting.

Later that afternoon we all went down to the Market Theatre, where I'd had some of my most memorable concerts. Alone on an empty stage, I played one of my old songs for the solitary member of the audience, Paul Erasmus.

A short while later I received an e-mail from Marie Korpe of Freemuse inviting me to the world première of the documentary to be screened at the 2nd World Conference on Music and Censorship in Copenhagen. Also attending would be my old friend and music producer/publisher David Marks, Michael Drewett and Paul Erasmus. It sounded like an event I'd be a fool to miss.

We landed in Copenhagen after a slightly boozy and uneventful flight and were surprised to be met by a man in a suit carrying a small South African flag. He turned out to be the first secretary of the SA embassy, Machiel van Niekerk. I remembered Machiel from the bad old days when he worked for a conservative Afrikaans daily newspaper in Johannesburg. Talk about the wonders of being a South African! With Machiel was a tall, slightly bohemian-looking man called John Hansen, originally from South Africa but who had gone into exile in the early seventies and was one of the movers and shakers of the early anti-apartheid movement. John took us on a tour of the delightful Christiana area of Copenhagen and he and I just couldn't stop yakking, about mutual friends from the old days, life in present-day SA, music, art. When I told him a few choice South African jokes he almost wet himself with laughter. We spent some great time with Machiel and John and even got to have lunch with the South African ambassador, a charming old man who had spent most of his life in exile in London.

The first event of the conference was the screening of *Stopping the Music*, the documentary about Paul and me. We arrived at the Royal Danish Film Institute after a short walk from the hotel and took our seats in the auditorium. I sat next to Paul. Ole Reitov of Freemuse said a few words; the lights went down and *Stopping the Music* started rolling. I won't say too much about my experience during that super-charged, roller-coaster ride of an hour, but even now, almost six months later, the memory of it sends shivers through my body.

And then came the conference and functions during which I met a whole array of truly wonderful people from every nook and cranny of this fascinating globe: listening to the stories of musicians in their quest for truth and justice and understanding the power of music and song; hearing the pure solo voice of Amal Murkus – even those of us from the southernmost tip of Africa could feel and understand the passion and pain that this great singer conveys; and Marcel Khalife, just him and his oud, with songs that silenced the hall, notwithstanding the fact that so few could speak the language of his songs. What a rare pleasure to share so much with so many people in so short a time, crossing so many barriers, connecting so many divergent points. And the nights of hard talking, hard laughing and hard drinking helped me to understand and put to bed the bad times that we came to talk about.

And so it was that Paul Erasmus and I ended up in Frankfurt with a day to spend before our connecting flight to Johannesburg. Many people are critical of the process of reconciliation that is taking place in SA at the moment. I personally have been criticized for my attitude towards Paul. Only this week, Robert Kirby, one of SA's leading columnists, wrote in the *Mail and Guardian*, 'Is it a hangover from the parent sentimentalities of the forgive and forget process of the Truth and Reconciliation Commission? Is it that, as a nation, we are so weary of guilt, resentment, and remorse, that in the face of crisis or terrible injury we elect appeasing denial? Where does it come from, this weird need to look the other way to ignore or excuse patent iniquity?'

During the many hours I spent with Paul, I got to see a man who has been haunted by the savagery of his past and who has gone to great lengths to put things right. I believe that he will always carry a huge burden. He has suffered and continues to suffer from the events of his past. If the truth be known, I developed a great deal of sympathy for him. He's just a guy like me who ended up on the wrong side.

I guess at the end of the day we all have to get on with our lives as best we can. Yes, we in South Africa have been through a savage and cruel time, and I have the greatest sympathy for those who will carry that pain with them to their graves.

My injuries were minor, although I still feel the loss of friends and colleagues who died at the hands of that terrible state. I believed Paul when he said he was sorry. For that I am thankful, and I'm now able to leave the past in its rightful place and move into a new part of my life, and hopefully find peace, creativity and love.

To all those wonderful musicians I met in Copenhagen: *A luta continua.*

# 9 | Roger, me and the scorpion: working for the South African security services during apartheid

PAUL ERASMUS

I was conscripted, as were all Caucasian South Africans of eighteen years old, into the South African Defence Force after matriculating in 1974. This entailed two years of military service and, more importantly, being away from the first love of my life, Colleen, and my family for most of this time.

The only alternative to this system was to volunteer for the SA Police (five months away from loved ones), and in December 1975 I graduated as a constable in the uniform branch, expecting to complete the year's mandatory service period and move on either to study fine art or find employment in an art-related field.

In June 1976, however, black students in Soweto rose up in revolt against the SA government's education policy and in the ensuing carnage some seven hundred people died – many of them children shot by the police. Like most South Africans I believed that this was godless satanic communism at work ... this had to be fought by every means possible. Prior to 16 June I had seen one or two bodies, people who had died through natural causes or from motor vehicle accidents. Nothing prepared me and many fellow policemen for the carnage that we witnessed in the first week of rioting, which was to continue sporadically for some time. I subsequently decided to remain in the police where, at the very least, I would be doing something noble with my life by combating this, the evil that was stalking our beloved country.

I applied for a posting to the Security Branch (SB), and in January 1975 I started work on the white (European) affairs desk at John Vorster Square, Johannesburg.

From the outset our commanders encouraged us field operatives to 'apply pressure' on our enemies, the enemies of the state – as this was clearly (ominously?) defined on an official intelligence course, any person/entity outside the 'national values' of pure Afrikaans, Calvinist, white Christendom. Any person, ideology or institution outside these parameters was 'suspect' and given varying degrees of attention by the security establishment – ranging from surveillance and reports from informers and agents to the bugging of premises, telephone taps, postal interceptions, and so on. The state's armoury further embraced a mass of 'security legislation' (including detention without trial, the prohibition of gatherings and the Internal Security Act). Where convictions could not be obtained, suspects' activities were restricted by placing them under house arrest, limiting associations and in some cases banishing people to a particular area.

This, however, was not enough! There were other options, and every time a suspect left SA and went into exile it was regarded as a victory, it being generally perceived that, in the case of the white suspects in my area of operation, these people were the enemy within – get them out of the country and we could deal with the rest, the black masses.

'Applying pressure' meant that we were given free rein to do to these people whatever we felt would disrupt their activities, and 'dirty tricks' was the order of the day – ranging from the ordering of unwanted supplies or services to shooting up vehicles and petrol-bombing homes. The only rule was quite simply don't get caught, although we all believed (and correctly so) that the state, and specifically the security establishment, would protect us to the hilt.

By 1984, and with the liberation war heating up on all fronts, the all-powerful State Security Council (SSC), chaired traditionally by the state president, had coined the acronym Stratcom (Strategic Communication), and reported to cabinet that 'Stratcom was one of the most powerful weapons in the state armoury', expressing concern that the various projects in operation should be better coordinated and structured. The fear was expressed that if any of the operations were traced back to the state the damage would be politically incalculable. The organs of state involved in the secret war (or Stratcom) were the SA Defence Force, National Intelligence, Foreign Affairs and the SA Police, whose function was determined, *inter alia*, as 'the identification and the eradication of enemies of the state'.

Prior to 1984 and this cabinet meeting many of the secret 'dirty tricks' were carried out by elements within the security branches – a core of 'naughty boys' who could be relied on to commit illegal acts against the left. Subsequently Stratcom units were formally constituted in every major city in South Africa and many of the ad hoc actions against the left were formally incorporated into Stratcom operations.

I had very quickly established something of a reputation with my own little portfolio of 'dirty tricks' and was regularly summoned to Security Branch Head Office in Pretoria to be given instructions on some 'Stratcom action' or other.

In June 1979 I had attended a show at His Majesty's Theatre in Johannesburg featuring a new personality on the South African music scene, Roger

Lucey, and his band the Zub Zub Marauders, who were making waves ... not only among the young white university liberals but also in Security Branch Head Office.

A set of Roger's music with an accompanying interview in which he aired his views about the SA political scene had been monitored during transmission on the Voice of America, and I was accordingly commissioned to open a personal file on him and see what could be done about 'stopping this filth'.

In due course I established that Roger was living at Peacock Cottage in Crown Mines, Johannesburg, and visited him officially one evening to obtain personal particulars – pretending to be a detective making enquiries about some minor matter or other. I also began attending Roger's shows, secretly recording his mainly haunting, plaintive ballads in which he sang about Steve Biko's death in Security Branch custody, state oppression and other 'unacceptable issues', faithfully transcribing the words and forwarding the whole lot to SB Head Office, who were incensed at the lyrics.

They were even more incensed when Roger's first album, *The Road Is Much Longer*, was cut, containing songs such as 'Longile Tabalaza' and 'You Only Need Say Nothing', which were forwarded to the Publications Control Board for consideration. Roger had not only attacked the state head on in 'Longile Tabalaza' but further made a direct reference to the Security Branch (Special Branch elite).

Longile Tabalaza was a young man only twenty
Lived in New Brighton Township just outside of Port Elizabeth
In a small house with his family
He lived through violations
Went to school in Kwa-Zakele
With the Bantu education
Yeah ... and they call it education.

Well the cops came Monday morning and they took him on suspicion
Of robbery and arson, the law makes no provision
So they handed him to plain clothes
The Special Branch elite
And it doesn't really matter how strong you are
They've got ways to make you speak
They going to make you speak if they really want to hear you speaking
They going to get it out of you, they're going to hear your voice.

Well whatever happened in that office God and the cops will only know

75

The law has ways of keeping it quiet so that nothing at all will show
But at three o'clock that same afternoon, Longile fell five floors
Lay dead below on the street outside
They quickly rushed his body behind closed doors
Some said it was murder and some said it was suicide.

But this is not the first time men have gone in there and died
And from New York and from London
Came angry cries and protests
But the overseers just carry on with their game ...

And from 'You Only Need Say Nothing':

And there's teargas at the funeral of a boy gunned down by cops
They say that there's too many mourners
And this is where it stops
And the moral of the episode
Is to do what you are told ...

'Stopping Roger' by any and all means possible were my instructions from head office, and while still awaiting the Publications Board's decision I contacted David Marks of WEA, arrived at his office and demanded to know how many albums had been pressed and to whom they had been distributed. I also planted the seed with David and others that Roger was a prime suspect connected with either the banned African National Congress or, worse, the South African Communist Party, and that he faced imminent arrest. WEA were aghast – obviously investing in and promoting Roger Lucey was not going to be a profitable venture and they assured me that they didn't want trouble with the Security Branch or the authorities. I then went to Hillbrow Records, South Africa's biggest music shop, and confiscated all the albums and tapes that were in their shop on a trial basis.

It was one thing to stop Roger's music being produced but stopping his live performances was a challenge of a different nature. I had earlier on instituted taps on Roger's telephone, arranged for interception of his mail and activated (to acquire information on him) the huge informer network. Having established that he was performing at Mangles (a bistro in Braamfontein), colleagues and I stopped his performance in mid-song by pouring CS (tear gas) powder into the air-conditioning unit and watching the ensuing evacuation from across the road, with great amusement.

This action was followed by a series of phone calls threatening to blow up the restaurant if they continued with his shows. Other potential venues were also told that what had happened at Mangles (or worse) would happen to them if Roger and his band were given gigs. Standard procedure was further to disseminate, via the informer network, the rumour that Roger was facing arrest for terrorist activities. He was also being harassed directly ... waking up one night to find his home full of armed policemen.

And so Roger's career slowly ground to a halt. *The Road Is Much Longer* barely received a hearing – 'Longile Tabalaza' was excised and replaced with a minute's silence. The album was totally ignored by radio stations, as was a second album, *Half Alive*, released in 1981.

I had by this stage moved on to other areas of intelligence operations, Roger becoming less of a priority, although I did hear from time to time about his activities and that his career as a recording and performing artist was on the rocks.

In 1986, during the first State of Emergency, I saw him manning a WTN camera during a UDF (United Democratic Front) demonstration in Commissioner Street, Johannesburg. The SB had by this time established a 'Cultural Affairs' desk, and his file and portfolio were being handled by colleagues.

The 'total onslaught' on South Africa, a term coined by the state president, P. W. Botha, was taking its toll – including in the cultural arena – and from time to time I conducted investigations in this regard, notably opening files on Johnny Clegg of Juluka/Savuka fame and E'void. During the late 1980s I transcribed (for submission to the Publications Board) some of U2's work, including their reference to Bishop Desmond Tutu and 'Apartheid's fence', against the backdrop of their widely publicized support for the Anti-Apartheid Movement. Unlike Roger's songs, however, U2's work was never banned by the state and the Publications Board, who were now realizing that in some instances (and most certainly U2's) banning was counter-productive in that it increased the popularity of the song concerned. This had happened with the banning of Pink Floyd's 'Another Brick in the Wall', when in the early 1980s it became the theme song of many South African school kids demonstrating against the state.

In transcribing the lyrics of Roger's music I had (grudgingly) become something of a fan – realizing his incredible talent and at the same time hating him for wasting this talent on anti-South African (as I saw it) 'filth'. I gave copies of Roger's music to friends and family and used to play 'Longile Tabalaza' in the cassette player of my Security Branch vehicle – sometimes to irritate colleagues or later in my career during episodes of depression when the lyrics seemed somehow to assume particular relevance.

In February 1990 the SA government released Nelson Mandela and revoked the ban on the liberation movements and negotiations began towards a new future for our country. The secret war and Stratcom continued, however, and with new impetus – while de Klerk's government had achieved respect with this incredible step into the future the same government had embarked, via the Stratcom 'vehicle', on a four-year programme (the estimated time to the country's first democratic elections) to reduce the ANC to 'just another political party'. In October 1990 I was functioning as a full-time Stratcom operative and deputy commander of Stratcom, Johannesburg. In August 1990 it was revealed that the government (via Stratcom) was secretly funding the Zulu trade union UWUSA, and like most of my colleagues I realized that the end of the road was in sight. Suffering from post-traumatic stress and major depression, I applied for and was given a transfer, to the Southern Cape, where I resolved never again to become involved in the corrupt filth that had become such a part of my life and career in Johannesburg.

I found myself in conflict with corrupt superior officers who were using the powerful security monitoring system to line their pockets, and it was not long before I realized that I was seen as a threat – it being considered at SB headquarters that I could possibly betray Stratcom. As head of 'Technical Services' for the Southern Cape I soon established that my telephone was tapped and that I was under surveillance ... like Roger's musical career, my career as an intelligence officer (is this a contradiction in terms?) began to grind to a halt.

While undergoing extensive treatment and hospitalization for post-traumatic stress disorder I was tipped off by a senior colleague at SB Head Office that the Commissioner of Police had ordered former colleague Colonel Eugene de Kock to blow me, my beloved wife Linda and my children Candice and Dylan to smithereens. Stratcom's aim was classically multi-objective – first to shut me up and second to provide de Klerk and the regime with much needed propaganda to discredit the ANC, suggesting that they were an uncontrollable and unmanageable bunch of murderous rabble that would, while negotiating politically, even resort to killing a stressed-out security policeman and his beautiful wife and children.

For this I was prepared! Now a victim of the ominous system I had worked for, I took preventive measures – spreading the story (true) that I had huge amounts of incriminating documentation which I had stashed away overseas with instructions that if I or any of my family were hurt in any way the documents should be made public. I also contacted the press – not revealing state secrets but sending out the message that I was suing the Minister of Police for the loss of my career. I was officially discharged from the SA Police on (ironically) Republic Day, 31 August 1993, being classed as medically unfit

5 **SAP minders at a Corporal Punishment concert at Pam Brink Stadium, Springs, late 1970s (photo: Robbie Bishop, Hidden Years Collection, copyright 3rd Ear Music/Robbie Bishop).**

(PTSD) and unfit for further service. In the ensuing stand-off Linda and I fled into hiding, first to Cape Town and then to Knysna, where we set about trying to rebuild our shattered lives. At the time I refused to read newspapers or watch TV coverage of the news, and news there was aplenty! SA was bleeding – massacres in KwaZulu Natal, Boipatong, talks suspended and negotiations resumed, de Klerk's denial of the 'third force', and the appointment of Judge Richard Goldstone to head a commission of inquiry into the 'third force'.

And so I shut myself off, living in idyllic Knysna and doing my best to cope with the ever present fear that my former colleagues or the emerging 'new dispensation' would find me – and the terrible reality of what I had done: served a fearful and terrible monster that would now attempt to rip me and my family to pieces. In a fit of drugged and drunken rage I had planned to assassinate de Klerk and my former commanding officer.

Following public revelations that three of my colleagues in the 'third force' were giving evidence to Judge Goldstone, I took the plunge, fearing imminent arrest, and volunteered information to the Goldstone Commission. Linda and I were placed on South Africa's first witness protection programme (WPP) and taken to the UK and Denmark, where I gave evidence to an international com-

79

mission. Much of the evidence formed the foundation of what was to follow – the Truth and Reconciliation Commission (TRC).

In 1995 I went public with my story, believing that elements of the old regime still permeated the justice and police system and that, despite my being on the WPP, the best safeguard for my family and me would be to publicize my story.

In the weeks that followed my revelations made headlines internationally. Many former adversaries contacted me – some told me they would never forgive me, some were supportive, and I formed friendships with some that will last for ever.

I had begun to put the many statements I had made on so many issues into the form of a manuscript and was approached by the *Weekly Mail* (now the *Mail and Guardian*) who wanted to publish excerpts – including a piece about Roger, whose music and lyrics have now become ever more relevant to my circumstances.

On publication of the article 'Music to Security Branch Fears' I was contacted by producer/musician David Marks of 3rd Ear Music and later spoke briefly to Roger on the phone. David supplied some of the missing pieces in terms of what had happened to Roger – I was only now beginning to understand just how ruthlessly effective the dirty tricks campaign against him had been. At its height, Roger had been reduced to working as a doorman and barman at one of the venues where he had once been the star performer! Recording contracts had been cancelled and, disillusioned, Roger had at times all but given up on his passion – music.

In November 2001 I was informed by the Amnesty Committee of the TRC that amnesty had been granted in respect of 'damage to property and harassment of Roger Lucey committed during 1979–1983'. After hearing about the devastation in Roger's life from David, I forwarded a letter to the TRC requesting that Roger be considered for compensation from the reparations committee of the TRC for the loss of his career.

I was only to meet Roger face to face after all these years in 2002 during production of the Freemuse/Michael Drewett (Rhodes University) documentary *Stopping the Music* – the story of Roger and me.

It is difficult to describe the emotions of the moment – certainly we both shared enormous trepidation. For my part I wouldn't have been too surprised if Roger had rejected or insulted me or worse ... but then again I didn't know the decency of the man and his capacity for forgiveness (which I still cannot fathom). During production of the documentary, Roger performed to a live audience of one person (me) at the Market Theatre in Johannesburg – singing 'those songs', an experience which I will cherish for ever.

*Stopping the Music* was to première in Denmark during the Freemuse conference in September 2002 with Roger and I forming part of the SA delegation. The whole experience of the Freemuse community – Roger performing at the Conservatory, receiving, I might add, a long-overdue standing ovation from a truly international audience – was a highlight of my life. I was further privileged to spend a day with Roger in Frankfurt en route back to SA – a special time during which my thoughts were consumed with regret at what I had done to this wonderful and caring person.

It is so trite, so futile, to talk of regret, of compensation, of reparation ... to apologize (which is nigh impossible) for denying Roger such a significant part of his life. I truly believe, with the benefit of hindsight, that an artist who cannot, with freedom from persecution and prejudice, give expression to his talent is being denied the very essence of his life – his God-given creativity.

I have agonized over Roger and my role in his life and so many others, and it is truly too late to say I'm sorry. No one can turn the clock back. The only measure of consolation, trite as this may seem, is that maybe, just maybe, our experiences will somehow contribute to others not repeating these injustices, making the same terrible mistakes.

The incredible Khalil Gibran summed it all up in *The Prophet* when he wrote, 'People of Orphalese, you can muffle the drum, and you can loosen the strings of the lyre, but who shall command the sky lark not to sing?'

Roger, my friend, I salute you for having the courage to sing those songs. Although I transcribed the words, I should really have heeded the message ...

# 10 | Encounters with a South African censor: confrontation and reconciliation

OLE REITOV

'Did banning songs include working with someone of another colour? I am still confused, because one of my songs was banned because I sang with a white person. Was that undesirable?' Ray Phiri is emotional; his face looks pained rather than angry. We're just a few minutes into the opening session of the 1st World Conference on Music and Censorship in Copenhagen. Sitting next to me on the podium is Ray, who became a global household name when he joined Paul Simon's controversial Graceland project. On the other side is Cecile Pracher, the former censor who a few months earlier revealed her story to me in a small side room adjoining the huge archive of the South African Broadcasting Corporation (SABC).

I sense Ray's frustration, but in my mind I'm back in Johannesburg. I remember that morning when I finally had the courage to ask Cecile about her role as a censor. She had just shown me the document I most wanted – the thirteen guidelines for censors at SABC, instructing them in general terms which music should be banned.

But Ray's voice takes me back to the session, and I ask him: 'What you are saying is that when things were banned you never got an explanation, is that correct?'

'Yes, that hurt a lot. You did not know whether you did something wrong or not and it stifled the growth of a creative person. It simply took away your dignity as a human being whereby you did not even know if you were doing the right thing or not. Somebody just decided that what you sing is undesirable without letting you know why your song was being banned. I am still hurting inside because I just want to know what it is that makes censorship members decide what is desirable and what is not. So we can also learn to understand how we can help others not to have to go through what we went through.'

Although it is a morning session, Ray has already set the agenda. We are here to learn, to understand and eventually reconcile, but Cecile's pending answer also illustrates the vast distance between the censored and the censor. For Ray this means life and death, days and nights of speculation, of unanswered questions. For Cecile – or rather for Cecile back in her role as a censor – banned songs were just part of a job that someone had to do.

Cecile is sitting upright, obviously well prepared, with a pile of documents in front of her. For the first time a former censor has agreed to be confronted in public with two of the artists she has censored – Ray Chikapa Phiri and his colleague Sipho 'Hotstix' Mabuse. She wants to be concise, and obviously in the beginning is not prepared to be swayed by emotion. She clarifies the workings of the censors, and her answer is unemotional. 'I would say it depended very much on what time we are referring to. But I think if we talk about between the 1970s and the 1990s the guidelines were to be interpreted by the heads of department of radio and TV in the broadcast environment.

'We did not have an open airwave in the sense that there were only two independent broadcasts and the rest belonged to the state broadcaster, which was the SABC. Therefore this committee consisted of all heads of department. The lyrics were scrutinized beforehand by the manager in the record library, which in this case was me, before it was somebody else.

'Those lyrics would be passed on to the meeting once a week. In the years between 1980 and 1990 there were generally about fifteen lyrics per week. If you take into account that we only in those days had about 480 LPs or CDs that came in per year then it was quite a substantial amount of lyrics that had to be checked and had to be voted upon. The voting system was open and my impression was that in those days virtually anything that was perceived as damaging to the state, to the SABC or to the National Party, was regarded as not acceptable and we would ban it. Being there was part of their mission in life – most people were Broederbond. My perception was: it was a job more than a mission.'

How the world conference audience reacted to this explanation I can't tell. As a moderator you have a certain agenda, certain questions you want to highlight, and eventually you know some of the answers to come.

Sipho 'Hotstix' Mabuse has taken the microphone. He tells the audience about how censorship kept musicians and audiences unaware of many new trends outside South Africa, not to mention the music produced by the many famous musicians who went into exile – the Masekelas, Makebas and Abdullah Ibrahims. But censorship equally stimulated the songwriters to include hidden meanings in their songs. 'Somehow we had to find a way in which we could convey such messages in our songs and we would normally use street language to communicate,' he explains. 'We would write songs in such a way that the officials could not detect what we meant in our songs. Because anything that would be seen as subversive would somehow be banned by the SABC, and it was the only form of communicating our music to the public.'

Ironically some of the best lyrics have been written during times of repression. 'Double entendre' or 'double meaning' became a refined art in South

Africa among black as well as white artists, and several songs slipped past the censors. On other occasions, with their well-developed paranoia, the censors saw hidden meanings everywhere, and thus many songs released by American artists were equally banned.

Mostly the record companies accepted the decisions, but when Tracy Chapman's *Crossroads* album was released and two tracks were banned, the chairman of the record company, being aware of the huge sales potential of the album, requested SABC to resubmit it. The answer from the chairman of the SABC committee was as follows: 'The two songs in question, "Freedom Now" and "Material World", were found undesirable because the committee was concerned that the songs would, for different reasons, offend certain sections of the community.' Concerts were stopped by the police. Bands were sometimes tear-gassed, beaten and humiliated in public. But the ways of the censors were unknown to the artists.

Ray had earlier been talking about dignity. 'Was it a constant feeling that someone is stepping on your dignity?' I ask him.

'Life is a precious gift and anything that construes life as not a precious gift is evil,' he says, and adds: 'The closest thing to religion happens to be music. When a child is born, at the celebration people are singing. At the funeral we sing hymns, so music plays a very important role in our lives and society's norms also. Each and every song is based either on your personal experiences or what the society is going through. That influences your way of thinking and writing. So when you are not given the right to express yourself then you start undermining yourself. It's like somebody is trampling on you.'

### 'The right thing to do'

I met Cecile Pracher for the first time in 1996. I was preparing a series of radio documentaries on South African music after apartheid but wanted to know more about the apartheid era. I realized that the SABC had loads of 'hidden documents' and I requested access. Being in charge of the archives, Cecile introduced me to the general manager, who asked me to send in an official request.

Two years later I was back where I started, in the archive with Cecile. My request had been wandering around the SABC bureaucracy, who forwarded it to a leading lawyer, a specialist in the Publications Act. Finally the head of SABC said over the phone from Johannesburg: 'OK. If Cecile agrees, you can come.'

Having looked into the files for a couple of days, and gradually realizing that Cecile really wanted to help, I finally dared ask her: 'What was your role in all this?'

> ### Thirteen reasons for censorship
>
> Guidelines for censors at the South African Broadcasting Corporation
>
> 1 Swearwords are unacceptable.
> 2 The lyrics contain blatant unacceptable sexual references, which will cause offence.
> 3 The lyrics are in bad taste and will cause offence.
> 4 The occult elements in the lyrics are unacceptable.
> 5 The lyrics may inflame public opinion.
> 6 Unfair promotion of a political party or movement is unacceptable.
> 7 Lyrics propagate the usage of drugs.
> 8 Glorification of the devil is unacceptable.
> 9 Blasphemy is unacceptable.
> 10 It is forbidden to use the national anthem in this way.
> 11 The SABC believes this song is open to misunderstanding. The song has no positive message or statement against AIDS.
> 12 The impression of a Christ-figure, different to Christ, is found in the lyrics and is therefore unacceptable.
> 13 The total nihilistic approach is unacceptable.

'Well, I was also sitting around that table,' she replied without hesitation.

A few minutes later, two floors underground in the gigantic SABC complex, I activated my tape recorder. The following ninety minutes took us on an emotional journey into the mechanisms and ugliness of a repressive society and its effects on the victims. Cecile noted that: 'When you're outside of it, it is very difficult to understand how one could be led by the nose – and it is the question we now ask ourselves over and over – why and how did we allow things to happen the way we did? And why didn't we do anything about it in a personal capacity? There were Afrikaners – I'm an Afrikaner – that saw the light, as it were, and protested. But I "was just doing a job" and I didn't see that much wrong in it. I just thought that it was the right thing to do.'

In the mid-1980s there were movements of people from within the Afrikaner community that started to rebel against the system and a few papers that started voicing criticism. Then a state of emergency was declared. Some people had – as Cecile would express it – the guts to say, 'Look, what you're doing is wrong.' 'They started opening up our eyes – it's the only way I can describe it,' says Cecile.

Her voice has gradually become more emotional. This talk hurts. But seemingly it also clarifies her mind. She is at the same time looking at herself as a distant person from the past and extremely well aware that she is still in the middle of the process of understanding what to outsiders may seem inexplicable. 'We were so polarized for such a long time and it is difficult now to understand. We ourselves have problems of coming to grips with what we went through. The mere fact that church for one has played a major, major role in the Afrikaners' history and how they were utilized almost in giving a particular message and leading people up the garden – and this is not the road to a garden, this is the road to hell as far as I'm concerned. And yet they would substantiate it by using the Bible.

'So you know, it's very complex. We grew up in conservative surroundings where you would belong to a church, a school and a community. Your entire world of reference was regulated by the Broederbond. There is no doubt about it because all those people, like the headmaster of the school, were Broederbond. The same people enhanced your whole world of reference, they used all communication routes. From that point I can only say we were led, we were led to believe that we were on the right path ... and you know ... the huge big bad wolf was communism.'

Cecile looks at me. She has gone from emotional to analytical, from present to past. She continues: 'If we were led to believe that what we do is the right thing, so could people living in a communistic country do exactly the same – it is a kind of a brainwash without questions to be asked. It was a very paternalistic and authoritarian society. The father is very strong – what he says you abide by.

'The brainwashing came through this whole authoritarian and paternalistic society where nothing gets questioned. You did while you were at university, although not in depth. And yet I always wonder: why is it that some people did see the light? Most of us didn't ... we somehow were more a group following the herd and not doing what was right at the time.'

*Black and white*

Close to the end of the Copenhagen session, Ray has recounted the story about the police operations against one of the concerts which his 1980s band Stimela gave with Johnny Clegg.

Cecile has once again used the word 'brainwashed' about herself and the majority of the Afrikaner community. Sipho adds: 'I think there's one other issue that we perhaps need to clarify as far as censorship in South Africa is concerned. I think it should be clear that it was not really a question of black and white. It was a system which was fearful, which was scared. That would censor everything that sings to oppose its legitimacy. So I think when you see us here, Cecile, Ray and me, the two black men and the one white woman, it is not really a true reflection of how censorship operated in SA. Of course the whites were in power but there were also white musicians who were affected by the censorship in SA. I think the fate of white musicians because of apartheid was more severe than it was for the black musicians.

'Fortunately for most of the black musicians we had a community that was very sympathetic. Of course the opposite was true for the white musicians because they were literally seen as white musicians. And if they had to sell records they would have to sell mostly to the white communities. One would understand that the white communities in SA at that particular time were averse to any musician who would seem to be on the opposite side.

'Basically most of the white musicians suffered more than we did. Because our position was that if we sang songs that were alluding to the struggle, our community was always there behind us, and we were always able to sell a significant number of records. For instance, the banning of Stimela's "Whispers in the Deep" and my own "Chant of the Marching" only propelled the interest from our communities. So we sympathized with [white artists like] Jennifer Ferguson and some of the musicians who suffered that fate.'

*Postscript*

In March 2001, Cecile, Ray, Sipho, Jennifer Ferguson and twenty other individuals invited by Freemuse gather in Johannesburg in one of its beautiful guest houses. The idea is to work out an action plan to present to the South African government.

For two days they reveal untold stories to each other and they come up with very concrete recommendations. The message is clear: Do not forget our past!

Cecile, fighting a deadly cancer, is seen hand in hand with Ray and Sipho. They have reconciled.

Cecile is part of a seminar group of researchers; their letter to the government states that: 'Archives are being lost (destroyed or thrown away) and people with valuable stories to tell are dying. There is an urgent need to interview as many relevant people as possible and to track down archival evidence and material.'

These are the stories of those who suffered, of those who raised world opinion against the apartheid regime more efficiently than many of the professional ANC leaders did.

One year later Cecile dies.

Two years later the government, led by former resistance politicians, still haven't answered the appeal.

# 11 | Remembering subversion: resisting censorship in apartheid South Africa

MICHAEL DREWETT

In the 1980s, as part of a campaign against the censorship of music in South Africa, independent Shifty Records subverted the well-known record industry warning: Home taping is killing music and it's illegal. They brought out a different warning: Censorship is killing music and it's legal. In another instance they changed the famous His Majesty's Voice with the dog-and-gramophone symbol to His Muzzled Voice, with a muzzled dog in the foreground.

When faced with severe state censorship by the Directorate of Publications, security regulations and the government-controlled South African Broadcasting Corporation (SABC), resistant musicians and others related to the music industry turned to innovative means of confronting and bypassing censorship. Censorship formed a considerable obstacle which undoubtedly constrained musicians, but it is argued here that repression gives rise to resistance. As a guide to musicians elsewhere, this chapter briefly works through instances of resistance arising out of various attempts to stop South African musicians from being heard during the apartheid era.

## Lyrical resistance

Both the Directorate of Publications (the official government censor) and the SABC focused primarily on the lyrics of songs when deciding whether or not to ban music. Knowing this, various musicians devised ways of overcoming censorial processes. While there were musicians who recorded overtly resistant songs (Roger Lucey and Mzwakhe Mbuli included), a number of musicians devised innovative ways of expressing lyrical resistance to injustice in South African society.

In some instances controversial lyrics were included in the recording, but the lyric sheet would be changed, in an attempt to fool the SABC censors. For example, in one song Carte Blanche changed the word 'policeman' to 'please man', and in David Kramer's 'Tjoepstil' the recorded line 'but when the shit starts to fly' was replaced on the lyric sheet by 'but when things turn sour'.

Shifty Records released a compilation album of rebel rhythms called *A naartjie in our sosatie* (Afrikaans for a 'tangerine in our kebab'), sounding like 'Anarchy in our society' without using an obviously subversive title which would surely have been banned. The title worked exceptionally well in diverting the suspicions of the censors, given that *naartjies* and *sosaties* are both an inherent part of Afrikaner culture: *naartjies* are often associated with rugby matches – the national Afrikaner sport – while *sosaties* are an essential component of a good South African *braaivleis* (barbecue). At face value the title of the album therefore seems to conjure well-intended and jovial images of important aspects of Afrikaner pastimes. Indeed, when the South African Police submitted the album to the Directorate of Publications it wasn't banned, and no mention at all was made of the album title in the explanation of the directorate's decision.

Many musicians tried to sneak controversial ideas into recordings and/or radio broadcasts using cryptic and symbolic references to the South African situation. A group who regularly did this was Juluka. For example, on their first album, *Universal Men*, they included a Zulu song (with Zulu lyrics) about two fighting bulls. One of the bulls is large with strong horns while the other is small with tiny horns. But when they fight the little one wins because of superior fighting knowledge. The battle against apartheid was thus encrypted through the use of a Zulu proverb (Marre and Charlton 1985: 39).

Left-wing band Bright Blue successfully bypassed the SABC's strict controls with their song 'Weeping', which contained symbolic lyrics about a man living in fear within a heavily repressive society. The lyrics were sung against the backdrop of a haunting version of 'Nkosi Sikeleli', the ANC national anthem. Nevertheless, the song became a major hit on SABC's Radio 5 music station. The disguised tune, if detected, heightened the symbolism of the lyrics, guiding the audience into a correct reading. Jazz musicians sometimes used strains of freedom songs within their music, allowing the audience to interpret their music radically.

An offshoot of the camouflaged or symbolic song is the satirical or ironic song. This is an auspicious means of bypassing censorship, and a clever medium of protest, given that the essence of the song is not immediately apparent. The greatest proponent of the satirical tradition in South Africa was David Kramer, who cleverly combined humour with critique, exposing the dark side of apartheid. For example, in his country-styled 'Hekke van Paradise' (Gates of Paradise) he describes a segregated apartheid town as being:

> Like a clean white shirt
> With gold cuff links
> It looks quite clean
> But the armpits stink.

The Kalahari Surfers cut up politicians' speeches, changed the meaning of

**6 Campaign poster against censorship (courtesy of Shifty Records)**

what they were saying and set the subverted speeches to a musical backing. For example, in 'Reasonable Men' a government minister's statement is cut up and mixed into the song in such a way that he appears to say 'It is the duty of the government to ensure that a normal community life can no longer be tolerated.' This technique very effectively put words into the mouths of apartheid politicians, who for far too long had controlled who said what on South African radio and television – interpreting people as best suited them, often putting words into the mouths of the opposition. Sampling of this type enables the musician-as-audience-to-government-speeches to become a producer, using studio technology to create something subversive. Although the Surfers were not played on South African radio, their music expressed a refusal to allow the government to issue statements that went unchecked, to speak unopposed, and to frame the world according to their perspective only.

### Subverting mainstream songs

The Kalahari Surfers made good use of existing songs to voice their protest by providing subtle renditions in order to change the political context of the song. These new versions were not just covers, although the tunes and words were not changed. An excellent example was their version of 'These Boots were Made for Walking' retitled 'Song for Magnus' (the apartheid regime's Minister of Defence, Magnus Malan). Sinister, menacing vocals completely transformed the meaning of the line 'They're gonna walk all over you'. By redeploying old songs in the present, the Surfers borrowed from socially shared memories and injected them with new meaning, causing the listener to focus on the lyrics, not to take them for granted, to suddenly realize that they said something about the South African situation. Very few bands used covers as a means of conveying protest, although on the folk circuit straightforward imitative covers of overseas protest songs were common.

### Formal links with political organizations

Musicians made good use of formal political organization to strengthen their position. They were able to perform on political platforms to show their commitment to the anti-apartheid cause in different formats. Musicians' interests were addressed with the formation of a union called the South African Musicians' Alliance (SAMA), which focused its efforts in particular around three basic freedoms central to the work of any musician: the freedom of association, the freedom of expression and the freedom of movement. SAMA's relationship with formal political organizations provided musicians with a framework through which they could channel their political commitment.

### Innovative indies: 3rd Ear and Shifty

1 Foreign funding: Shifty Records avoided the commercial necessity of obtaining radio play to pay for recording costs by getting overseas sponsors to pay for the records it produced. This enabled Shifty to record many marginal artists and musicians with a political message. As a result they made a major and crucial contribution to archiving resistance and other alternative music.

2 Mobile studio: Shifty's most innovative strategy was the use of a mobile studio in a caravan, which travelled to various locations to record musicians, most famously to Lesotho (an independent country landlocked by South Africa) to record Sankomota, who weren't allowed into South Africa because of their message. 3rd Ear also went out into the field to record music, taping hundreds of hours of live music from rock and folk concerts to church and trade union choirs and political rallies.

3 Self-production: Warrick Sony (1991), who worked with Shifty, bypassed the major pressing plants by releasing his first album on cassettes, produced at home and distributed personally. Cassettes and CDs are small, cheap and easy-to-use formats which provide important opportunities for tiny production companies.

The Kalahari Surfers circumvented restrictive South African pressing plants by signing a contract with Recommended Records in England, who pressed two of their albums. And of course, some musicians went one step farther by actually going into exile to sing protest music.

4 Release of resistance compilation albums: In the mid-1980s Shifty were pivotal in focusing the direction of resistance music that might otherwise have remained isolated by means of two compilation albums. This was at a time when major companies were hesitant to record a single political song on any of their albums. The first of these albums was put together with the End Conscription Campaign and called *Forces Favourites*, a compilation of anti-military and anti-conscription songs. The second was *A naartjie in our sosatie*, already referred to. In addition, in 1989 Shifty released a compilation *Voëlvry* album of Afrikaner resistance music.

*Organizing concerts and tours*

Musician Jennifer Ferguson (personal interview with author, 1999) commented that live performance was important because 'there was so much repression on many other levels that the theatres and cabaret venues were often the only place where any kind of truth could be uttered'. Given the lack of radio exposure, concerts offered an excellent opportunity for musicians to get their message across to audiences and to have their music heard. Ray Phiri (personal interview with author, 2001) has also spoken about black musicians getting airplay in shebeens and nightclubs as an alternative to radio play. Juluka's 'Woza Friday', which was banned by the SABC, became a major hit in the townships in this way.

*Conclusion*

It would be appropriate to end this chapter with an image provided by Juluka, performing live in apartheid South Africa, to an audience taught that inter-racial mixing was wrong. This image illustrates the power of innovative musical performance in the face of a repressive system of music censorship.

Juluka wore animal skins, beads and bangles, and the front musicians (particularly Clegg and Mchunu) engaged in Zulu dance and stick fighting to heavy drumbeats and sang in Zulu and English to a cross-over between African and European musical styles. White youth in particular was drawn to Juluka, precisely because the image on show contrasted with the bourgeois and racist respectability of their parents' generation. Juluka's openness in collaboratively exploring a black culture in the South African context where for a long time it was illegal for white and black even to share a park bench communicated a vision of a different South Africa to the mixed audience. Music was used to prepare Juluka audiences (through the image of inter-racial collaboration and freedom of association) for a post-apartheid future. The very justification and legitimization of apartheid inequality were threatened by Juluka's demonstration of an alternative way, which not only challenged apartheid's values but which, in every instance, reflected a freedom more alluring and liberating than the claustrophobia and colloquialism of racial separateness.

This powerful image resulting from Juluka's stance, as well as the other strategies discussed in this chapter, captures the way in which musicians can indeed be heard in many different ways in the face of heavy repression and censorship.

## Note

Sections of this paper have previously appeared in Drewitt 2003 and 2004.

## References

Drewett, M. (2003) 'Music in the atruggle to end apartheid: South Africa', in M. Cloonan and R. Garafalo (eds), *Policing Pop*, Philadelphia: Temple University Press.

— (2004) 'Aesopian strategies of textual resistance in the struggle to overcome the censorship of popular music in apartheid South Africa', in B. Muller (ed.), *Censorship and Regulation: Cultural Regulation in the Modern Age*, Amsterdam: Rodopi Press.

Marre, J. and H. Charlton (1985) *Beats of the Heart: Popular Music of the World*, London: Pluto Press.

Sony, W. (1991) 'Strange business: the independent music culture in South Africa', *Staffrider*, 9(4).

# 12 | Playing with fire: manipulation of music and musicians in Zimbabwe

BANNING EYRE

Zimbabwe is home to a rich array of traditional and popular music. But in recent years, as the country's government has struggled to retain power, musicians have become targets and tools in a hard-fought campaign to boost support for the ruling party and quell voices of opposition. Long depended upon to express the suffering, hopes, fears and aspirations of their people, Zimbabwean musicians have now endured years of government scrutiny, intimidation, unofficial censorship and, most recently, pressure – both carrot and stick – to distort and transform their art from free expression to outright state propaganda.

While censorship laws and the mechanisms to enforce them have always existed in Zimbabwe, official censorship of music occurs rarely, if ever. Such direct measures are simply not needed. A climate of caution affects composers, singers, DJs, journalists and writers alike, muting and even silencing artistic voices. Broadcasters are closely watched and often scripted to ensure they avoid criticism of the state. Some have lost their jobs when judged to have crossed the line. At the Zimbabwe Broadcasting Corporation (ZBC) – still the only legal broadcaster in the country – the practice of posting lists of banned songs is now a thing of the past, but DJs there know well that they can lose their jobs or even face physical harm if they offend the sensitivities of the ruling party, ZANU-PF.

Since 2000, and the rise of the Movement for Democratic Change (MDC), ZANU-PF's first credible political opposition during more than two decades in power, ZBC has abandoned even the appearance of balance and devoted its entire range of activities to the task of supporting and defending the government. Meanwhile, artists have been cajoled with financial favours and have participated in recording projects overseen by the Minister of State for Information and Publicity, Jonathan Moyo. Throughout the 2002 presidential election campaign, and for almost a year afterwards, ZBC radio listeners were subjected to a barrage of propaganda jingles, under the banner of Chave Chimurenga, or 'Now it is war'. Although contributing to this initiative has reportedly hurt the reputations of prominent musicians, such as Dick 'Comrade Chinx' Chingaira, Andy Brown, Chiwoniso Maraire, Busi Ncube, Sister

Flame and Brian Taurai Mteki, these and other artists have nevertheless participated.

As economic conditions have worsened in Zimbabwe, many musicians have felt strongly motivated to address political realities in their music. Today, those who dare to do so take enormous risks. Musicians have been interrogated and threatened. Thomas Mapfumo, consistently the most outspoken popular singer in the country's history, has had many songs restricted from radio play, beginning in the aftermath of the 2000 elections, in which the MDC won over a third of the seats in parliament. Mapfumo moved his family to the United States in September 2002, citing concerns for their security and his own. He continues to record and release songs filled with direct and indirect criticism of the regime, although these songs receive little or no airplay on ZBC. He also returns to Zimbabwe to perform traditional year-end concerts. He has faced only minor harassment during these visits, but they have been brief.

Another veteran singer, Oliver Mtukudzi, attracted substantial heat in 2001 when one of his songs, 'Wasakara', was widely interpreted as a call for ageing President Robert Mugabe to resign. Mtukudzi repeatedly denied this intention behind his song, but was forced to do a lot of explaining, and his fans were victimized, sometimes brutally.

Random violence carried out by trained youth gangs and liberation war veterans has remained a fact of life in the townships of Harare, the nation's capital, and throughout Zimbabwe's rural areas, for years now. Although Robert Mugabe won re-election in March 2002, in an election condemned as illegitimate by most international observers, the government's campaign of violence and intimidation continues today. Property destruction, beatings and killings are reported daily in the nation's opposition newspapers, and routinely overlooked by its state-controlled press. Meanwhile, the government appears more concerned with curtailing the power of the judiciary and parliament to intervene in these matters, and with amending the constitution to allow the president a free hand to interfere in all branches of government, than with halting violence or restoring the rule of law.

At the heart of all this lies the burning issue of land reform. Beginning with the arrival of Cecil Rhodes and his followers around 1880, and continuing up until Zimbabwe's independence in 1979, the best land in this agriculturally rich nation was systematically appropriated by the white colonial government and put into the hands of commercial farmers. Although retrieving this stolen land was the central objective of the Zimbabwean liberation struggle, little progress was made during the first twenty years of President Mugabe's rule. The reasons for this are complex and beyond the scope of this chapter. In brief, the 1979 Lancaster House accord that paved the way for independence embraced a 'willing seller, willing buyer' approach to land reform, requiring British and American financial support for the process. Progress declined from tepid during the Thatcher and Major eras to non-existent under Tony Blair, in part because Mugabe's government never made land acquisition a priority. (Since independence, 80 per cent of the country's farms have changed hands, but as the government chose not to exercise its option to buy, most of them went from white hands to other white hands.) Addressing the land question belatedly in 2000, the Zimbabwean government began to encourage youth gangs led by war veterans to occupy farms by force. Objections by voices in the press, in the arts, in Zimbabwe's own courts and in governments around the world have not halted the government's initiative, and by now most of the farms have been seized by the government, although few are operational or productive. Mugabe has staked his career and reputation on retrieving the land, by any means necessary, and he has done so at terrible cost to the country.

If the violent and unregulated seizure of white farms were the only crime and excess of the Mugabe regime, most Zimbabweans would probably support it eagerly, such is the depth of passion the question of land stirs. As it is, many educated and well-informed Zimbabweans are willing to forgive all the government's misdeeds out of respect for its willingness to act boldly and seize white-owned land. The fear that electing an MDC government would mark a stealthy return to a form of colonialism and foreign domination is very real, and Mugabe's government has manipulated this fear masterfully. Unfortunately, in the process, it has done deep damage to Zimbabwe's institutions and political culture, as well as its economy and civil society.

This chapter explores the effects of these events on the art and careers of prominent musicians. Focusing on censorship and intimidation, it summarizes and updates the case histories at the centre of my Freemuse report, *Playing with Fire: Fear and Self-Censorship in Zimbabwean Music* (October 2001). The concluding section outlines the Zimbabwean government's subsequent use of musicians as agents of propaganda.

### Censorship

The Censorship and Entertainments Control Act dates back to the Rhodesian era, when by all accounts censorship of many kinds was common. It has been amended at least twice since independence, in 1981 and 1997. The act provides for the formation of a Board of Censors, defines its make-up and responsibilities, and goes into considerable detail about the characteristics of films and publications that can be censored. In general, concerns about

**Thomas Mapfumo**
**and The Blacks Unlimited**

*Chimurenga Explosion*

7   **Thomas Mapfumo left Zimbabwe after having experienced threats and the censorship of several his songs on the CD *Chimurenga Explosion* (courtesy of Anonymous Records).**

lewdness, obscenity and personal defamation, rather than political content, seem to be paramount.

The Board of Censors has rarely been used since independence, virtually not at all where music is concerned. It seems to have played no role in the events surrounding Thomas Mapfumo's most controversial songs – 'Corruption' (1988), 'Mamvemve' and 'Disaster' (both 1999) and a number of other songs since then – nor Oliver Mtukudzi's 'Wasakara' (2000) or any other locally produced music. Julian Howard, the head of Gramma/ZMC – the conglomerate holds an effective monopoly in the country's recording industry – acknowledged in 2001 that he himself has decided not to release material because he felt it was too sexually explicit. But he claims that the Board of Censors has never told him he could not release a record.

Here, as in the realm of broadcasting, direct censorship is not the modus operandi favoured by the Zimbabwean regime. Given that all legal broadcasting takes place under government control, overt acts of censorship are unnecessary. In 1999, a report by the Media Monitoring Project Zimbabwe cited the continuing attitude on the part of government that ZBC is its mouthpiece rather than a vehicle for general matters of public interest. This could be seen in the intermittent sacking and suspension of broadcasters who display a degree of independence: from TV newsreader Derek Sones in the early years after independence, to Nyika Bara and Brian Shava in 1989, who interviewed a critic of government economic policy, to Geraldine Jackson in 1997, who took listeners' phone-in calls on police brutality in the food price riots in Harare. It could be seen in the notices pinned on ZBC noticeboards prohibiting the broadcasting of interviews with certain critical public figures, such as independent MP Margaret Dongo and businessperson Strive Masiyiwa. And most of all it could be seen in the almost total absence of alternative voices on the airwaves themselves.

It could also be seen in the subtle ways in which DJs have been discouraged from playing songs critical of the government. As one veteran DJ told me in 2001, 'Self-censoring is huge here, and huge on radio. It's very hard to describe that unless you've been involved in it. As you drive in ZBC, there are guys with guns at the gate. And you walk through and the receptionist just looks at you, and you go in and there's this sort of deathly silence, and you open the microphone, there's this, like, fog that envelops you and you just know what you can't say. No one has to tell you.'

Another long-time DJ confirmed this: 'When I was at ZBC, it's not like anyone ever came and told you, "No, you cannot say this." But you just felt it. You just felt it. They were so paranoid. They are so afraid of different voices.'

With regard to the restriction of Mapfumo's songs, and others – a central theme of my 2001 Freemuse report – the bottom line was best summed up in this statement by a ZBC official, a man in a good position to know what really went on. He said, 'It's left to the discretion of the DJs to do what they want. But it's true that there was word that flew around: Don't play those songs. But it was not written down, and the official position then becomes, no one has stopped these songs from being played. You are told, "Please, don't play that song." Just that. And so, what I am saying actually is that if you were to say there was restriction of his songs on ZBC, they would say, "There was no restriction. Officially, there was no restriction."'

## Intimidation

Thomas Mapfumo cleared the way for songs critical of the government with his 1988 hit 'Corruption'. Within a few years after that, lesser singers who followed in his footsteps were interrogated by officials. A prominent example comes from a singer who was on his way to becoming a major star. A song on his debut album talked about the unfair treatment of workers, and was interpreted as political. Recalling the experience in 2001, this artist said:

> I was asked twice. Once in Southerton there, by the guys. 'Who are you singing?' I said, 'I don't sing a person. I sing music. I compose a song about the situation that I experienced ... I don't sing against the government. I don't do that.'
>
> You know, these guys, they are not in uniform, but they said, 'You know, we can deal with you, and we can silence you.'
>
> And I said, 'Well, of course. But what I am telling you is the truth. Listen to the song. It doesn't talk about anyone in particular. I'm just singing my experiences.' But after that event, some came to me and said, 'Who has asked you about this song?'
>
> I said, 'Nobody.' I used to refuse because if it was the CIO [Central Intelligence Organization], and you speak out about whether you were asked or not, you will be creating more problems for yourself. So whoever asks me, I tell them nothing has happened.

Later on, this artist found himself being singled out for harsh criticism in the government-owned newspapers, the *Herald* and the *Sunday Mail*. They accused him of singing political songs, venturing into realms an entertainer should avoid. Stung by these attacks, the artist began refusing interview requests. As he tells it, a writer for one of these publications then told him, 'Do you know that the press can build you and the press can destroy you? If you try to go against the press, my friend, I tell you, your career is coming to an end.'

A few years later, another emerging artist was questioned about lyrics on his debut release. Like many singers in the late 1990s, he was giving voice to people's frustration with rising prices. This artist told me in 2001:

> The first person called me on the phone and said, 'Look, I am also an ex-combatant. Why are you singing such type of music?'
>
> I said, 'Look, I am talking the straight point here. Are you arguing with the point that I'm saying?' He said, 'Ah no, [artist's first name].' Then he started laughing. That was on the phone. The second time they approached me, there were two, here in town. They said, 'Ah, we are very much interested to hear. We are from ZBC.' That's what he was saying. 'We are from ZBC, but we are in the investigation team. We want to know what you were trying to say.'

Although these enquiries were followed by no further action, this artist said that he did take it as a warning, and has since been careful not to write lyrics that are overtly critical of the government.

The case of Oliver Mtukudzi and the song 'Wasakara' looks in retrospect like a great fuss over a relatively small matter. Many observers contend to this day that there is no escaping the fact that the song implicitly suggested that it was time for President Mugabe to step aside and cede power to someone younger. Mtukudzi steadfastly refused to embrace this interpretation, and he himself was never subjected to official interrogation and intimidation. Interviewed in 2001, as the controversy was dying down, Mtukudzi furthermore denied that artists in Zimbabwe are afraid. He said,

> No fellow artist has ever come to me to say that I want to say this, but I am afraid ... There are a lot of ways of speaking out in our culture. If people are scared to criticize, I don't know. But I've been criticizing left and right ... In my Shona culture, criticizing is not illegal, not at all ... Leaders can be criticized. That's how they learn in our culture. Criticizing in Shona culture – it's done, but we have channels. There is some degree of respect. You can criticize, but it has to be respectful.

Many fans who came to Mtukudzi's concerts during the 2000 parliamentary elections campaign took the singing of 'Wasakara' as an occasion to demonstrate support for the MDC by waving an open hand, the symbol of the party. At some concerts, those who did so were singled out for severe beatings by Central Intelligence Organization (CIO) men in the crowd. Apparently waving an open hand was not a sufficiently 'respectful' form of criticism.

Two points emerge from this story. First, the exaggerated response to a song as indirectly suggestive as 'Wasakara' clearly shows the public's appetite for music that voices their dissatisfaction with the Mugabe regime and their desire for change. Many informants I spoke to in Zimbabwe in 2001 acknowledged this appetite. Some even expressed surprise that fewer artists sought to satisfy it; these, like Mtukudzi, seemed unaware of the atmosphere of fear that exists, especially among smaller artists. The second point is that Mtukudzi, unlike Thomas Mapfumo, is absolutely unwilling to identify himself publicly as anti-government. If his songs contain coded messages of protest, he will never acknowledge them, and he remains highly circumspect in his comments on politics. For example, I interviewed him shortly after the 2002 presidential election and he took pains to avoid criticizing the highly suspect manner in which this election was carried out. Despite widespread reports of irregularities, violence, voters being turned away from polls, and so on, Mtukudzi characterized these allegations as 'rumours'. He said, 'For the two voting days, there was so much quietness, and it was cool and people just voted. But what happened during the campaigning period up to the time of voting, I don't have first hand ... I wasn't at home. I don't know what really happened there. We were all out, and we were also out for the voting period. We were in South Africa. So when we came back, you get these people saying this, that, and what I read from the media. It's very confusing. So you don't argue. You don't know.'

While Mtukudzi doesn't argue, doesn't know and isn't afraid, many artists I spoke to in 2001 admitted that they were afraid to sing or speak about the political situation. The comments of a veteran guitarist and singer/songwriter are typical. I asked him whether he thought singers wanted to address political themes in their work. 'Of course,' he replied. 'They would like to do that, but they can't do that because they are afraid of the government. If you say something direct to the government, something bad, you disappear. The only guy who doesn't disappear for saying something is Thomas. They are not afraid of Thomas, but Thomas is a public figure. If they do something wrong to Thomas, there will be a noise.'

Thomas Mapfumo came to prominence by singing bold, political songs during the liberation struggle in the 1970s, and enjoyed the status of a national hero for some time afterwards. The notion that he is therefore immune from intimidation, effectively allowed to criticize the government, came up often in my 2001 interviews. Clearly Mapfumo is not afraid to speak his mind freely, and never has been. And yet, he was threatened by anonymous phone calls. In 2000, the police did confiscate four prized cars from him, and later accused him of having bought them with the knowledge that they had been stolen. In this context, Mapfumo moved his family out of Zimbabwe, and although he continues to sing songs against the government, he no longer plays all-night concerts four nights a week all over the country. Through all these events, his voice has undeniably been muted in the national conversation.

Since 2001, whenever Mapfumo has released music in Zimbabwe, ZBC has shown no qualms about avoiding songs with critical messages. After his album *Chimurenga Rebel* was released in December 2002, Mapfumo spoke to a DJ friend in Harare. The DJ told him that Minister Moyo had called a meeting at ZBC to denounce Mapfumo. 'He was saying a lot of things about my music,' Mapfumo recounted. '"This is why this guy named his music *Chimurenga Rebel*, because he's a rebel. He's just like a terrorist." They were trying to deny, to say that my music was not banned, but it was banned.'

No doubt there are some artists in the present context who genuinely support the government. The highest-ranking ZBC official I spoke to in 2001 professed to be a huge Mapfumo fan, and was among those who bemoaned the fact that more artists were not following his lead. Bypassing the possibility that artists are afraid to do so, he said:

They are so quiet. Or they completely ignore [politics] altogether. I don't know. I don't have an answer to that. But perhaps. Perhaps. Just perhaps, it's just a possible explanation. I suppose it has to do with this overriding issue. I think it has to do with the land. Let me explain. No matter how much you maybe disagree with the government, with the way it is handling the issue, for instance. But then, somewhere in your mind, it is an issue that is so close to your heart actually, that you end up just saying, I don't know. I don't know. It's so close to everyone's heart that there is a real possibility of forgiving people for the manner in which they are handling it. You end up agreeing with them.

In 2001, I spoke to one young traditional pop artist who has since joined the ranks of those singing in favour of the Mugabe regime. He found himself in an awkward position. Thomas Mapfumo was his friend and role model, and yet, unbeknownst to me at the time, he was recording music in defence of Mugabe's land seizure policy, a policy Mapfumo has attacked in no uncertain terms. At the time, this artist's puzzling response to my questions looked like fear. He was unwilling to acknowledge his mentor's plain distaste for the regime. In retrospect, the answer may offer insight into the self-deception required of an artist who would, as the ZBC official put it, 'end up agreeing with them'. I asked this young musician whether he ever felt inspired to criticize the government as Mapfumo does. He said:

> I don't want to touch much on that area ... Normally these are newspapers saying this and that, and you know what some of these journalists do. They don't ask you what to write about, but they simply write of whatever they think is OK, so I can't say Thomas is against the government or the government was against Thomas because this is secondary information. Maybe Thomas is very close to the government and maybe the government is very close to him.

Puzzled by this 'see no evil' attitude, I pointed out that Mapfumo had made very strong public statements against the government. The artist replied: 'Some of these things are propaganda because they want to sell newspapers ... I'm not saying they are talking lies, but I want to just say that Thomas is a musician and the government is a government, I don't see there's anywhere they can merge ... So there is no one who is wrong or no one is right, but we are just in between. I am someone who takes life as it is. I don't want to complicate situations.'

According to Maxwell Sibanda, an exemplary music critic for the opposition newspaper the *Daily News*, this artist's subsequent participation in the government's musical propaganda campaign has nipped a promising career in the bud.

In 2001, the Zimbabwean government was catching on fast that music could be a powerful means for it to manipulate hearts and minds. A number of my informants characterized the Zimbabwean public as 'docile', cowed first by the colonial experience in Rhodesia, and now by years living under an increasingly oppressive state. One veteran ZBC DJ referred to the widespread 'belief that you as an individual cannot make a difference'. This DJ recounted an argument he had recently had with someone in the government. The DJ had complained that anyone who voices a criticism of Mugabe's policies is immediately dubbed as a puppet of foreign powers, 'in cahoots with the Americans and the British'. The government official had an interesting response. 'He said, "Because, you see, the whole Zimbabwe population is like sheep. They have to be herded. So if somebody comes and tries to wrestle from us the nose ring by which we are pulling, we will fight hard to get it back so we can pull this way."'

## Propaganda

The government's use of musicians to help it pull the public nose ring came into clear view in the months that followed Freemuse's publication of *Playing with Fire* in October 2001. That autumn, a singer named Bekithemba Khumalo made international news when Zimbabwean producers refused to record his album because it contained a song called 'The President is a Thief'. Khumalo eventually made his recording, but then shops in his home town of Bulawayo refused to sell it. But not content with an atmosphere of fear that makes censors of producers and shopkeepers, the government then went farther.

In 2001, Zimbabwe at last enacted a long-debated broadcast reform act. In theory, the law would lay out the ground rules for private broadcasting in the country. In fact, it created a whole new set of obstacles to that development. A July 2001 press release from the Media Institute of Southern Africa (MISA) stated that 'The Broadcasting Authority of Zimbabwe (BAZ), the broadcasting regulatory authority set up under the new broadcasting law, has been mired in controversy following revelations that it is funding musicians to compile songs in support of the ruling party, ZANU-PF.' Zimbabwe's Minister of State for Information and Publicity, Jonathan Moyo, had championed the new law's provision for 75 per cent local content, but with Moyo retaining the sole right to appoint members to the BAZ, and the BAZ now funding local artists, it was becoming clear, as Maxwell Sibanda later wrote in the *Daily News*, that '"local content" meant ZANU-PF propaganda songs'.

No case more vividly illustrates the corrupting power of the BAZ's undertaking than that of veteran pop singer Andy Brown. Brown had long been a strong, independent voice in Zimbabwean music. His 2001 song 'Nation of Thieves' was banned on state media alongside Thomas Mapfumo's anti-government songs of that era, and Brown defended himself defiantly, telling a reporter, 'We are now a nation of thieves. They have been stealing all the money, so as a result the whole infrastructure is beginning to fall apart.'

In March 2001, Brown told this writer about his run-ins with the government media, specifically about being escorted out of a ZBC radio interview by policemen because the authorities did not like the way the conversation was going. But by July 2001, just a few months after we spoke, Brown's manager was conceding publicly that Brown had received money from the BAZ, reportedly to help him build a recording studio, and the artist was speaking out strongly *for* the regime, especially its land seizure policy. In September 2001, Brown made news when he physically threatened *Daily News* photographer Aaron Ufumeli and confiscated film from his camera. Ufumeli had photographed Brown, presumably intending to illustrate a story about the singer's sudden conversion. Brown had by then dedicated his new album, *Tongogara*, to Mugabe's land seizure policy, telling a reporter, 'If the white settler fast-tracked himself on our land, why not us? We have to fast-track the programme and sort out everything else after that.'

Brown's about-face is nothing short of stunning. The most charitable interpretation would be the ZBC official's statement that, given the moral clarity of the land issue, you 'end up agreeing with them'. But given the suddenness and severity of the change, it seems more likely to be an example of the government manipulating the art and career of a major artist in the crudest possible manner, through bribery.

By the time of the presidential election in March 2002, Maxwell Sibanda was reporting in the *Daily News* that four propaganda albums had been recorded since Minister Moyo began his musicians campaign. Sibanda wrote, 'Andy Brown, Chinx Chingaira, Marko Sibanda and Mechanic Manyeruke recorded the first release *Hondo YeMinda*, a double album with 18 songs. The album was recorded under the guidance of Moyo. Brian Mteki recorded the second album, *Mwana Wevhu*, under the guidance of Minister Elliot Manyika, followed by Andy Brown's *More Fire* with eight tracks. Simon Chimbetu recently recorded the album *Hokoyo*.'

Speaking in January 2003, Thomas Mapfumo made it clear what he thought about these developments. 'It is sad,' he told the *Daily News*, 'that promising musicians have fallen for money and politicians are using them to promote their policies which are not in line with the people's expectations ... It is by choice that people like Andy Brown have lost their respect. Surely he would have made more money as a musician in his own right than trying to earn a living out of ZANU-PF projects.'

By this time, Zimbabweans had been subjected to almost a year of Minister

Moyo's Chave Chimurenga ('Now it is war') jingles campaign, which ran relentlessly in Shona, Ndebele and English on state radio and television, often featuring prominent artists. Andy Brown's wife Chiwoniso Maraire had resisted following her husband's lead, but early in 2003 she contributed to Chave Chimurenga and its companion Machembere commercials, thus publicly declaring herself a ZANU-PF artist.

Many observers felt that these advertisements were fanning the flames of racial hatred in Zimbabwe. Voicing widespread public irritation with the government campaign, MISA opined that 'the ads are discriminatory in their use of language and derogatory of those with dissenting views. The ads in fact violate norms governing language use, especially in an African context. The jingles violate the expectations of viewers and affect their receptivity, hence the outcry by listeners and viewers ... This has disastrous results for our politics and economy.' In March 2003, ZBC at last stopped broadcasting these much resented advertisements.

## Conclusion

As Zimbabwe faces dire food shortages, triple-digit inflation and a relentless campaign of violence that aims to stifle all public opposition, a campaign that includes the arrest, torture and killing of MDC officials, it might seem banal to focus on the censorship, intimidation and corruption of musicians as a significant issue. But music lies at the heart of a people's culture and sense of identity, and nowhere is this more true than in Africa. In southern Africa specifically, music has been a part of all significant movements, from ancient battles to modern liberation struggles. In South Africa, freedom songs probably counted as much as any other form of resistance in ending apartheid. Recent developments in Zimbabwe must be seen as part of an ongoing assault on artistic expression in this country, an assault that begins with Rhodesian missionaries attempting to stigmatize ancient religious music, continues with the white colonial regime's efforts to suppress music associated with protest and nationalist ambitions, and now leads to a black government's desperate and heavy-handed efforts to manipulate free artistic expression simply to preserve its own power. Of course, there are still artists such as Thomas Mapfumo who continue to speak out bravely, and others like Oliver Mtukudzi who skilfully avoid attempts to politicize their work in any way. When Robert Mugabe's government does finally end, we must hope not only that the country recovers some of its squandered material and human wealth, but also that musicians as a whole can regain their right to free expression and again become voices of the people, rather than tools of the powerful.

# 13 | Guerrilla of pop: Matoub Lounès and the struggle for Berber identity in Algeria

ANDY MORGAN

'Silence is death and yet if you speak you die. If you keep quiet you die. So then speak and die.' *Tahar Djaout*

'I want to speak and I don't want to die.' *Matoub Lounès*

## A grave between an olive and a cherry tree

Death finally caught up with him on the lonely bend of a mountain road. The bullet-strafed car was still smoking and the pools of blood on the asphalt were still warm when the news broke. Telephones lines crackled and the Internet came alive. 'They've killed him.' 'He was with his wife and two sisters-in-law.' 'They were hit too.' 'It happened just after 1 p.m.' 'On the Tizi Ouzou road.' 'It was a false roadblock.' 'It was an ambush.' 'It was the GIA.' 'It was Chenoui's men.' 'It was the government.' 'He's dead.' 'He's gone.' 'Matoub has gone.' Some even whispered, 'It had to happen.'

Within hours angry mourners in their thousands had gathered around the Mohammed Nedir hospital in Tizi Ouzou, where Matoub Lounès's bloodied remains were taken after the attack. Their shouts boomed like mixed-shot salvoes of anger, desperation and grief. 'Government ... Assassin!' 'Zéroual ... Assassin!' 'Islamists ... Assassins!' 'The generals ... Assassins!' Over the next few days youths took to the streets of Tizi Ouzou, Akbou, Sidi Aïch, Bejaia, Aïn el Hammam and Tizi Guénif and unleashed their rage on government buildings, party offices, banks and shops. The police and security forces retaliated nervously with water cannon, tear gas and bullets. Three protesters were killed. Prime Minister Ahmed Ouyahia appealed feebly for calm. Kabylia was burning.

In Paris, thousands gathered in Place de la République, in front of an immense black-and-white portrait of Matoub. Actors, politicians, community leaders, writers and musicians took to the stage to say a few words or sing a song. The great Berber singer Idir denounced the new Arabization law which was due to be passed on 5 July, making Arabic the compulsory language of almost every official or semi-official transaction in Algeria. The crowd stood smouldering under the fluttering yellow, blue and green flags of Kabylia, arms raised to the skies, chanting his songs. 'Matoub was the Bard of Kabylia. They wanted to shut him up so they killed him,' said one mourner. 'He sang for freedom, our freedom, Berber freedom,' said another. 'He was our Che Guevara,' said a third.

The Berber Cultural Movement (MCB) called for a general strike and the response was overwhelming. Tizi Ouzou, the capital of Kabylia, was enveloped in a sepulchral silence on Sunday, 28 June 1998, three days after Matoub's murder. Boarded-up shops and businesses looked like mausoleums lining the paths of a huge cemetery. Many of the city's inhabitants had left before dawn and made their way up the mountain to Taourirt Moussa, the village where Matoub was born. They stuffed themselves in cars or braved the 25 kilometres on foot. The roads were hopelessly jammed. This, for once, was a real roadblock. In every hollow, on every ridge, down every street or path and on every rooftop around the Matoub villa, as far as the eye could see, a sea of mourners stood simmering under a hot and ripening sun. The presence of women, dressed defiantly in their colourful traditional dress or Western threads, all of them unveiled, surprised many. Traditionally, funerals in Algeria are all-male affairs.

The heat was intense, the atmosphere even more so, and many fainted. Militants from the various Berber political groups and local village defence associations policed the gathering. Their work was light because no one was in the mood for troublemaking. Placards bearing Matoub's intense and anxious features were held aloft. Banners broke the silence and the sobs. 'Remember and Revenge!' 'No Peace without Tamazight.' 'Arabo-Islamism, the shortest way to HELL.' Eventually Matoub's body was brought out, wrapped only in an Algerian flag, and laid tenderly in a grave just in front of his family home, between an olive and a cherry tree, facing the majestic Djurdjura Mountains which he had loved with such a passion. His mother Aldjia fired two shots in the air and his sister Malika made a short speech which ended, 'The face of Lounès will be missed but his songs will dwell for ever in our hearts. Today is a day of great joy. We are celebrating the birth of Matoub Lounès.'

*One God? One nation? One people?*

Like a young adult who has just broken free from parental chains, any newborn nation-state must grapple with the fundamental questions 'Who am I? What is my identity?' Sometimes the answer comes easily. Countries whose territory is already blessed with linguistic and cultural coherence have little trouble establishing a national identity. But for many of the huge, amorphous nations of Africa, which were often carelessly cobbled together from a chaotic patchwork of tribes and ethnicities by civil servants in the oak-panelled ministries of Paris or London, the question of identity has always posed huge problems. Proud, defiant but still politically immature, the new leaders of these fledgling states find they cannot entertain progressive notions of federalism and live-and-let-live cohabitation for fear that the weak mortar that binds their nation together will just crumble into dust and anarchy. The grail of national unity becomes an end that justifies the most violent and oppressive means.

Algeria's birth pains were brutal and severe. The war of independence that ended in 1962 was one of extreme hatred and extreme violence. It combined a Gestapo-like approach to civilian control – many former resistance fighters turned French army officers were all too familiar with the Gestapo's methods – with the kind of all-terrain guerrilla shock tactics that would later find favour with the Vietcong, the Mau Mau and many other popular people's armies. The French used napalm, torture, mass civilian executions and a scorched-earth strategy, anything to defeat their invisible opponents. The rebel mujahidin answered in kind. Europeans killed Muslims. Muslims killed Europeans. Muslims killed Muslims and eventually Europeans killed Europeans. The scars went very deep. The war ended with the birth of an independent Algeria and one of the greatest mass exoduses of the twentieth century. Over one million people of European descent left the country in the few months before independence; businessmen, doctors, lawyers, teachers, engineers and civil servants, taking with them the very foundations of a functioning civil society. The country's new leaders were left with hopes and ideas but few of the skills necessary to turn them into reality.

As long as the war was taking its murderous course, the rebel nationalist movement managed to maintain at least an outward appearance of unity. But beneath this veneer there were deep divisions which began to surface even before the ink was dry on the Evian Accords of March 1962 which guaranteed Algeria its independence. Various factions had very different answers to that 'Who are we?' question. The émigré revolutionary council led by Ahmed Ben Bella, who eventually managed to seize power and become Algeria's first effective head of state, was inspired by three overarching ideologies. The first was command-and-control socialism, Soviet style. The army and the state had a duty to commandeer the economic, social and natural resources of the country and manage them for the good of the people. The second was more a reaction than an ideology. Algeria would slowly and surely purge French civilization, the French language and French cultural values from society. In time, Arabic would take over as the language of education, the judiciary, science, technology, culture and commerce. French notions of *égalité*, *fraternité* and *liberté* would be strictly controlled and curtailed. Muslim Algerian intellectuals and thinkers, who had all hitherto used the French language as their vehicle of expression, would now have to think, dream and cry in Arabic.

The third ideology was Arab nationalism. Ben Bella and his crew had delved deep into the same well of political inspiration as Nasser in Egypt, Assad in Syria or the Ba'athists in Iraq. They all believed that if a nation-state in North Africa or the Middle East was to stand proud, defiant and spiritually self-sufficient in a post-colonial world, then it must draw on the glorious history and culture of Arabic civilization, the unifying power of classical Middle Eastern Arabic and the bedrock of Islam in order to succeed. 'Petty' regional and ethnic differences must be buried or obliterated. Unity was paramount.

These ideologies only began to make a small difference to daily life in Algeria during the short reign of Ben Bella, who was ousted in a military coup by his nemesis and erstwhile comrade Colonel Houari Boumédienne in 1965. Boumédienne was an Arabic literature teacher turned steely military leader and staunch command-and-control socialist. He was also a diehard Arab nationalist, and it was during his reign that the process of Arabicizing and nationalizing the country really gained momentum. Apart from his agrarian and industrial revolutions he also instigated a cultural revolution with the aim of 'decolonizing the mind'. He knew that Algerian society was fundamentally fractious and partisan with a historic tendency to splinter and implode. Only the discipline of the great revolutionary army and unifying forces of Islam, state socialism and the Arabic language could hold the nation together. His programme of Arabicizing all walks of Algerian life was continued after his death in 1978 by the new president, Chadli Bendjedid, and into the 1990s by President Lamine Zéroual and even the present incumbent, Adelaziz Bouteflika. All these men were loosely affiliated to the nationalist clan which took power in 1962. Their ideas have softened and shifted over the decades but many of their core beliefs about identity have remained unchanged.

There was, however, a very different answer to the question 'Who are we?' The problem with this pan-Arabic, nationalist, 'Ba'athist'-inspired vision of Algeria was that at least 25 per cent of the country didn't speak Arabic at all. They spoke Berber. Instead of looking to the Middle East for an answer to the country's identity, these Berbers looked to their own past. They saw that their ancestors, the original inhabitants of North Africa, had a heroic tradition of defying the might of successive invaders – Romans, Visigoths, Arabs, Spaniards, Turks and French – even though they never prevailed long enough to establish their own Berber nation. They revered their own heroes like Jugurtha, Massinissa, Kahena and Koceila, and took an intense pride in the riches of their own poetic and musical traditions. Their vision of Algeria was that of a multi-ethnic, multi-lingual Mediterranean country, which possessed more affinity with neighbours like Spain, Greece or Yugoslavia than far-flung

Middle Eastern nations like Egypt, Syria or Iraq. They recognized the fact that the Algerian territory had long been home to a highly nuanced patchwork of different cultures – Berber, Arab, Spanish, Turkish, Jewish and French – and that the local Arabic dialect reflected this mongrel past. This was something to be cherished and preserved, not brutally eradicated by the artificial imposition of the classical Arabic of the Koran, a language that hardly any Algerian speaks in daily discourse to this day. Their proposed solution was to establish Algerian Arabic, Berber and French as the three official languages of the nation, and to let each be used according to habit, convenience or necessity.

There are Berber communities with different social and cultural characteristics dotted all over Algeria, and North Africa as a whole, but the largest and most significant are the Kabyles, who inhabit a mountainous region of unparalleled beauty called Kabylia, which is situated south-east of the capital, Algiers. Dour, rugged, tough, free, ungovernable, honour-obsessed, dignified, homesick, democratic, music-loving – these are some of the characteristics, some would say clichés, perennially associated with the Kabyles. For a long time their idyllic country has been neither large nor fertile enough to support all its sons, and emigration is hard-wired into the Kabyle experience. The first Algerian Muslims to emigrate to France at the beginning of the twentieth century were Kabyles, and they became the largest North African immigrant group in France before the 1960s. Consequently it was the Kabyles who adapted quickest to the French language, to French ideas of egalitarianism, socialism, democracy and nationhood. The first recognizable Algerian nationalist movement, the Étoile Nord-Africaine founded by Messali el Hadj in the 1920s, comprised mostly men of Kabyle origin. The movement went through several tortuous mutations to emerge eventually as the Front de Libération National or FLN in the 1950s. Kabyles played pivotal roles in this evolutionary process. They fought hard in the war of independence. Kabylia itself, with its remote valleys, ravines and mountaintops, is classic guerrilla country, and as such it suffered some of the worst brutalities of the conflict. A body with its throat slit is said to be wearing a 'Kabyle smile' to this day.

Nevertheless, it soon became apparent that many Kabyles in the nationalist movement had fundamental disagreements with their Arabic co-revolutionaries. They were not prepared to see their Berber identity and their own dialect of the Berber language, known as Tamazight, disappear under the authoritarian umbrella of an Arabic socialist über-state. They also had very different ideas about democracy and the future shape of Algeria's government. The traditional system of Kabyle village and clan politics, with its *djemaat* or village councils and *aarouch* or tribal councils, instilled a raw but visceral feeling for democracy and the values of community involvement and egalitarianism in many Kabyles. This went against the grain of the authoritarian, centralized and top-down ethos of Arab nationalism. Many Kabyles also recognized the importance of Islam, but they preferred to let faith be a personal matter, between the individual and God, rather than something decreed and formulated by the state. They increasingly feared that state-sanctioned Islam and an insistence on Arabic, the language of the Koran, as the only vehicle for education, would roll out a red carpet for extreme political Muslim fundamentalism, which was already making its presence felt in Egypt, the Middle East and Algeria by the 1960s. The fundamentalist Muslim ulema or 'scholars', a revolutionary movement founded by Sheikh Abdelhamid Ben Badis in the 1920s, had already denounced Kabyle and Berber aspirations as 'a reactionary doctrine born of imperialism'. All in all, the answer of many Kabyles and, it has to be said, a fair number of other non-Berber Algerians to the question 'Who are we?' could not have been more divergent from that supplied either by Ben Bella and his allies or the fundamentalist Islamic revolutionaries for whom an Islamic state was the be-all and end-all.

Almost as soon as the independent flag of Algeria was fluttering freely over the skies of Algiers, the Kabyles were on the move. There was a gradual purge of dissident Kabyle elements in the nationalist movement already under way by 1962, but a year later a senior Kabyle revolutionary called Hocine Aït Ahmed formed the Front des Forces Socialistes (FFS), as a vehicle to promote social democratic ideas and the rights of Berber minorities. A full-scale revolt flared up in Kabylia against Ben Bella's government, with skirmishes and reprisals as bloody and brutal as anything that had been seen during the war of independence. Eventually Aït Ahmed was captured, sentenced to death, reprieved and exiled. With his departure the entire Berber movement in Algeria collapsed or went underground. The emphasis of the struggle moved to France, where gradually throughout the 1960s and 1970s Berber cultural awareness grew like a storm cloud in the expat Algerian community. Thanks to the activities of numerous Berber cultural groups, notably the Mouvement Culturel Berbère (MCB), the language, history, literature and music of the Berbers started to become a major force in the diaspora.

What is striking about this struggle is its essentially cultural nature. Most Berbers aren't fighting for autonomy or an outright Berber Algeria. Nor is their struggle predominantly about trade union rights, women's rights, cheap food, better schools and hospitals and an end to corruption, although, like most other Algerians, they long for these things too. Their overriding cause is simple: first and foremost the recognition of Tamazight as an official national

111

language, suitable for use in schools, commerce and government business; and second, a general acceptance that Algeria should be governed along secular, egalitariañ, multi-cultural and democratic lines. That in a nutshell is the Berber struggle.

## Childhood and strange fruit

Musing on his early childhood in the pages of his autobiography *Rebelle* (1995), Matoub Lounès wrote, 'I was turbulent, I still am. I'll be a rebel for the rest of my life.' In many ways his beginnings were that of the Kabyle Everyman. He was born in 1956, in the middle of a bitingly cold Kabyle winter, in Taourirt Moussa, a village of great beauty on the northern flanks of the Djurdjura Mountains. His father had been living and working in France for the past ten years and so he grew up among women, strong women, the kind who can bear the responsibility of raising a family and keeping a home without their men around in the midst of a full-blown war. It was also the women of Matoub's childhood, especially his mother Aldja and his grandmother, who mixed music with the blood in his veins. Music-making went on everywhere, at work in the fields during the day, at home in the evenings, at weddings, henna feasts, parties; music and old Berber tales of kings and princes, heroes and villains. Matoub's mother was illiterate, but like many Kabyles she possessed a treasure trove of rich and evocative words with which to depict the world.

From the start 'trouble' was Matoub's middle name. School was death by boredom and he preferred to be off in the fields with his mates, trapping rabbits and running wild. 'I made the bush school into a way of life,' he wrote. Nevertheless, he did appreciate the way in which the French Christian Fathers, who ran many rural schools in Kabylia, would inculcate a sense of Berber history and identity, along with many of the positive aspects of French culture and thought, into the minds of their young charges. Matoub's schooling was entirely in French, and at home he spoke only Tamazight. He never learned more than a few words of Arabic in his whole life. This preponderance of French teachers in Kabylia, and the fact that it was French historians and French philologists who did much to revive the study of Berber poetry, languages and the ancient Tifinagh alphabet in the nineteenth and early twentieth centuries, led many a staunch Arab nationalist to claim that 'the Berber is a creation of colonialism'. Despite his respect for certain French teachers, however, and like many a young boy in the Djurdjura Mountains, Matoub venerated the freedom fighters, the mujahidin of the independence struggle, who would sneak into the village late at night. They were heroes, and the war of liberation was a heroic struggle. There was no doubt about that in Matoub's

8 Thousands of people demonstrated for the release of Lounès Matoub while he was imprisoned in Algeria in the beginning of the 1990s. He survived several brutal attacks, but was murdered in 1998 (© Ouahad, Sipa Press).

mind. The shelter that the impenetrable contours of their territory gave to the freedom fighters was Kabylia's pride.

One day, on his way back from school, the young Matoub saw the bodies of three men hanging from a tree. They were *harkis*, the name given by Algerians to traitors who collaborated with the French, and they had been executed by the mujahidin. Their skin was already black and sun-cracked. Flies covered their eyes and faces, buzzing morosely in the evening heat. The image stayed lodged in Matoub's mind for the rest of his life. It was his first encounter with death; close, intimate and real. A haunting lifelong flirtation had begun.

Matoub belonged to the generation of Algerians who grew up believing that their revolution was a beacon for the world. It was one of the greatest victories of a colonized people over its colonizers that the late twentieth century ever saw. During the 1960s, Algeria seduced many into thinking it was a model socialist state, a dynamo of new thinking and new ideas and a natural leader, along with Cuba, of non-aligned nations everywhere. Che Guevara and Fidel Castro came to visit. The youth were proud to be Algerian and free. But under the surface, trouble was brewing. For many Kabyles, Aït Ahmed's uprising of 1964 had a traumatic effect, radicalizing them and making them reject all things Arabic. The result of this failed adventure was that Berbers became pariahs in their own country, afraid to speak their own language except in staunchly Berber enclaves. The forced Arabization of schools in 1968 was also traumatic. Many who spoke only Berber or French, like Matoub, were effectively robbed of their education. In order to fill the vacancies left by sacked French teachers, the state had to import thousands of second-rate teachers from Egypt and Syria, who taught in a Middle Eastern form of Arabic, which hardly anyone understood. This blind and destructive policy broke the momentum of a generation. 'It was then that Algeria's descent into hell began,' wrote Matoub.

Matoub's own revolutionary dream finally turned into a nightmare when he was sent to Oran for his compulsory military service in 1975. Algeria had just provoked a war with Morocco over the question of the Western Sahara. Matoub saw Moroccan families, with many fellow Berbers among them, being rounded up and forcibly evicted from their homes in Oran and western Algeria and sent back over the border. The treatment they received disgusted him. Army life itself was a nightmare. Matoub witnessed the cynical corruption of the high command and officer ranks. He also suffered the prejudice of his fellow Arab conscripts. His lack of Arabic and his Kabyle origins marked him out and attracted a plethora of insults: 'peasant', 'yokel', 'backwoods kid', 'enemy of national unity', 'traitor' and 'idiot'. Boumediénne's secret police lurked in every dingy hole and corner. The heroic vision of the great Algerian revolutionary army, scourge of the colonizer, liberator of the people, father and unifier of the nation, dissolved into nothing. Matoub came away more disgusted, disillusioned and rebellious than ever.

For solace and mental survival, Matoub began to compose poems. Back in Taourirt Moussa he had already made himself a guitar out of an old oil can, a length of wood and some fishing tackle. He mastered a few songs and even started playing at parties and gatherings. When Matoub's father eventually came back from years of economic exile to settle down with his family, he bought with him a beautiful *mandole*, a kind of large, elongated mandolin popular in modern Kabyle music, as a gift for his son. It had been bought with Matoub senior's hard-earned cash at the Paul Beuscher music shop in Paris. Matoub was so awed by this splendid object that he didn't even dare touch it for a while. Eventually, with the help of some older local musicians, he began to master the instrument and even built a lively local reputation as a party and café entertainer. However, Matoub was also a regular at the card table, and after a particularly bad run at poker he lost the *mandole* on a busted flush. The shame was excruciating, but honour bound him to pay the debt. His father was broken by the news.

This one dolorous little tale paints Matoub in all his vividness and darkness. His wayward heart ruled his hand, and his mouth too. In fact 'Big Mouth' was a title that would attach itself doggedly to him throughout his life. His mouth made him many enemies, but it was also the vehicle of his greatness. For him, pain, shame, danger and fear were there to be tested, confronted and then just brushed aside if they became too much of a barrier to living a full life. An almost savage passion drove Matoub's inner engine, spurred by a quick-fire temper.

In *Rebelle*, Matoub talks of an incident in a barber's shop, when he sliced someone with a razor for some insult. He was given two nights' detention in a local jail and then brought in front of the magistrate. 'Because you are a minor I will release you, but I never want to see you again. Have you anything to say for yourself?' said the magistrate. 'Have you got a spare cigarette?' asked Matoub. The answer was one month in jail for contempt of court. That was Matoub, a rare combination of intensity, cheek, courage and foolishness. *Rebelle* is a striking self-portrait inasmuch as Matoub's failings and weaknesses are never glossed over but constantly revealed and even underlined with a kind of devil-may-care honesty.

## Exile in Paris and the Berber spring

After the army had crushed his dreams, and life in Kabylia seemed to offer no future for a young man with a stunted education and a head full of songs and poems – all in Tamazight too, which ruled out a career as a public performer in Algeria – Matoub did what so many Kabyles had done before: he left for France. In the town of Annemasse in the French Alps he was astonished to discover that he could earn money, good money, by playing his songs in émigré cafés. Soon afterwards he moved to Paris, where he slowly became a fixture in the cultural life of the expat Kabyle community, playing in cafés and hanging out. Idir, who was probably the most famous Kabyle singer alive at the time thanks to his enormous international hit 'A Vava Inouva', took Matoub under his wing, showed him the ropes and even gave him shelter when it was needed.

In a recent interview Idir gave an intriguing character assessment of his former protégé:

115

It wasn't so much his activist side which interested me. It was above all his intimate side, the suffering and the inner pain. That's the part of him I liked. I saw that he was a man, more in the ilk of Verlaine, in his non-conformism and in his ambiguities too. Later he came to be considered a myth, hero, a brigade commander. But that intimate side of him could be felt in certain songs, a side that had nothing to do with being militant and everything to do with the wounds of the heart. He had this sensitive streak which was the root of his talent.

Not long after he arrived in Paris, Matoub attended a concert of Kabyle music at La Mutualité. There he met one of his great heroes, the singer Slimane Azem, who, along with Cheikh El Hasnaoui, was responsible for laying the foundations of modern popular Kabyle music in the 1950s and 1960s. Like most Kabyles of his generation, Matoub had grown up in thrall of these two singers, and his meeting with Azem was charged with emotion and wonder. The foundation of Matoub's music is the Kabyle songs of Azem and Hasnaoui, among others, and *chaabi*, or the popular music of Algiers which dominated Muslim tastes in Algeria until the 1970s and even beyond. 'I'm following in the steps of Cheikh El Hasnaoui,' he once told the *Le Matin* newspaper. 'The precision, the accuracy in his tempo and scales dazzles me. Technically I belong to him. But in terms of the message, I'm closer to Slimane Azem and to the spirit of rebellion in his music. Chaabi was also the music of my childhood. I feel myself gliding when I hear El Anka or Fadila Dziriya.'[1]

But the truth was that no previous Kabyle singer had gone as far as Matoub wanted to go in terms of the simplicity, power and provocation of his lyrics. 'When I started, modern songs didn't carry that need to express anger,' he once said. 'They didn't have any convincing protest lyrics. I shouted out my anger in my songs. Music is my anger.' Many Algerian journalists who wrote about Matoub's music often referred to the 'violence' of his songs. To a Western ear his lyrics don't seem violent, just challenging in the manner of early Bob Dylan or Billy Bragg. But their bare-knuckled spirit of confrontation is extreme in a North African context, where musicians and songwriters had always previously pulled back from head-on confrontation, and couched their protest in rich and symbolic imagery. That wasn't Matoub's style. His words came from his own mountain world, simple, unadorned, rich in their colours and allusions, but often stark in their meaning. 'I don't censor myself,' he once said bluntly.

Fame followed fast on the heels of the release of Matoub's first album, *Ay Izem* (The Lion), in 1978. By 1980, he was already headlining Paris's legendary venue L'Olympia, scene of memorable visits by the Rolling Stones, James Brown, Edith Piaf and Genesis among many others. It was almost as if the timing of the concert was divinely ordained. Trouble had been brewing back home in Kabylia towards the end of 1979 and the early part of 1980. The political submissiveness that had descended like a blanket of lead on the territory after the defeat of the uprising in 1964 was finally beginning to lift and crack. In the end, typically, it was a cultural contretemps which lit the fuse.

The revered Kabyle writer and Berberist Mouloud Mammeri was due to give a lecture on traditional Berber poetry at the University of Tizi Ouzou. At the last moment the authorities smelled Berberist subversion and banned the lecture. The resulting student protests grew into an all-out revolt, which was brutally repressed by the security forces and denounced by the new president, Chadli Benjedid. Over thirty people were killed and more than two hundred injured. This uprising, which became known as the 'Berber Spring', was enormously significant. It was the first overtly popular large-scale show of dissent since Algerian independence. It radicalized a generation, and the anniversary of the uprising on 20 April each year, known as 'Tafsut' in Berber, has been a day of protests, marches, parties, gatherings and celebrations ever since. Kabyles felt that they were the conscience of the Algerian nation, expressing the anger and frustration not only of Berbers but of all Algerians. Like Bloody Sunday in Northern Ireland or the Soweto uprising in South Africa, the Berber Spring was a pivotal event which strengthened the political sinews of the Kabyle nation and boiled the passions of its people.

In the midst of the uprising Matoub took the stage at L'Olympia dressed in army fatigues, thereby expressing his solidarity with the 'war' that was raging in his homeland. The event was highly charged. The Berber Spring elevated the new breed of Kabyle singers, 'the guerrillas of song' as the Kabyle writer Kateb Yacine called them, to a status of extraordinary power. Owing to the lack of any credible coverage or analysis of events in the state-controlled Algerian media, Kabyles in France were forced to rely on expat Berber publications and the odd radio station to keep them abreast of the unfolding drama. But for inspiration, insight, zeal and courage they turned to singers like Matoub Lounès, Ferhat Mehenni, Aït Menguellet, Djamel Allam and Idir. They were the bards of the gathering revolt. They were the pied pipers of the movement. After Mitterrand's election as president of France in 1980, a new system of political and cultural associations became available to immigrant populations. This new opportunity spawned the 'Beur' movement, a flowering of North African culture, politics and media in the old colonial power, France. New radio stations, newspapers, theatre groups, publishing houses, sporting clubs, record labels and community groups appeared like blooms after a flash flood, offering new channels of information and cultural education which allowed Algerians to circumvent the oppressive state control of culture and media back at home.

Matoub Lounès rode this wave like a rebel surfer. His plainly spoken words of revolt hit the bull's-eye of the times. His message was clear and passionate. North Africans, especially young Berbers, fed on that clarity and that passion. A reviewer who attended one of a series of nine Matoub Lounès concerts at L'Atlas in Paris in the early 1990s wrote in *Parcours Maghrebin*,

> How does one describe the perfect symbiosis between the artist on stage with an audience completely dedicated to a cause ... The concerts of Lounès have the grandeur of a rite, a rite full of flowers which are offered every ten minutes by overwhelmed fans. The presence of Matoub at L'Atlas, a total event in itself, has brought a ray of hope to people crushed by the cost of living, the riots, the deadly raids, corruption and the proliferation of ills in our country. Cheikh Lounès sings about their pains and their hopes which have been tragically blighted thanks to a system made gangrenous by a bunch of criminals.

As the eighties progressed Matoub's big mouth also had occasion to make life intensely exciting and dangerous for all the wrong reasons. Once he picked a fight with a music producer who owed him money. The producer's insults had to be avenged – Kabylia and Corsica have worryingly similar attitudes to revenge and retribution. Matoub rushed up to his hotel room and fetched a knife while the producer ranted in the lobby. During the ensuing street brawl Matoub stabbed the producer in the abdomen. He thought he'd killed him. He was arrested, beaten, showered with racist abuse by the police and spent one month in La Santé prison in Paris. A few years later Matoub wrote a song denouncing the London Accords between Ben Bella and Aït Ahmed, two men who had fought each other mercilessly in the early sixties but had now decided to make up for purely pragmatic reasons. Matoub felt that this 'false reconciliation' was a betrayal. The left-wing *Libération* newspaper called Matoub a fascist and accused him of wanting to throw the Arabs into the sea. Matoub couldn't find a single producer in the North African music community who would release the album featuring the song. All of them received threats not to touch it. In the end a Tunisian Jew agreed to put it out. It was deleted soon afterwards and has never been available since. A few weeks later Matoub was shot at by a group of North Africans in a passing car in the Rue d'Amsterdam.

### Five bullets and the dangers of homesickness

Despite these unnerving incidents, Matoub Lounès might still be alive today if he had only desisted from visiting Algeria. But homesickness was an unbearable affliction, as it was for many Kabyles. 'That country is my refuge, my bolt hole, my consolation and the only place where I feel really good,' he wrote (Matoub 1995). The problem with going back, however, was that Matoub was now famous in his home country, despite the fact that RTA, the national Algerian state-owned radio and TV company, never broadcast his music until the day of his death, when they suddenly realized that they didn't possess a single piece of live footage, studio recording or taped interview of one of the greatest Algerian singers who ever lived. However, thanks to the 'alternative' media of cheap cassettes and French associative radio stations, Matoub's fan base among young Kabyles and other Algerians in Algeria itself was now huge. But fame in Algeria was a dangerous, even deadly curse when it brought you notoriety among the security forces, the government and the Islamists as a troublemaker, a shit-stirrer and a no-good protest singer.

Matoub experienced the downside of his fame in a very dramatic way in October 1988. It was a time of radical unrest, when the tectonic plates of Algerian society were shifting in the most explosive way and immense geysers of dissent were spurting up everywhere. On 9 October, Matoub decided to join a group of students in front of Tizi Ouzou University to distribute flyers calling for a two-day national strike in support of rioting students and workers in Algiers. Together with a couple of students, Matoub then decided to drive to the nearby town of Aïn el Hammam to distribute more flyers there. On the way they stopped passing trucks and cars to hand out more flyers. All of a sudden a police car appeared in front of them, raced past and then turned and sped after them. After a brief chase along the snaking mountain roads, Matoub, innocently expecting nothing more than a verbal drubbing or a bit of rough stuff at the local gendarmerie, stopped the car and confronted his pursuers. When he saw that they were from the quasi-military Défense Nationale, rather than the somewhat more lenient local police, he began to worry. He was handcuffed and treated to a broadside of abuse from his furious pursuers. Then suddenly, without any clear cause or reason, one of the policemen took out his revolver and shot Matoub in the arm, after which he emptied four more rounds into the body of the horrified and astounded singer. Matoub collapsed. He was taken to Aïn el Hammam, every bump in the road doubling his agony, and then to the hospital in Tizi Ouzou. After three days he was evacuated to the Clinique des Orangers in Algiers, a city still smouldering with unrest.

Matoub's body was a wreck. One of the bullets had sliced through his intestine and shattered his right femur. The under-equipped and hygienically atrocious Algerian health service was in no position to put him back together again and their interventions often made matters worse. Infections multiplied and Matoub spent his days in constant and excruciating pain. The nurses started to administer Dolossal, a morphine-based painkiller, to which Matoub eventually became addicted. He also had to cope with deep depression and moments when he just wanted to destroy everything in sight. Eventually, after tortuous bureaucratic wranglings and needless, not to say intentional, delays, Matoub was given a permit to leave for Paris. There, with better treatment, his recovery gathered momentum, although morphine deprivation drove him to the brink of despair. His scars were atrocious. One of his legs was badly set after an operation in Algiers and it ended up measuring five centimetres shorter than the other. He would limp for the rest of his life. And to cap it all, his bowels and intestine were permanently damaged, forcing him to carry around a colostomy bag, an indignity that the proud and sensitive Matoub bore with extreme difficulty. It was only the ardent and sustained support of Matoub's family and his fans, together with the time spent singing and composing songs, which saved his sanity through the long months of recuperation. In Algiers he received literally hundreds of well-wishers by his bedside, and many more letters and gifts from far and wide.

Those five bullets exalted his reputation, turning him from a popular singer with a big mouth into an existential hero, a man who had danced cheek to cheek with death, and whose words thereafter carried special magnetism and power. As murder and violence became daily facts of Algerian life, Matoub was the one singer who could speak of its horrors from direct personal experience. People loved and venerated him for that. He was no longer a theoretical artist, but one who knew pain and suffering as intimately as it was possible to do so without losing your life. 'When one has flirted so closely with death,' he wrote, 'you feel this kind of debt which obliges you to respect life. Suffering, it's true, helps you to appreciate happiness' (Matoub 1995).

After six weeks at the Beaujon hospital in Paris, Matoub discharged himself and went back to Kabylia with his crutches and colostomy bag, to perform at an emotional concert in Tizi Ouzou's football stadium. Such was his defiant, headstrong gluttony for life and its inevitable punishments. 'Aggression, which could have annihilated me, ended up reinforcing me. That day I knew that the five bullets of Aïn El Hamman were defeated,' he wrote. Needless to say, the cop who had almost murdered Matoub was never brought to trial.

### Fundamentalism and the descent into hell

Meanwhile Algeria was plunging into hell. When oil and gas prices plummeted in the mid-1980s, the country's only real source of hard currency dwindled. The state could no longer pay its bills and what had always been a fragile society, even at the best of times, began to disintegrate. Forced by the massive nationwide unrest of 1988 to take drastic measures, President Chadli Benjedid announced the first free multi-party presidential and parliamentary elections since independence. The first round was held in December 1991. The voter turnout was low, with many Algerians decidedly unenthused by the choices on offer. The Front Islamique du Salud (FIS), an ascendant fundamentalist Islamic party led by the imprisoned Abassi Madani and Ali Benhadj, won an overwhelming victory.

Like many extremist political organizations, the FIS offered simplistic, starry-eyed solutions to complex, deep-rooted problems. Their ultimate goal was clear: an Islamic state run according to the precepts of shariah law in which democracy, the rights of women and the aspirations of ethnic minorities would have absolutely no place at all. This programme held definite attractions for certain sections of a population crushed by years of poverty, corruption and the mismanagement of the one-party FLN state. It also seemed to provide an alternative to failed Western ideologies such as socialism and communism, an alternative that was defiantly Arabic and Islamic. The more oppressed and socially deprived a people, the more inclined they are to cling to the rock of an unambiguous and proud identity, however bogus it may be. The FIS seemed to provide the answer to people's needs, although many votes cast in their favour were more like gut rejections of the previous regime than positive endorsements of their programme. The FIS were also masters of grass-roots organization, and they used mosques and religiously inspired welfare programmes to seduce the populace.

But in the fundamentalist mind, democracy is a heresy and a sin against God. The first-round victory of the FIS presented the army generals, who still held ultimate power in Algeria, with an excruciating dilemma. Should they allow the second round of the elections to go ahead and thereby herald a fully fledged Islamic state in Algeria? Should they let democracy destroy democracy? Was it worth sacrificing their own political dominance for a democracy that they had never felt comfortable with anyway? The strongman of the ruling army council, Major-General Khaled Nezzar, had little doubt in his mind. He purposely provoked a constitutional crisis by forcing Chadli Benjedid to resign and appointed a High State Council to rule in his place. Their first act in office was to annul the second round of elections. It was a military coup d'état, all in the name of democracy. The FIS and their followers felt cheated and robbed. The political system had betrayed them. The time had come for direct action. The gun, the bomb and the knife took over from the ballot box and the Islamic movement went underground.

Matoub had even less love for fundamentalist Islam than he did for Arabic nationalism. 'I'm neither an Arab nor a Muslim,' he once famously said in a TV documentary, in a blatant refutation of the FLN's rallying cry at independence: 'One Nation – Algeria! One People – The Arabs! One Faith – Islam!' As far as Matoub was concerned, the fundamentalists wanted to destroy anything that might help society evolve: intellectuals, doctors, journalists, teachers, young women who refused the veil and, of course, musicians. The FIS and the Armed Islamic Group (GIA) were unequivocal in their view that music was a sin and musicians enemies of God. Furthermore, Matoub liked to drink. He loved spending time in cafés, chatting to friends. It was his way of keeping in touch with the people he loved most. None of this helped to improve his image as a good Muslim. In any case, he had never had any time for the marabouts, or holy men, who controlled traditional Kabyle society, preying on the simple faith of the people and enriching themselves in the process. He suspected them of aiding and abetting Islamic terrorism in Kabylia and beyond. 'Religion exploits consciences,' he wrote. 'I don't want it to exploit mine.'

### The only one who lived to tell the tale

Although Matoub spent a lot of his time in France and touring abroad with the help of an international network of Berber groups and activists, he could never stay away from Kabylia for long, and he always tried to be there for the annual 'Tafsut' celebrations commemorating the Berber Spring. In 1994, when fundamentalist terrorist violence was reaching its murderous apogee, Matoub began to hear rumours that he was on the terrorists' blacklist. Friends urged him to go back to the safety of Paris. Posters began to appear in Tizi Ouzou proclaiming that Matoub was next. But he bluntly and stubbornly refused to leave. It would look too much like a climb-down, a loss of courage and a defeat. Instead he took the precaution of avoiding main roads, where the GIA often set up false roadblocks. But he still went to cafés to talk and drink late into the night with friends.

One night in later September, Matoub and a couple of friends were driving back to Tizi Ouzou when they decided to stop off at a roadside café for a pick-me-up. All of a sudden, fifteen men armed with knives, hunting rifles and sawn-off shotguns burst into the bar. They searched the place, pistol-whipping the proprietor with the warning that if he continued to run such an ungodly business he would be shot. Eventually they found the gun that Matoub kept for self-protection in his belt. The cry went up. 'It's him. It's Matoub!' Their leader, whose war name was Hamza, said to Matoub, 'Now you're getting ready to die, have you decided to pray?' 'Obviously,' replied Matoub. 'Lounès,' came the stern answer, 'it's better to be alive and scared than heroic and dead.' After taking the proceeds of the till and beating some of the other clients, the guerrillas departed into the rainy night with Matoub.

No one had ever survived being kidnapped by the GIA. Throughout the two weeks of Matoub's captivity, death was a constant presence. His own execution seemed to be forever only a few hours away. The young members of the GIA group who were holding him captive spoke about death all the time. They revelled in it, boasted about it and glorified it. They were also completely resigned to the idea of their own martyrdom in the cause of Islam and subsequent entry into paradise. Matoub was astounded by how little political analysis or discourse went on in the stinking remote mountain camps of the GIA. The will of God was the simple motivation behind their every thought and the justification of their every action. Matoub felt his only possible survival strategies were wit and cunning. He even joined in with the tearful prayer sessions which the guerrillas held five times a day.

Eventually Matoub was tried by two 'Emirs', or GIA leaders, and sentenced to death. His trial was recorded on tape, so that his own expedient contradictions of his core beliefs could be used later to discredit him. His judges had an intimate knowledge of his poems and lyrics, even though they claimed that they never listened to his music, or any music for that matter. 'You are the enemy of God,' they told him. 'Because of you and your songs, Kabylia is wallowing in darkness.' Their arguments were simple and without nuance. They urged him to follow the example of Cat Stevens, aka Youssef Islam, who had renounced the ungodly life of a musician and embraced the true faith. Paradise awaited him if he started praying and adopted Islam. Looking down the barrel of a gun, proverbially and literally, Matoub said anything to stay alive. He promised to give up singing and open a respectable business, to which end the guerrillas in turn offered to lend him some money. He also promised that he would try to persuade the Berber movement to give up its political aims.

In the second week of his captivity Matoub began to hear rumours that he might be released. He refused to believe them, and kept telling himself that death was nothing to fear because he was dead already. Part of him suspected that the GIA might be planning to manipulate his popularity and use his taped promises and declarations to influence his fans. As part of this scheme they might just want him alive. But mostly it was death which dominated his thoughts. He pictured his own end obsessively, in the minutest detail. 'I imagined my assassination one hundred times,' he wrote. 'One hundred times, I lived my own death.' A captured policeman was executed only ten feet away

123

from him. His captors considered Matoub responsible for the moral degenera-tion of Kabylia and they had fun playing games with his state of mind.

Eventually, on 10 October, Matoub was driven to the village of Ath Yenni and released. His joy and relief were unbounded. After rejoining his family in Taourirt Moussa, where thousands of well-wishers gathered to greet him, Matoub began to find out what had happened during his absence. The Mouve-ment Cultural Berbère (MCB) had sent an ultimatum to the GIA, threatening all-out war if Matoub were killed. Groups of youths had braved the dangers of the remote mountain areas to look for him. Tens of thousands took to the streets of Tizi Ouzou and Algiers chanting 'Matoub or the Gun!' In the end, his execution was too hot even for the GIA to handle. Matoub was unequivocal about the significance of his own escape from the clutches of the fanatics. 'My liberation was their first setback,' he wrote. 'The terrorists freed me because they had no choice ... For the first time a whole region mobilized, arms in hand, to show that they would not give in to intimidation ... My songs, my music, my struggle will be even stronger now.'

### The chronicle of a death foretold

Soon afterwards, Matoub released his album *Kenza*. It was dedicated to the daughter of the Kabyle writer Tahar Djaout, a close friend of Matoub's, who was murdered by the GIA in 1993. Life, precarious as it was, went on. Matoub now suffered from regular panic attacks for which he took Valium. Composing songs and writing his autobiography were the only forms of therapy he allowed himself. Of course, his traumatic encounter with the GIA had been far from unique. It is estimated that almost 200,000 people were murdered in Algeria in the decade after 1992. But the fact that he was able to express his experiences and feelings in songs of such clarity and power set him apart. 'The essential thing for me is to fulfil the link between my life and my ideas, my struggle and my songs,' he wrote. 'My life is a permanent search for that equilibrium, from which I take my strength and my inspiration.'

Nothing in Algerian politics is simple, and pure, unsullied Algerian heroes are almost non-existent. Matoub had his doubters and his enemies. In the early 1990s the Berber movement had split into two factions. One supported Aït Ahmed's FFS party and the other a new political movement called Rassemble-ment pour la Culture et la Démocratie (RCD). The FFS believed that ultimately peace and stability could be won only through dialogue with the FIS and other fundamentalist groups. The RCD rejected this notion outright, and even went so far as to ally itself with President Abdelaziz Bouteflika and the army generals in favour of an all-out war on religious fanaticism and terrorism. Kabyle society split along these party lines, turning neighbour against neighbour and friend against friend. Matoub always claimed that he was a poet and that political machinations held no interest for him. Nevertheless, he was a fervent and declared admirer of Saïd Sadi, the man who had founded the MCB in the late 1960s and was also behind the creation of the RCD in the late 1980s. Matoub was an MCB loyalist through and through. 'It represents that which is most important for us Kabyles: our identity,' he declared. By association, he was also considered to be an RCD supporter, and this dragged him into the political fray, despite himself.

Soon after Matoub was released by the GIA and the joyous celebrations in Kabylia, Algiers, Paris and the rest of the diaspora had died down, dark mutterings began to be heard. Certain parties accused Matoub of 'staging' his own kidnap, in order to enhance his reputation and that of the RCD. For them it was the only logical explanation for Matoub's escape from the GIA, an organization whose record of murdering all their kidnap victims had been hitherto watertight. The singer Ferhat expressed his own doubts publicly, and many others did so privately. With great insight, the journalist Catherine Simon, writing in *Libération*, pointed out that doubt was one of the few political reactions left to the Algerian people. 'In this theatre of shadows into which evil has plunged the country,' she wrote, 'the only freedom left to the populace, pressured to choose between one camp or another, is to doubt, without let-up, everything and everybody.'

Aït Meguellet, a singer revered by many Kabyles and Algerians, refused to comment on Matoub's kidnapping when pressed by journalists. For Matoub, his silence was a grave insult. He went on Beur FM, the biggest North African radio station in France, and accused Aït Meguellet, who continued to reside in Kabylia throughout the troubles, of buying his own protection from the GIA. Matoub even claimed to have proof of this arrangement. The normally reserved Aït Meguellet went public and denounced Matoub, accusing him of mythomania and megalomania. 'In the future, for each proffered lie, ten truths will be told about this person,' he said.

This sorry débâcle became known as the Matoub affair. Claim and counter-claim dogged him right up until the day of his death and beyond. The French TV channel Canal+ even broadcast a documentary casting doubt on the assumption that the GIA were Matoub's killers. Matoub's sister Malika and the Matoub Lounès Foundation are still trying to expose the dark forces that they claim were responsible for his eventual murder. Ironically, her suspicions are focused on the RCD, the one political party that Matoub was supposed to have supported during his life. Her argument is that since the RCD allied itself with the regime, it had the means and the motivation to eradicate her brother. The party was only doing the government's dirty business for them. Once again Malika claims to have evidence to back up her accusations. The RCD are suing her and the Matoub Lounès Foundation. The case continues.

It is easy to imagine the army generals, the mafia who rule Algeria, rubbing their hands in glee at all this fractious infighting at the heart of the Berber movement. And despite his natural tendency to mouth off and call a spade a spade, it is equally hard to imagine that Matoub himself would have looked on this controversy with anything other than frustration and despair. All Kabyles, whether FFS or RCD, share a similar dream, and ultimately it is the dream which suffers while the accusations fly. But that's the nature of crime and punishment in modern Algeria. Army, FIS, government, GIA, this party, that party – they all sometimes blend into one deathly and impenetrable medusa. As the great Polish journalist Ryszard Kapuscinski wrote way back in the 1960s: 'Algeria is unique. At every moment it reveals its contrasts, its contradictions and its conflicts. Nothing is unambiguous and nothing fits into a formula.'

A perspicacious journalist once wrote that Matoub's end was like 'the chronicle of a death foretold'. People thought he was mad even to contemplate returning to Algeria. They even told him so. But Matoub couldn't stay away from his beloved Kabylia for very long. After he had put the final touches to what became his last album, *Lettre ouverte aux* ... , the thirty-sixth of his career, he decided to accompany his new wife Nadja back home, in order to help her get a visa. He knew the risks he was taking. 'I know I have been reprieved,' he wrote. 'Popular pressure saved me from the nightmare. Next time my kidnappers will have my skin, and without any warning, of that I'm certain.' But in the end, for Matoub risks were just like red rags to a bull. Contrary and stubborn to the last, Matoub turned a deaf ear to all the warnings and travelled back home for his final rendezvous with death. Only a poet could attempt to capture the tangled web of fate and foreboding that dogged his steps as he climbed into the car with his wife and her two sisters, and drove off up that lonely mountain road.

*Note*

1. Mohammed Hadj El Anka and Fadila Dziriya are among the greatest *chaabi* singers ever.

*Reference*

Matoub, Lounès (1995) *Rebelle*, Paris: Editions Stock.

FOUR | **The Middle East**

# 14 | Singing in a theocracy: female musicians in Iran

AMENEH YOUSSEFZADEH

In 1979 the Islamic revolution established a theocracy in Iran – a theocratic state that imposed religion as the sole authority for legal, cultural, economic and political aspects of society, and which was regarded as a legitimate means to integrate Islam into all aspects of human life. For example, the laws voted by the National Assembly are not effective unless they are approved by the *Shorâ-ye negahbân* (a kind of constitutional court composed entirely of religious men). This body reviews all the laws and interprets whether or not the political decisions are in accordance with Islamic principles, and is in a position to make decisions regarding censorship and anything that does not respect these principles. Although it is claimed that Iran is a democracy, it is the clergy who hold the power.

Each moment of daily life in Iran is supposed to conform to Islamic laws as decreed and defined by clerics. However, one should always keep in mind that there is a considerable difference between what is theoretically allowed in official declarations and what people actually do in private.

In Iran female public entertainment, which includes both singing and dancing, has been forbidden since 1997. Official policy states that women are not allowed to sing solo before a male audience; they can sing only in a choir, since it then becomes impossible clearly to distinguish individual women's voices.

Although the Koran does not contain one single word in condemnation of music, Islam has always approached music with a certain mistrust, believing it to be endowed with a magical power liable to exert a strong influence and produce great excitement. In fact music is thought to cause the listener to lose control of his reason and behaviour and consequently to govern his passions (Shiloah 1995: 34). Thus the Prophet, and his companions after him, sought to keep the mind of man away from what was termed *malâhi* – the 'forbidden pleasures' – which, aside from music, included wine and women (Farmer 1979: 427).

Throughout the ages, Islamic jurisprudence has attempted to elaborate on what constitutes temptation. For instance, it seems that a woman's voice reflects her most 'intimate sphere' (*awra*) (Chehabi 2000: 151). In Egypt, as in many Muslim countries, women cannot recite the Koran in public, since it is said that 'a woman's voice makes one think of things other than Allah' (Nelson 2001: 202, note 2).[1]

In Iran, up to the beginning of the twentieth century, upon answering the door to a male visitor, women would either have to distort their voices or clap their hands, instead of asking 'Who is it?' Indeed, a woman's voice could not be heard by any male who was not a close relative.

Women's sexuality is commonly linked to women's role in musical activities. In most societies where men claim women for heterosexual activity, women assume musical roles that either heighten their sexuality – and consequently their implied or real association with prostitution – or restrict its display (see Koskoff 1987: 1–23). Iran constitutes an excellent example of this.

In her article 'Prostitutes, Courtesans, and Dancing Girls: Women Entertainers in Safavid Iran', Rudi Matthee (2000) documents how female performers were an integral part of court life and how prostitution was commonly associated with public entertainment in the form of singing and dancing. Such phenomena continued up to the beginning of the twentieth century, in the Qâjâr period (see Youssefzadeh 1999).

On the other hand, the phenomenon of women singing for other women, especially in the realm of traditional music, continues to be widespread. Wedding ceremonies and other life-cycle celebrations continue to be the customary circumstances in which such performances take place.

*Before the 1979 revolution*

At the onset of the twentieth century, and particularly under the Pahlavi rule in Iran (1925–79), women increasingly entered public life. Public singing by women emerged from the tradition of religious music (*rowze-khâni*), which, with the constitutional revolution of 1906 and the lifting of the veil by Reza Shah (the founder of the Pahlavi dynasty) in 1936, evolved into more open and public performances of classical singing by women. The genre of classical music that was traditionally performed by men emerged as a medium through which women could perform without the veil in public.

The pioneering women singers gained fame not only because of their talent, but also because of the fact that they were women with enough courage to perform in public. Women gradually performed openly in all genres of music: Western classical music (by the 1960s, Iranian women were singing major parts in Western operas), Persian classical and popular music, and Westernized pop music. By the 1970s there was a classical ballet company in Tehran whose British ballet master came from the Royal Ballet.

In 1970, more than 90 per cent of national radio and television programmes broadcast music appealing to the masses; this music mainly consisted of imitations of Western pop tunes sung by Iranian 'pop' stars. Such a phenomenon may be considered as one of the major reasons for the violent reaction of the 1979 revolution and its 'back to our roots' movement. In fact Westernized pop was decried as a manifestation of Western 'corruption' (see Youssefzadeh 2000).

The majority of these pop singers, especially females, left the country soon after the revolution. They now live in exile, mostly in Los Angeles. Today, Persian pop music is thriving in the diaspora, and is still popular within Iran, where it has became a new genre, labelled 'Los-Angelesi', because most of it is made by Los Angeles-based Iranians.

## Revolution and women

Indeed, even though women participated en masse in the 1979 revolution, a systematic campaign designed to 'purify the public space of women' began soon after Ayatollah Khomeini came to power. For a lot of women, this meant either early retirement, losing their jobs or exile. Very quickly, women disappeared as entertainers. In movies, they appeared only as mothers or wives. Regardless of their faith, women were forced to cover themselves (*hejâb-e eslâmi*). The veil is the most distinct expression of gender separation in many Islamic societies.[2] Thus in post-revolutionary Iran, in order to prevent any chance of sexual temptation, women were segregated in public spaces – mosques, universities, beaches, buses (see Milani 2001: 406–11).

## Revolution and music

Again, what happened to women at the beginning of the Islamic revolution resembles what occurred to the standing of music in Iranian society. For instance, a contract could no longer feature the term 'music' without being illegal. Instruments were collected and destroyed, and musicians often had to answer to police authorities (Youssefzadeh 2000).

After the end of the Iran–Iraq war (1980–88), and following Khomeini's 1989 fatwa (a religious decree establishing the licit or illicit character of an act) authorizing the purchase and sale of instruments serving a 'licit purpose', little by little some concerts were authorized, although remaining under certain restrictions, such as a ban against 'sensually arousing rhythms' and on women singing before a male audience. As is the case with literature and movies, any suggestion or actual display of what was deemed 'erotic' was forbidden. Government authorities, even the current so-called 'reform-minded' ones, have never moved on this issue, since it relates to what they view as one of Islam's fundamental tenets. For example, on a set of three cassettes of music recorded in Khorasan – a region in the north-east of Iran – the voices of women performing various folk tunes such as lullabies and harvest songs were obscured by a male voice declaiming some explanatory text (Darvishi and Tavahodi 1992).

## Today

Today, however, more than two decades after their revolutionary triumph, the Islamic fundamentalists have not been able entirely to mould society according to their views and suppress the aspirations of Iranian women. Moreover, the very intention of abolishing music in public life unexpectedly led to increasing musical expression within the family circle on the part of the younger generation of all social classes, especially women.

The triumphal election in 1997 of President Khâtami, who promised moderation and less social control over women, led to a revived official interest in music, through, for example, the *Fajr* festival. Originally, this festival was established as a pure celebration of the revolution; nowadays it is also a major cultural event. Since 1997 a new section has been added to the festival, dedicated to both traditional and regional music – sung for and by women.

It should be noted that twenty-two years after the establishment of the Islamic republic, Iran remains the focus of struggles between various socio-religious tendencies, even among the highest authorities of the country. These conflicts naturally affect music, and the organizations in charge of representing and supervising it. Thus, even a powerful government organization such as the *Vezârat-e farhang va ershâd-e eslâmi* (Ministry of Culture and Islamic Guidance) has to negotiate with other political authorities, which sometimes disregard its decisions. For example, Mr Morâdkhâni is the musical director of this organization, one of whose roles is to issue permits (*mojavez*) for all sound recordings (cassettes or CDs), teaching of music, concerts, etc.[3] Considered an ally of the 'reformists', he told me during an interview in the summer of 2002 that, as head of the musical department, he had been summoned two months earlier to court, where he had to explain why he had issued one of these *mojavez* for the recording of *Âhuy-e vahshi* (Wild Gazelle) by Ms Malihe Milâni (composer and director of the Tehran Conservatory of Music for Girls). Indeed, this recording features the easily distinguishable voice of a woman singing, and illustrates the phenomenon mentioned earlier – the large gap that exists between what is officially forbidden and what is actually allowed.

Furthermore, women themselves have managed to play a more active role in the musical field. It is thus now possible to hear female performers abroad, on tours organized with or without the authorization of the Islamic republic.

And in Iran itself women's voices are more distinctive than ever in the choirs during public performances.

Mr Morâdkhâni also showed me the law governing musical performances and female voices in Iran, as it was signed into effect by the Guide (*Rahbar*) of the revolution, the Ayatollah Khâmenei, in 2002. It states that 'Music which is not *motrebi* [merely entertaining] nor conducive to debauchery is licit. Should the audience not find it offensive, then it is not so. The listener's responsibility is engaged in determining the actual nature of the music played. The same goes for a woman's voice. As long as the song is not arousing [*tahrik âmiz*], no restrictions are applied. The very fact that the singing is done by a woman does not make it automatically illicit.'[4]

The above statements represent a radical change from what used to be the official policy regarding both the nature of music and women as public performers. Indeed, Mr Morâdkhâni concurs when he adds that: 'The problem is not with the voices of women; the problem is with our men.'

Another example of the constant attitude changes and contradictions within the regime is offered by the recent troubles of a young female researcher, Ms Toka Maleki, author of *Women and Music in Iran, from Mythological Times to Today*. The book, published in 2001, was banned a few months later, following the publication of a critical account in the newspaper *Iran*, because it contained a chapter dedicated to the Islamic era which the authorities deemed to be blasphemous. In the book, the author, using different historical sources, established that the Prophet himself is said to have enjoyed music as performed by singing girls. The author was not the only one to suffer from making such a statement; publication of the weekly supplement in which the article appeared was stopped and the chief editor was fired and, together with the journalist (a woman), fined a considerable sum. They also became *mamnu'ol qalam*: no longer allowed to publish.

This unfortunate case illustrates how, more than two decades after the revolution, the gaps between legislation and social practices are widening rapidly and becoming more and more confused. On the one hand, tough legal restrictions are still in place, while on the other substantial transformations have started to affect gender relations as well as the legitimacy of music.

The contradictory situation of women and music in Iran continues to be the subject of intense political and religious debate in the country. In the musical field, women are still subjected to various restrictions and threats because of their alleged seductive power.

*Notes*

1 However, in Indonesia and Malaysia, where Koranic recitation has been greatly influenced by the Egyptian male tradition, women cantors do become public figures (see Nelson 2001).

2 For a study of women and gender in Islam, see Ahmed (1992).

3 On the role of official organizations in the musical life of post-revolutionary Iran, see Youssefzadeh (2000).

4 Personal communication with Mr Morâdkhâni, summer 2002.

*References*

Ahmed, L. (1992) *Women and Gender in Islam. Historical Roots of a Modern Debate*, New Haven and London: Yale University Press.

Chehabi, H. E. (2000) 'Voices Unveiled: Women Singers in Iran', in *Iran and Beyond. Essays in Middle Eastern History, in Honor of N. R. Keddie*, Mazda, CA, pp. 151–66.

Darvishi, M. R. and K. Tavahodi (1992) *Musiqi-ye. shomâl-e Khorâsân* [Music of northern Khorasan], set of three cassettes, Tehran: Hôze-ye honari-e tabliqât-e eslâmi.

Farmer, H. G. (1979) 'The Music of Islam', in *The New Oxford History of Music : Ancient and Oriental Music*, vol. 1, London: Oxford University Press, pp. 421–77.

Koskoff, E. (1987) 'An Introduction to Women, Music, and Culture', in Ellen Koskoff (ed.), *Women and Music in Cross-Cultural Perspective*, Urbana and Chicago: University of Illinois Press.

Maleki T. (2001) *Zanân-e musiqi-ye Irân: az osture tâ emruz,* Tehran: Khorshid.

Matthee, R. (2000) 'Prostitutes, Courtesans, and Dancing Girls: Women Entertainers in Safavid Iran', in *Iran and Beyond. Essays in Middle Eastern History in Honor of N. R. Keddie*, Mazda, CA, pp. 121–50.

Milani, F. (2001) 'Gender Relations in Persia. i. In modern Persia', in *Encyclopaedia Iranica*, vol. X, pp. 405–11.

Nelson, K. (2001) *The Art of Reciting the Qur'an*, Cairo and New York: American University in Cairo Press.

Shiloah, A. (1995) *Music in the World of Islam, a Socio-Cultural Study*, Scolar Press.

Youssefzadeh, A. (1999) 'Negâhi be vaz'e musiqi dar dowre-ye Qâjâr' [A Short Survey of Qâjâr Music], *Irân Nâme* 17(3): 453–67.

— (2000) 'Music in Iran Since the Revolution: the Role of Official Organizations', *British Journal of Ethnomuscology* 9(2): 35–61.

# 15 | Defending freedom: blasphemy trials and censorship in Lebanon

MARCEL KHALIFE

*Introduction: by Marie Korpe*

On 3 November 1999, Marcel Khalife appeared before the Beirut Court of First Instance, accused of blasphemy, charges that can bring him six months' to six years' imprisonment. The charge against him relates to the song 'Oh My Father, I am Yusuf', based on a poem by the Palestinian poet and writer Mahmoud Darwish. The song, from the album *Arabic Coffeepot*, released in 1995, is inspired by the story of Yusuf (Joseph) and his brothers which quotes a verse from the Koran. The song's vague citation of a Quranic verse drew hostile attention from Dar-al-Fatwa, Lebanon's highest Sunni religious authority.

A month earlier, the appointed investigating judge recommended that prosecutors bring criminal charges against Khalife for 'insulting religious values' by using a verse from the chapter of the Holy Qur'an in a song'. Sunni clerics ruled that singing verses from the Koran was 'absolutely banned and not accepted'. On 21 October the highest Sunni religious authority in Lebanon, Grand Mufti Sheikh Muhamed Rashid Qabbani, stated: 'There is a limit to freedom of expression. One limit is that it should not infringe on people's religious beliefs.'

According to Article 473 of Lebanon's penal code, blasphemy in public is punishable by one month to one year in prison. Article 474 of the penal code authorizes imprisonment of six months to three years for publicly insulting a religion.

Prominent Lebanese intellectual, political and religious figures rallied to Khalife's defence in Beirut on 5 October, where he performed the song to a standing ovation. Some fifty lawyers volunteered to defend the musician and thousands of people and organizations, including the Lebanese Bar Association, signed petitions urging the Lebanese authorities to respect the right to freedom of expression and drop the charges against Khalife.

This was the second time in three years that Marcel Khalife had been accused of blaspheming Islam for singing the same song. The first proceedings against him in 1996 were halted after intervention by then Prime Minister Rafik al-Hariri.

On 14 December 1999, a Lebanese court found Marcel Khalife innocent of blasphemy.

The text below constitutes his addresses to the two court sessions and his statement upon receiving the verdict.

*Address to the first court session*

Today, I am heading to court to defend myself against an incomprehensible charge. I do not think I am going alone. I am accompanied by a rich tradition of artistic and cultural expression, past and present, the fruit of more than one generation. This tradition arises out of an overwhelming yearning for freedom, a deep desire to free the human mind from forces bent on deforming and distorting human thoughts. Yet, as I head to court, I am troubled by an inescapable feeling of dread which lies heavily upon my spirit and existence, a feeling of human sadness and cultural disgrace.

I am sad because in this part of the world there is a force that can take an artist to court and indict him, not for a crime he committed, a harm he caused, a disloyalty or treason, but for singing of love and freedom and trying earnestly to convey the conditions and concerns of his society.

I am sad because I have always based both my work and my private life on a love of freedom. I believed this goal to be common to all human beings, except for those that are perverted and ill natured.

I am sad because I assumed that the appreciation and support I received throughout the entire Arab world were a testimony to my success in expressing my nation's spirit in striving for freedom. This support reveals a nation whose conscience has been enriched by a religious tradition that has provided its people with a depth of intellectual and cultural dimensions.

The appreciation and love showered on me resulted from my advocating my people's concerns, ambitions, hopes and their longings for a better future while maintaining their connection to their past and without losing their authenticity.

My faith in my nation remains unshaken, as does my belief in its basic elements – the spiritual, cultural and moral, as well as the aspiration for a well-deserved place in this world.

As I head to court, I am not only saddened but also feel a profound cultural shame and great disappointment, shame and disappointment for a country that indicts an artist at the dawn of a new century. The accusation against me stems merely from relating passionately to a Quranic verse which opened my soul to vast horizons in ways no other text is capable of doing. I stand accused because I believed that the spirit of religion was more broad and tolerant than the interpretations by those who appoint themselves as guardians of our faith and morality. I also believed that inquisition courts were things of the past.

I am heading to court, burdened with pain because this trial may degrade the moral heritage of which I am proud. I took such care that my works should unify people – my people – and not divide them. I addressed people's sense of dignity and resistance, and was strengthened by their faith and their rightful claim to their land. I am going to court without the slightest feeling of guilt, though I do not know whether I am entering a triumphal arch of freedom or a monument of defeat for the future. I am going, not only to defend myself, but also to defend freedom. (Translated from the Arabic by Manal Swairjo)

*Address to the second court session*

First, I would like to ask a simple question:

Why is it that the Palace of Justice, which, in fulfilment of its basic purpose, opens the session in the name of the people and issues its verdicts in the name of the people, has its gates closed in the face of the people?

Is it because a creative artist has been dragged to the defendant's cage, while we stand on the cusp of a new century, that we found it necessary to lock all entrances to the Palace of Justice, more accurately the Palace of the People?

In any case, we are all here perhaps because we still believe in freedom and justice.

Why do you prosecute me?

I shall not believe that quoting or incorporating a fragment of a Koranic verse in a poem, and reciting it with reverence and spiritual sensitivity, justifies this lawsuit, this dubious decision, this rabid campaign, this prosecution.

Why do you prosecute me?

Is it because I have so keenly embarked upon a quest to elevate Arab music to a cultural status that empowers Arabs to address themselves – and the world around them – with eloquence that befits this nation?

Is it because I have protested in a civilized manner against the banality and stagnation in which the Arab individual blissfully lives day and night, exposed to the 'artistic' creations transmitted and aired by the Arab terrestrial stations and satellite networks?

Is this why I have been found liable to face an accusation as cold as a murderer's blood?

One would suppose that drug dealers, currency traders and merchants of electoral votes would be dragged to court to be questioned about their deeds which wound our national and religious dignity. But to drag the song 'Oh Father, I am Yusuf', along with its singer to the defendant's cage is the height of effrontery against the rights of the mind to conceive as it may conceive and to interpret its own consciousness.

What have I done to deserve this whirlwind? I have no need for it. I have formulated the song 'Oh My Father, I am Yusuf', written by the poet Mahmoud Darwish, with a densely symbolic texture in which Joseph represents innocence, beauty, truth and sacrifice, contrary to what was stated in the bill of charges.

Even if we abandon this conservative approach and consider the matter directly connected to the Quranic text, 'Surat Yusuf', what harm would befall a poet if his poem, his creative text, included a fragment of a scriptural verse?

Did I commit an outrageous precedent when I recited this refrain and thus deserved all this woe? Quranic citations and allusions have been a constant cultural and literary tradition that Arabs have kept alive from the time of the emigration to Yathrib to our time of emigration to the unknown in the twentieth century.

Have we become so desperately lost that the song 'Oh My Father, I am Yusuf', so full of truth, reverence and sensitivity, turns into a bombshell that threatens to shatter and destroy our whole edifice?

Have we so misread each other's faces that a song of resistance becomes a 'devil' that poisons our sacred texts, that we, who are the guardians of identity and integrity, would rob others of the ecstasy of gazing upon whatever makes them feel that they are a people with a mission on earth?

Who would believe that we, in an unguarded moment, would, just like that, be targeted by the law, when it was we who restored the law to its place on earth amid the debris of that chaos of banality, futility and war?

Who would believe that we would be prosecuted by a state whose right we defended to emerge from the age of militias as the phoenix emerges from its ashes?

And who would believe that a song that represents a burning moment of the collective Lebanese, even Arab, conscience would be condemned?

Can any human being imagine Lebanon putting its artists on trial? Lebanon would then be putting itself on trial. For who would dare judge the conscience of the people without subjecting the whole nation to a loss of self-confidence?

Lebanon erred against itself when it waged war against itself for fifteen years, producing an abundance of gratuitous death, far exceeding the bounds of self-sufficiency. It is our hope that it will not err once more against its image as a fulcrum of freedom where ideas, opinions and symbols are exchanged without having to pay political tariffs (in the name of religion or anything else). It is our hope that Lebanon will not succumb to insulting itself and insulting Arab culture by insulting the song 'Oh My Father, I am Yusuf'.

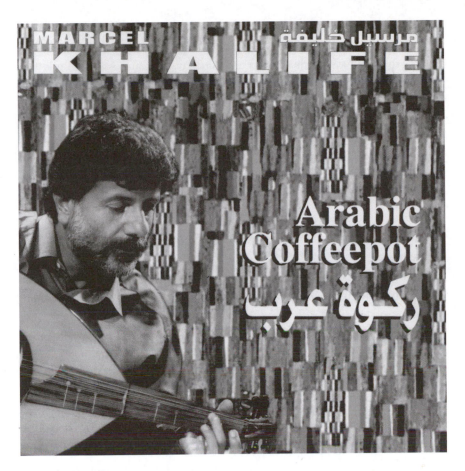

MARCEL KHALIFE    مرسيل خليفة

Arabic Coffeepot

ركوة عرب

9   *Arabic Coffeepot* **was first released in 1995 (CD cover designed by Emile Menhem, courtesy of Nagam records).**

The public has expressed its opinion regarding this unjust accusation which has been opposed by the forces of civil society (labour, students, the legal profession, the press corps, and proponents of culture), in magnificent initiatives of solidarity that embodied one of the most beautiful and powerful scenes of awakening of the collective Lebanese conscience. In this great torrent of initiatives of support launched by the vibrant social forces throughout the country, the objective was not only to defend Marcel Khalife, but also to defend Lebanon and its great national gains and assets. Once again, I salute those who created this scene of mass solidarity and defended the home country by defending justice against injustice. I am grateful to the outstanding moral support they have all demonstrated and in whose warmth I bask today amid the chill of this court of law.

In the end, my concern is to exercise my sacred natural and legal right to defend myself against this false accusation as a Lebanese citizen. It was never an ambition of mine to stand in a defendant's cage in my own country, accused of a charge that I know has a bigger and further aim than what it claims. This false, unrighteous accusation that has been levelled against me represents the worst personal offence that I have ever sustained in my life and the most vengeful attack against my artistic works by any entity. This offence, which I consider of dubious intent and malevolent nature, is an affront towards me and towards all those who have embraced these songs and this music from the Gulf to the Pacific Ocean. Indeed, this accusation is an insult to the national spirit. (Translated from the Arabic by Fuad Yahya)

*Statement upon receiving the verdict*

Having been notified of the judgment issued in my case, I feel happy for the Lebanese justice system for having cleansed itself of the previous questionable decision, which had placed it in the defendant's cage as a suppressor of freedom, culture and art.

I would like to thank all the people in Lebanon, the Arab world and the whole world who have supported my case and in doing so defended the human rights of freedom, culture and art. (Translated from the Arabic by Fuad Yahya)

# 16 | Songs of freedom: cultural resistance in Palestine

RANIA ELIAS-KHOURY

In South Africa they sang and danced against apartheid. In Chile they sang against dictatorship. In Palestine we shall sing for our freedom, to our own tunes and to those of the friends of freedom.

In Palestine we are struggling to maintain our presence in the prevailing circumstances, believing that our cultural heritage is being targeted as it represents the essence of a nation and its enduring ability to resist occupation and to keep on going. Our culture is reflected in our identity and is the means through which we confront crisis. It was for this reason that Yabous Productions was founded in 1995.

Yabous Productions is a non-profit Palestinian organization, initially founded in 1995 and based in the city of Jerusalem. Yabous organizes festivals and concerts, promotes Palestinian groups and artists working mainly in the field of the performing arts, and in the distribution of albums. The Jerusalem festival is the main annual activity of Yabous.

Each year we organize the different activities in modern and innovative forms as we assess the available artists, the closed borders, issues of timing and the capabilities of the organization and the people. Our ambition is to continue our cultural work free of any external influence, to plan and to implement, to organize and to delight people. Yet how can we achieve such a dream, knowing that our work is intimately affected by the surrounding social, political and economic situation?

Organizing a concert in Palestine these days is no easy task. In fact it is a very tough job unless you have hope, power and others contributing to your efforts. Let us look at the facts.

The political situation influences our goals, our programmes and our entire presence as it deprives us of our ability to move and work freely, hence to lead a normal life like all human beings. In 2001 Yabous Productions had to cancel two festivals and several concerts for reasons relating to the general political situation and the difficulties of issuing permits to groups and musicians, especially those from the Arab world. Even Palestinian artists living in West Bank towns such as Ramallah, which is nine kilometres from Jerusalem, are not allowed to travel to Jerusalem and vice versa.

Israeli occupation prevents international artists and musicians from participating in cultural events in Palestine. Maestro Daniel Barenboim was prevented by the Israeli occupation forces from travelling from Jerusalem to Ramallah to hold master classes at the Friends' Boys' School with the students of the National Conservatory of Music. Marwan Abado, the Palestinian oud player living in Vienna, was invited to perform in Jerusalem and Ramallah but he was stopped and detained for forty-eight hours at Ben Gurion Airport and was then sent back to Vienna. He has been blacklisted and is no longer allowed to enter Palestine.

The year 1998 marked the fiftieth anniversary of the Nakba 'cataclysm'. In human terms, that year saw the mass deportation of a million Palestinians from their cities and villages. In commemoration of these events in Palestinian history, Yabous Productions planned to organize a series of concerts called Songs of Freedom.

The Inti-Illimani group from Chile was invited to Songs of Freedom 2002. One of the Cuban artists was denied entry, being detained for twenty-four hours at the airport in Tel Aviv before being sent back on the first flight to Chile.

My husband Suhail Khoury – a Palestinian musician and composer and director of the National Conservatory of Music – was arrested and spent several months in an Israeli prison after he was caught at a checkpoint during the Intifada, transporting hundreds of cassettes of his music calling for freedom and struggle against Israeli occupation.

I remember a statement by the Palestinian author Tawfiq Zayad, saying: 'I never carried a rifle on my shoulder or pulled a trigger. All I have is a *nay*'s [flute's] melody, a brush to paint my dreams, a bottle of ink. All I have is unshakeable faith and an infinite love for my people in pain.' And this is what my husband is always carrying in his heart.

During the incursion of the Israeli occupation forces into Ramallah on 9 March 2002, several cultural premises were invaded, including the National Conservatory of Music (NCM), the Peace Centre in Bethlehem, the Sakakini Cultural Centre, and the Popular Art Centre in Ramallah. The main door of the NCM was opened using explosives, which caused major damage. They broke all the drawers and threw all the contents around. Cellos and other instruments were broken, as well as music CDs. Books were thrown on the floor and trampled upon. Ahmad Al Khatib, head of the Oriental Music Department at the NCM, was arrested on 8 April. He was used as a human shield by the Israeli occupation forces and later released.

The political situation controls all the news. Little coverage is given to cultural events if any. Official Palestinian TV stations and radio stations have been bombed and completely destroyed, as Israel claims that these stations encourage people to resist occupation.

In several cities, such as Ramallah, concerts are not organized nowadays. A curfew is imposed every day after six o'clock. People are occupied in taking care of their daily lives, finding work and food. There is no social life – nothing. In Nablus, they have been under curfew for three months. There are no schools, no work, not even a chance to bury the dead and give them respect. People are burying their beloved in their own courtyards!

As regards travel and visas, it is difficult for us as Palestinians to move – borders are closed, we are not allowed to travel through Ben Gurion Airport in Israel, and there are strict rules regarding travel through Jordan. This year I had to apologize for not being able to take part in twelve conferences and events in different parts of the world.

Given the difficult economic situation in which we are living, musical events are not among people's major priorities. Besides, people are afraid to move during the night-time. East Jerusalem is a ghost town at night. Come and visit Jerusalem and you can decide for yourselves.

Limited funding for musical events and the Jerusalem issue complicate matters greatly. Donors hesitate nowadays to fund musical events, as they are more focused on funding emergency measures such as rebuilding homes in Jenin and Nablus which have been destroyed by the Israeli army. This has left hundreds of refugees homeless, refugees twice over in their own homes.

How can we be expected to build our musical life under such conditions?

# 17 | The sound of silence: conformist musicians in Israel

NOAM BEN-ZEEV

When I told colleagues and friends I was flying to Copenhagen to participate in a conference on music and censorship, my statement met with genuine surprise. What? Music censorship? You mean in Israel, now? Surely there are no blacklists, I was told, no secret committees, no evil governmental schemes in our country. Surely the secret service does not chase up our musicians and silence them; so what will you talk about?

Some distant memories did arise while conversing, and my friends started vaguely remembering – the Beatles were not allowed here in the sixties, for example, and some of playwright Hanoch Levin's songs were banned. The forbidden 'Song for Peace' was mentioned, and likewise some daring fringe musicians who are being silenced. But these were but anecdotal occurrences, they said; how can you compare them with real censorship, such as that exercised in the totalitarian regimes of the world? No, this is not part of the culture of the 'the only democracy in the Middle East', as we proudly call ourselves, where one abides by the Declaration of Independence in terms of the absolute equality of all people in the face of the law.

The rich Israeli musical life, it seems, pulls a veil over our eyes – that is, the eyes of the Jewish-Israeli community, an 80 per cent majority in Israel. Twelve hundred classical music concerts a season, numerous festivals for vocal music, jazz, ethnic music, rock and pop, radio stations, TV programmes – all make us oblivious to the Palestinian music perspective, where a real, cruel censorship is taking place. These sounds – in halls and open-air venues, in parties and discos – shut our ears to the hardships of the 'other': where you must send your songs to broadcast committees for authorization, where you have no broadcasting opportunities, where record companies are not interested in you, where there is no infrastructure for music marketing, no music education system and neither governmental budgets nor copyright protection.

Still, my colleagues were absolutely right. From the point of view of the Jewish community, no music censorship does exist in Israel. We are as free as birds to play and sing whatever we choose.

But this is not good news.

Unfortunately, the absence of music censorship in the Israeli Jewish com-

144

munity comes about for the wrong reasons. Because to create a system of persecution the establishment needs a motivation. It needs to be threatened somehow. Someone should be very angry at it, protest against it, resent it strongly, even strive to overturn it.

But in today's Israeli music world, even as we watch democracy collapsing, there is only silence. The silence of Israeli artists and intellectuals during these past two years has been deafening. And this is frightening.

Musical instruments in Ramallah were destroyed by Israeli soldiers in the notorious 'Defence Shield' operation in March and April 2002 – and there's silence.

When holiday music festivities are taking place, the whole Palestinian population in the occupied territories is placed under curfew in order to protect the musicians and audience from a potential danger. Has any musician cancelled his appearance because of that? Protested against it? Commented upon it? Written a song about it?

No, there's silence.

Human rights organizations in Israel are vocal and active, uncompromisingly resisting this alarming escalation; but not musicians, composers, instrumentalists, conductors. So there's no one to persecute.

I would like to point out two rare exceptions to this rule.

In March 2002, the singer Yafa Yarkoni, as Israel Prize winner and an advocate of the consensus – she is known as the 'War Singer', having entertained soldiers in the front for more than half a century – declared that the images she saw of 'Defence Shield' reminded her of the Jews in the Holocaust. She saw Palestinians made to walk in file, tied and blindfolded. She didn't see the killing of civilians, the pulling down of houses on their inhabitants, the abuse at the roadblocks. These the papers didn't show. Still, it reminded her of the Holocaust; and she declared that she backed those soldiers who refused to serve in the occupied territories.

The reaction was swift. Her status in Israeli life didn't help her – she was dethroned in a day. All her concerts were immediately cancelled, including one organized by the Union of Israeli Artists. Threats made against her life obliged her family to hire private bodyguards. The media were outraged, and for more than a year now one has hardly heard her on the radio.

That means censorship is there. It is lurking. But it doesn't need the Establishment to exercise it. The job is being done from within. For example, Daniel Barenboim, the conductor and pianist, in protest at Sharon's regime goes to Ramallah to play and hear children play. He makes known his relations with Palestinians and has created a Jewish–Arab orchestra, as he believes that

145

having young people from opposite sides striving for the same artistic ends helps contribute to change. This has drawn criticism from within Israel. Another example is the Israeli conductor Uri Segal, who lives abroad, and who declared at the beginning of hostilities that he would not perform in Israel due to its behaviour in the occupied territories. He has not been seen in our country since.

These rare examples, of two musicians, one who lives abroad and one who is no longer active, only serve to underline the terrible silence of those musicians who are here now, and active. How can this be when artists and intellectuals in Israel are known to be so liberal and humane.

Is it fear?

I would say it is conformism. And conformism is not only the enemy of human rights; it is also the worst enemy of art.

Conformist musicians make things even worse by letting music itself down. They diminish it, and they hurt something very valuable and authentic that prevailed among Israeli and Palestinian musicians: their thirst to cooperate.

This cooperation occurs naturally in Israel, based less on ideology than on mutual need, on the common musical grounds that are present in the country. But it has been receiving blow after blow in the last two years, since more Israeli musicians have been turning their backs on their Palestinian colleagues.

My last example refers to a very dear friend, a Palestinian children's choir conductor from Jerusalem, a model of this cooperation. I heard her choir, singing with an Israeli one, both in Palestine and in Israel. The two choirs travelled together in both countries; you couldn't distinguish between the children, of course, and they were utterly happy, the Palestinians travelling abroad for the first time, visiting a town by the Mediterranean coast, and the Israelis venturing for the first time into the unknown Palestinian terrain, a forty-minute drive from their homes.

This is happening no more. For fear of roadblocks and raids, trapped in her home, my friend can no longer think of cooperation. This is now the stuff of future dreams.

I told her in a telephone conversation, 'We are lucky that you are such forgiving people, this is the only hope I have left.'

She said: 'We are too forgiving, too often.'

FIVE | **The Americas**

# 18 | Crash into me, baby: America's implicit music censorship since 11 September

ERIC NUZUM

'Freedom has been attacked, but freedom will be defended.' These were the words of President George Bush shortly after the 11 September terrorist attacks on the United States. Bush went on to say that the terrorists 'cannot touch the foundation of America' and 'we go forward to defend freedom'.[1] Despite Bush's rhetoric, the actions of the US government demonstrated a slightly different tactic for protecting the American way of life.

Within hours of the attacks, the Federal Bureau of Investigation (FBI) installed its controversial Carnivore system at some Internet providers to monitor and eavesdrop on electronic communications, especially those to and from accounts with Arabic names and words in the user IDs. Within two days, the US Senate had adopted legislation making it easier for the FBI to obtain warrants. Also, within a week of the attacks, many elected representatives were promoting 'anti-terrorism' legislation designed to allow law enforcement to gather private financial and education records and information, to expand the definition of 'terrorist' to anyone who knows or should know that an organization they support in any way is a terrorist organization, and to seize the property of those so suspected.[2]

The words of other politicians didn't match those of their commander-in-chief. US Senators Jon Kyl (Republican, Arizona) and Trent Lott (Republican, Mississippi), and House Democratic Leader Richard Gephardt (Democrat, Missouri), all said that the erosion of civil liberties was 'inevitable'. 'We're in a new world,' Gephardt said, 'we have to rebalance freedom and security.' Vermont's governor, Howard Dean, said the crisis would require 'a re-evaluation of the importance of some of our specific civil liberties'.

The American people seemed to get the message sent by their government: in order for us to protect you, you'll need to give up some of your freedom. The message resonated with the public, with an ABC-*Washington Post* poll finding 66 per cent of Americans willing to give up some civil liberties to combat terrorism.

Further complicating the protection of civil rights in the United States was the myopic jingoism permeating America, creating an atmosphere of visceral intolerance. Peace activists and civil libertarians were branded as 'un-American' and 'crazy communists'. Displays of American flags in public places became an expectation. One national talk-show host referred to the American Civil Liberties Union as 'the American version of al-Qaeda'. Many unpopular and dissenting opinions were dismissed as 'unpatriotic'.

This put the American music industry, traditionally a voice for almost all political and ideological persuasions, in a difficult position. Many artists and music companies felt the need to display some new-found sensitivity: Dave Matthews nixed plans to release 'When the World Ends' as his next single, Bush changed the title of their new single from 'Speed Kills' to 'The People that We Love', the Cranberries pulled their video for 'Analyse' because of its repeated images of skyscrapers and aircraft, Dream Theater changed the artwork from their three-disc live album to remove its renditions of burning New York buildings, and Sheryl Crow rewrote several lyrics for her most recent album.

While many of these gestures were simple exercises in latent taste, others were not. For example, The Strokes removed the song 'New York City Cops' from the US version of their album *Is This It*. Like so many pop songs, the theme of 'New York City Cops' is a relationship, but it does contain some lyrics, such as 'New York City cops – they ain't too smart', that could cause potential consternation in a post-11 September America.[3]

The official website for the group Rage Against the Machine – a high-profile virtual soapbox and town square for social and political discussion and debate among the group's fans – shut down its discussion boards shortly after the attacks following queries to the band and site's management by federal officials.

Further, the hip-hop group The Coup was forced by their record label, 75 Ark, to change the artwork for their album *Party Music*. The original cover featured the group standing in front of an exploding World Trade Center. While admittedly eerie in the wake of the attacks, the artwork (originally created eighteen months earlier) bore no direct connection to the attacks. The cover had not been printed but had been distributed electronically to the media in anticipation of the album's release. Shortly after the attacks, the group's leader, Boots Riley, told *Wired.com* that the design 'was supposed to be a metaphor for the capitalist state being destroyed through music'. Although he had initially expressed hope that the strong imagery would remain, Riley backed down under pressure from his record company. 'Two hours after the thing happened, we got the call saying, "OK, you've got to have another album cover. No discussion,"' Riley remembers. 'That was it. It was one of the first things that I saw in a series of censorship.'[4] The only further public comment on the cover came via a press statement released by the label, which read, '75 Ark recognizes and supports the artistic freedom of its artists, however recent extraordinary events demand that we create new artwork for the album.'[5]

But the incident that received the most attention was a rumoured list of songs banned from the radio, each containing literal or metaphorical references a bit too close to recent events. The list, containing more than 150 songs described as 'lyrically questionable', started as a grass-roots effort by local programmers, then was redistributed to all programmers by a senior executive at Clear Channel, the largest owner of radio stations in the United States. Among the listed songs were 'Fly', 'Jet Airliner', 'Head Like a Hole', 'Only the Good Die Young', 'Great Balls of Fire', 'Crash Into Me', 'It's the End of the World as We Know It', and many more.[6]

When the story hit the mainstream press, most journalists got it wrong. In a series of lapsed journalistic judgements, reporters were quick to believe that the list existed, then quick to believe it was a hoax.

It was widely reported that Clear Channel overtly banned the songs to avoid consternation and controversy, which wasn't true. The list was compiled by a senior vice-president of programming at Clear Channel, and then e-mailed from corporate management to the more than 1,100 individual stations under Clear Channel's ownership. While the management e-mail did not call for an overt ban on songs, it did ask that programmers use 'restraint' when selecting songs for airplay.

The story was initially reported on several radio industry websites on 14 September,[7] hitting the mainstream media on 17 September, led by a story on Slate.com.[8] When the story spread through the media, Clear Channel released a cleverly worded press statement headed 'Clear Channel Says National "Banned Playlist" Does Not Exist'. In the release, the company stated, 'Clear Channel Radio has not banned any songs from any of its radio stations.'[9] While the statement might seem to end the matter, it is just as telling for what it doesn't say as for what it does. Clear Channel correctly pointed out that the original e-mail didn't order anyone to ban any songs, but nowhere in the statement does the company deny that a list of 'lyrically questionable' songs was created, edited by management, redistributed by management, and then acted upon by its employees. The statement denies the existence of an explicit ban, which is accurate, but does not deny the existence of the list. Further, the statement does not deny any censorious actions by its employees.

While Clear Channel is quick to point out that there was no explicit censorship connected with the list, it is a perfect example of music censorship at its most implicit. Regardless of Clear Channel's intentions, censorship did occur. While many Clear Channel programmers were quoted in the media as saying

151

that they did not follow the suggestions of the e-mail, many times more said that they did indeed remove songs from broadcast because of the list or its suggested sense of restraint.[10]

Unfortunately, the media didn't apply the necessary scrutiny to Clear Channel's statement. Just as quickly as the media were swept into the controversy, the entire incident was written off as a 'hoax', disappearing from public discussion. Thanks to Clear Channel's savvy statement, the company had convinced the press that the list didn't exist at all; that earlier reports were no more credible than any other Internet hoax, such as get-rich-quick chain e-mail schemes or tales of sick children needing correspondence. Arguments over the complicated truth of various accusations and denials surrounding the Clear Channel list tend to distort the most troubling aspects of the incident. The real issue lies in the list's content, leading one to wonder exactly what Clear Channel's executives and programmers were trying to restrain.

While the list was mainly comprised of songs bearing lyrical references to burning, death and aircraft, it also advocated censure for 'Peace Train' by Cat Stevens, John Lennon's 'Imagine', and all songs by Rage Against the Machine. What do these songs have to do with flying aircraft into buildings? Absolutely nothing, but in the past each of these artists has expressed controversial political sentiments that buck mainstream beliefs.

'If our songs are "questionable" in any way, it is that they encourage people to question the kind of ignorance that breeds intolerance,' said Rage Against the Machine's Tom Morello in an e-mail statement. 'Intolerance which can lead to censorship and the extinguishing of our civil liberties, or at its extremes can lead to the kind of violence we witnessed.'[11]

The inclusion of many of the songs on the list shows a troubling degree of literalism and prejudice when examining lyrical imagery. For example, 'I Go to Pieces' was one of two songs by Peter and Gordon included. 'I suppose a song about someone going to pieces could be upsetting if someone took it literally,' said the group's Peter Asher. 'But "I can't live without love" is a sentiment that's as true in crisis as it is in normal times. It's a totally pro-love sentiment and could only be helpful right now.'[12]

The list's existence and the actions it prompted are a perfect example of how a well-intentioned attempt at 'sensitivity' can quickly careen down the slippery slope towards stifled free expression. This is hardly the first time American radio has taken such well-intentioned, yet censorious, action.

Back in 1940, the NBC radio network banned 147 popular songs containing potential sexual innuendo, including Billie Holiday's version of 'Love for Sale', calling these songs 'obscene'. In 1942, the United States government sent radio broadcasters a list of wartime practices, including a ban on weather forecasts (which might help enemies plan air attacks), and a suspension of listener requests (fearing it might allow the transmission of coded messages). In order to safeguard the morality of America's youth, *Billboard* magazine got behind a 1954 effort to rid radio of black R&B artists, claiming they 'show bad taste and a disregard for recognized moral standards'. In 1967, the ABC radio network and a group called the American Mothers' Committee tried to remove all songs from airplay that 'glorify sex, blasphemy, and drugs'. In 1970, the Federal Communications Commission – under pressure from the Nixon administration and working with a list of songs compiled by the US Army – sent a telegram to all radio owners warning them to remove all songs condoning drug use. Their list of songs included 'Yellow Submarine', 'Eight Miles High', and 'Puff (The Magic Dragon)'.

The idea of what was considered offensive or dangerous may have been different back then, but the reason such potential censorship needs to be resisted is the same. When we open up the question of 'tasteful' or 'appropriate' censorship – even a little – we turn rights into permissions. This month, radio might not want to offend those affected by tragedy or jeopardize domestic security; next time they may not want to play music that criticizes the government. You can imagine where this ends up.

Unfortunately, defending music is easily dismissed by some Americans as comparatively trivial in the wake of these horrible and gruesome tragedies. But should artistic liberties be cast aside in a time of national crisis? That depends on what you define as freedom. Music's reach and pervasiveness puts it on the cutting edge of that definition.

Defence of artistic rights is a multifarious example of the importance of protecting civil liberties – even on their periphery. While electronic wire-tapping and the boundaries of search-and-seizure laws may not excite or directly impact on a large number of Americans, the ability to hear 'Stairway to Heaven' or 'Lucy in the Sky with Diamonds' does.

In America, we are exposed to more music in a day than any other art form, perhaps more than all other forms of art combined. We use music in the most significant and most mundane of our activities, both to focus intense feelings and to distract us from the occasional dullness of life. While censors justify their actions based on music's suggested provocative potential, their actions completely disregard music's demonstrated evocative nature. Thus, as we impede music, we inhibit our ability to be fully human.

Music doesn't have to be patriotic, sensitive or even make sense. Music, at its most fundamental, is freedom. It just needs to be there.

*Iraq, 2003*

Since this chapter was first written in September 2002, the United States has initiated a military campaign in Iraq aimed at toppling the regime of Saddam Hussein and ridding the country of its alleged weapons of mass destruction. Debate over the justifications for this military action has been intense, both domestically and globally.

As in past military conflicts involving the United States, musicians attempted to play a central role in opposition to the war as well as, to a far lesser extent, opposing efforts organized to show support for the government's action and for US troops serving overseas. Unfortunately, and almost unilaterally, music failed to make much of a significant impact on the discussion in the United States.[13] Although a significant roster of musicians recorded and released anti-war songs,[14] only one (System of a Down's 'Boom') saw significant distribution and airplay. While some suggested that the limited effect of anti-war music was due in part to the decidedly pro-war stance taken by many large entertainment and media companies, the selection of anti-war music failed to ignite much interest among anti-war advocates at even the most grass-roots level.

Leading up to and during the military campaign, incidents of direct music censorship were few. However, many musicians who were focal points of the anti-war movement (or even *perceived* to be associated with the anti-war movement) received harsh and vituperative treatment in the media and from the public supporting the war. Those in support of the war seemed to have a short fuse as regards any anti-war statement made by celebrities in any media. Websites,[15] newspaper editorials and many current-events radio and television programmmes were devoted to efforts to keep musicians, actors and writers from using their celebrity and public status to discuss the war. Specific to music: Lenny Kravitz was widely chastised for his open opposition to the war, reporting that he received countless letters and phone calls rebuking him for releasing an anti-war song that featured an exiled Iraqi pop singer. The *New York Post* referred to Kravitz as the 'enemy's pal'.[16]

During a 1 April concert by the rock group Pearl Jam, singer Eddie Vedder placed a mask of US President George W. Bush on a microphone stand, then knocked it to the ground and repeatedly jumped on it. While some fans did cheer the actions, others booed and left the concert, demanding their money back. The incident was a discussion point in the American media for several days following the concert.[17]

Sensing the brewing hostility towards anti-war music, Madonna edited then later pulled her video for 'American Life'. The video's strong anti-war imagery included Madonna tossing a live grenade to a George Bush lookalike.

10 Dixie Chicks Destruction Day rally sponsored by Louisiana radio station KRMD-FM (at the time of going to press all efforts have been made to locate the copyright holder of this photograph).

According to a statement released by the singer: 'Due to the volatile state of the world and out of sensitivity and respect for the armed forces, who I support and pray for, I do not want to risk offending anyone who might misinterpret the meaning of the video.'[18]

The most troubling and widespread of the few censorious acts taken against anti-war musicians involved the country group the Dixie Chicks. In-between songs during a 10 March concert in London, Dixie Chick lead singer Natalie Maines said, 'Just so you know, we're ashamed the President of the United States is from Texas.'

However large a controversy the comment eventually created back home, the incident did not seem to make much of an immediate impact. Six London papers reviewed the show and none made any reference to the comment. Further, the American ambassador to Britain – who was in attendance at the concert – came backstage afterwards to greet the group and made no reference to the remark. The quote did not show up in the press at all until two days later, when the *Guardian* published a lukewarm review of the show, including a mention of the comment and how unusual it was. A few days later the *Guardian* article was posted on the ultra-conservative website <freerepublic.com>[19] (ground zero for conservative talk shows in America – information posted on the site is usually that day's lead discussion topic on most conservative talk radio and television programmes).

Once the controversy erupted, Maines did offer an apology, claiming her remark was 'disrespectful'. However, the apology didn't seem to register with those angered by her remark. Even though news of the comment coincided with the launch of the US invasion of Iraq, the reactions were quick and angry. With little concern for verifying the accuracy of the statement, war supporters were swift to call for harsh sanctions against the group. Within a day of the incident's mention on Free Republic, dozens of radio stations (and several radio networks) pulled all Dixie Chicks songs from their playlists. In South Carolina, the state legislature approved a resolution calling for the Dixie Chicks to play a benefit concert for military families.[20] In Kansas City, Missouri, local patriots staged a 'Chicken Toss' – inviting their America-loving friends and neighbours to toss Dixie Chicks CDs and tapes into the trash. In Louisiana, concerned citizens held a demonstration that involved a mass destruction of the group's CDs.[21] One radio station in Dallas logged 700 calls on the day the story broke, calling the group 'anti-Bush', 'anti-American' and 'anti-troop'.

Although the number of censorship incidents is relatively small (especially considering the level of political dialogue concerning the war), the heated reactions of many Americans to *any* dissenting opinion have had a chilling effect, both inside music and out. The real impact of anti-war vilification may not be apparent in the context of the Iraqi war, but rather in how it affects American musicians' willingness to provide a voice for unpopular expression in the future.

## Notes

1 'Poll: Americans Back Bush; Expect War', Reuters, 16 September 2001.

2 Jean Patman, 'First Amendment advocates fear erosion of rights in aftermath of attacks', *The Freedom Forum,* 14 September 2001. Internet:<http://www.freedomforum.org>.

3 Quote from the lyrics to 'New York City Cops' by The Strokes:

The authorities they've seen
Darling I'm somewhere in between
I said everynight everynight, I just can't stop sayin'
New York City cops
They ain't too smart

4 Soren Baker, 'Coup Change Blowing-Up-WTC Cover Art, But Keep Revolutionary Message Intact', *MTV Online,* 7 November 2001. Internet:<http://www.mtv.com/news/articles/1450559/20011107/story.jhtml>.

5 Internet: <http://www.75ark.com>.

6 The list, as reported in the press, contains the following songs (list rearranged alphabetically by title, original spellings left intact): '99 Luft Balloons/99 Red Balloons', Nina; 'A Day in the Life', The Beatles; 'A Sign of the Times', Petula Clark; 'A World without Love', Peter and Gordon; 'Aeroplane', Red Hot Chili Peppers; 'America', Neil Diamond; 'American Pie', Don McLean; 'And When I Die', Blood Sweat and Tears; 'Another One Bites the Dust', Queen; 'Bad Day', Fuel; 'Bad Religion', Godsmack; 'Benny & The Jets', Elton John; 'Big Bang Baby', Stone Temple Pilots; 'Bits and Pieces', Dave Clark Five; 'Black is Black', Los Bravos; 'Blow Up the Outside World', Soundgarden; 'Blowin' in the Wind', Peter Paul and Mary; 'Bodies', Drowning Pool; 'Boom', P.O.D.; 'Bound for the Floor', Local H; 'Brain Stew', Green Day; 'Break Stuff', Limp Bizkit; 'Bridge over Troubled Water', Simon and Garfunkel; 'Bullet with Butterfly Wings', Smashing Pumpkins; 'Burnin' for You', Blue Oyster Cult; 'Burning Down the House', Talking Heads; 'Chop Suey!', System of a Down; 'Click Click Boom', Saliva; 'Crash and Burn', Savage Garden; 'Crash into Me', Dave Matthews Band; 'Crumbling Down', John Mellencamp; 'Dancing in the Streets', Martha and the Vandellas/Van Halen; 'Daniel', Elton John; 'Dead Man's Curve', Jan and Dean; 'Dead Man's Party', Oingo Boingo; 'Death Blooms', Mudvayne; 'Devil in Disguise', Elvis Presley; 'Devil with the Blue Dress', Mitch Ryder and the Detroit Wheels; 'Dirty Deeds', AC/DC; 'Disco Inferno', Tramps; 'Doctor My Eyes', Jackson Brown; 'Down', 311; 'Down in a Hole', Alice in Chains; 'Dread and the Fugitive', Megadeth; 'Duck and Run', 3 Doors Down; 'Dust in the Wind', Kansas; 'End of the World', Skeeter Davis; 'Enter Sandman', Metallica; 'Eve of Destruction', Barry McGuire; 'Evil Ways', Santana; 'Fade to Black', Metallica; 'Falling Away from Me', Korn; 'Falling for the First Time', Barenaked Ladies; 'Fell on Black Days', Soundgarden; 'Fire', Arthur Brown; 'Fire and Rain', James Taylor; 'Fire Woman', The Cult; 'Fly Away', Lenny Kravitz; 'Fly', Sugar Ray; 'Free Fallin'', Tom Petty; 'Get Together', Youngbloods; 'Goin' Down', Bruce Springsteen; 'Great Balls of Fire', Jerry Lee Lewis; 'Harvester or Sorrow', Metallica; 'Have You Seen Her', Chi-Lites; 'He Ain't Heavy, He's My Brother', Hollies; 'Head Like a Hole', Nine Inch Nails; 'Hell's Bells', AC/DC; 'Hey Joe', Jimi Hendrix; 'Hey Man, Nice Shot', Filter; 'Highway to Hell', AC/DC; 'Hit Me with Your Best Shot', Pat Benatar; 'Holy Diver', Dio; 'I Feel the Earth Move', Carole King; 'I Go to Pieces', Peter and Gordon; 'I'm on Fire', Bruce Springsteen; 'I'm on Fire', John Mellencamp; 'Imagine', John Lennon; 'In the Air Tonight', Phil Collins; 'In the Year 2525', Yager and Evans; 'Intolerance', Tool; 'Ironic', Alanis Morissette; 'It's the End of the World as We Know It', REM; 'Jet Airliner', Steve Miller; 'Johnny Angel', Shelly Fabares; 'Jump', Van Halen; 'Jumper', Third Eye Blind; 'Killer Queen', Queen;

'Knockin' on Heaven's Door', Bob Dylan/Guns N Roses; 'Last Kiss', J. Frank Wilson; 'Learn to Fly', Foo Fighters; 'Leavin' on a Jet Plane', Peter Paul and Mary; 'Left Behind, Wait and Bleed', Slipknot; 'Live and Let Die', Paul McCartney and Wings; 'Love Is a Battlefield', Pat Benatar; 'Lucy in the Sky with Diamonds', The Beatles; 'Mack the Knife', Bobby Darin; 'Morning Has Broken', Cat Stevens; 'Mother', Pink Floyd; 'My City was Gone', Pretenders; 'Na Na Na Na Hey Hey', Steam; 'New York, New York', Frank Sinatra; 'Nowhere to Run', Martha & the Vandellas; 'Obla Di, Obla Da', The Beatles; 'On Broadway', Drifters; 'Only the Good Die Young', Billy Joel; 'Peace Train', Cat Stevens; 'Rescue Me', Fontella Bass; 'Rock the Casbah', The Clash; 'Rocket Man', Elton John; 'Rooster', Alice in Chains; 'Ruby Tuesday', Rolling Stones; 'Run Like Hell', Pink Floyd; 'Sabbath Bloody Sabbath', Black Sabbath; 'Sabotage', Beastie Boys; 'Safe in New York City', AC/DC; 'Santa Monica', Everclear; 'Say Hello to Heaven', Temple of the Dog; 'Sea of Sorrow', Alice in Chains; 'See You in September', Happenings; 'Seek and Destroy', Metallica; 'She's Not There', Zombies; 'Shoot to Thrill', AC/DC; 'Shot Down in Flames', AC/DC; 'Smokin', Boston; 'Smooth Criminal', Alien Ant Farm; 'Some Heads are Gonna Roll', Judas Priest; 'Speed Kills', Bush; 'Spirit in the Sky', Norman Greenbaum; 'St Elmo's Fire', John Parr; 'Stairway to Heaven', Led Zeppelin; 'Suicide Solution', Black Sabbath; 'Sunday Bloody Sunday', U2; 'Sure Shot', Beastie Boys; 'Sweating Bullets', Megadeth; 'That'll be the Day', Buddy Holly and the Crickets; 'The Boy from New York City', Ad Libs; 'The End', The Doors; 'The Night Chicago Died', Paper Lace; 'Them Bones', Alice in Chains; 'Ticket to Ride', The Beatles; 'TNT', AC/DC; 'Travelin' Band', Creedence Clearwater Revival; 'Travelin' Man', Rick Nelson; 'Tuesday's Gone', Lynyrd Skynyrd; 'Under the Bridge', Red Hot Chili Peppers; 'Walk Like an Egyptian', Bangles; 'War Pigs', Black Sabbath; 'War', Edwin Starr/Bruce Springstein; 'We Gotta Get Out of This Place', Animals; 'What a Wonderful World', Louis Armstrong; 'When Will I See You Again', Three Degrees; 'When You're Falling', Peter Gabriel; 'Wipeout', Surfaris; 'Wonder World', Sam Cooke/Herman's Hermits; 'Worst that Could Happen', Brooklyn Bridge; 'You Dropped a Bomb on Me', The Gap Band; All Rage Against the Machine songs.

7  'The Reactions Keep Coming', *Hits Daily*, 14 September 2001. Internet: <http://www.hitsdailydouble.com/news/newsPage.cgi?news02701m01>.

8  Eliza Truitt, 'It's the End of the World as Clear Channel Knows It', *Slate.com*, 17 September 2001. Internet:<http://slate.msn.com/?id=1008314>.

9  Full text of the Clear Channel press statement:

Clear Channel says National 'Banned Playlist' does not exist

For Immediate Release

San Antonio, TX, September 18, 2001 ... Clear Channel Communications, Inc. (NYSE: CCU) today issued the following statement as a result of numerous stories, emails and calls concerning an alleged 'list of banned songs' on its U.S. radio stations following last week's tragedy in New York, Washington and Pennsylvania:

'Clear Channel Radio has not banned any songs from any of its radio stations. Clear Channel believes that radio is a local medium. It is up to every radio station program director and general manager to understand their market, listen to their listeners and guide their station's music selections according to local sensitivities. Each program director and general manager must take the pulse of his or her market to determine if play lists should be altered, and if so, for how long.

'"In the wake of this terrible tragedy, the nation's business community is responding with a degree of hypersensitivity," explained Mark P. Mays, President and Chief Operating Officer of Clear Channel. "Even some movie companies have altered some of their release schedules in light of the mood in America today.  Clear Channel strongly believes in the First Amendment and freedom of speech. We value and support the artist community. And we support our radio station programming staff and management team in their responsibility to respond to their local markets.'"

10  James Sullivan, 'Radio employee circulates don't-play list', *San Francisco Chronicle*, 18 September 2001. Internet: <www.sfgate.com/cgi- in/article.cgi?file=/ chronicle/archive/2001/09/18/DD228327.DTL>; Mark Armstrong, '"Imagine" All the Inappropriate Songs', *E Online*, 18 September 2001. Internet: <http: //www.eonline.com/News/Items/0,1,8842,00.html>; Frank Ahrens, 'After Heroics, Russian Reporter Stricken', *Washington Post*, 18 September 2001. Internet: <http:// www.washingtonpost.com/ac2/wp-dyn?pagename=article&node=&contentId=A47168- 2001Sep17>; Brad King, 'Radio Sings Self-Censorship Tune', *Wired.com*, 18 September 2001. Internet: <http://www.wired.com/news/culture/0,1284,46925,00.html>; Douglas Wol, 'And the Banned Play On', *The Village Voice*, 26 September 2001. Internet: <http: //www.villagevoice.com/issues/0139/wolk.php>.

11  Neil Strauss, 'After the Horror, Radio Stations Pull Some Songs', *New York Times*, 19 September 2001. Internet: <http://www.nytimes.com/2001/09/19/arts/music/ 19POPL.html?ex=1001895812&ei=1&en=2e0d16964ae0c1ea>.

12  Ibid.

13  Internet: <http://www.nytimes.com/2003/02/20/opinion/20THU4.html>.

14  Anti-war songs released before the start of the Iraq war: Zack de la Rocha, 'March of Death'; System of a Down, 'Boom'; REM, 'The Final Straw'; Lenny Kravitz, 'We Want Peace'; Billy Bragg, 'The Price of Oil'; Beastie Boys, 'In a World Gone Mad'; John Mellencamp, 'To Washington'; Mick Jones, 'Why Do Men Fight?'; Cat Stevens, 'Peace Train'.

15  Internet:<http://www.ipetitions.com/campaigns/hollywoodceleb/>.

16  Sarah Gilbert, 'Peace of the Rock', *New York Post*, 27 March 2003, p. 55.

17  Jenny Eliscu, 'War On Protest', *Rolling Stone*, 1 May 2003, p. 9.

18  Jon Wiederhorn, 'Madonna Yanks Controversial "American Life" Video', *MTV News*, 31 March 2003. Internet: <http://www.mtv.com/news/articles/1470876/ 20030331/madonna.jhtml?headlines>.

19  Internet: <http://www.freerepublic.com>.

20  Associated Press, 'Lawmakers: Chicks Should Do Free Concert', 20 March 2003.

21  Warren St John, 'The Backlash Grows against Celebrity Activists', *New York Times*, 23 March 2003, pp. B1, B12.

# 19 | Havana and Miami: a music censorship sandwich

ERIC SILVA BRENNEMAN

Freemuse has become increasingly preoccupied with the recent crack-down on dissidents in Cuba. Along with the arrests of journalists, academics and affiliates to religious and non-governmental organizations, Freemuse is most concerned with the censorship and/or imprisonment of Cuban musicians for performances or lyrical content deemed subversive by the Castro government. To further complicate the situation for musicians, freedom of musical expression is not suppressed just in Havana. The anti-Castro exile community in Miami, particularly Dade County, has imposed its own forms of music censorship on Cuban musicians. Thus, an almost 'lose-lose' situation exists for Cuban musicians, sandwiched between the two locations.

This study was conducted mostly through Internet research as well as e-mail contact with journalists and academics.

## Crack-down 2003

In March 2003, with US preparations to invade Iraq being finalized and concern throughout the world that other states accused of aiding terrorists might also be targeted, around seventy-five Cuban citizens accused of conspiring with the USA were arrested, subjected to quick trials and sentenced to terms of up to twenty-eight years. Wayne Smith, head of the US government's Cuban interests section in the Carter administration, stated, 'The Cubans saw it [the Iraq war] as a signal that the United States was determined to throw its weight around and to blow away anyone it doesn't like through the unilateral use of force.'[1] Amnesty International (AI) notes this as the most severe crack-down on the dissident movement since the years after the 1959 revolution. AI also considers the detainees prisoners of conscience and thus demands their immediate release.[2] Ironically, the round-up occurred as Cuban relations with the international community were improving. There was open dialogue with the EU (blocked for five years) and meetings with EU representatives were scheduled. For the eleventh consecutive year, the UN called on the USA to end its embargo. Cuba's relations with Canada improved. Along with the worry of another US invasion, Cuban authorities observed the arrival in Havana and the subsequent actions of James Cason, head of the US interests section in the Bush administration, as a threat to the Cuban government. It was reported that Cason spent a lot of time travelling around the island meeting religious leaders and journalists, and even allowing dissidents to use his residence for events.[3]

Freedom of expression has been limited by the Cuban constitution since the revolution. Freedom of speech is recognized 'in conformity with the objectives of the socialist society'.[4] As such, speech observed as hostile to the Cuban government is not constitutionally protected – thus Article 91 of the Cuban Penal Code and Law 88, which together were used against fifty-one of the dissidents and have the potential to be used against musicians as well. Article 91 states: 'He who, in the interest of a foreign state, commits an act with the objective of damaging the independence or territorial integrity of the Cuban state, incurs the penalty of ten to twenty years, imprisonment, or death.'[5] Law 88, the Law of Protection of the National Independence and Economy of Cuba, came into existence in February 1999 as a direct reaction to the US Helms-Burton Law.[6] Perhaps the most relevant articles of Law 88 in terms of freedom of musical expression are Articles 7 and 8. Article 7 prescribes imprisonment of up to five years for anyone collaborating with radio, TV or other media deemed to be promoting US policy (the penalty increases if the individual profits through the activity). Article 8 prescribes up to five years for disturbing the public order for the benefit of the US economic war on Cuba.[7] It has been established by Article 19 of the International Covenant on Civil and Political Rights that any restriction on freedom of expression must be strictly proportionate to the threat posed to national security and may not exceed what is necessary to fulfil that aim. Owing to the fact that Cuba has faced no military aggression since the crack-down, and dissidents including musicians are still threatened, one may conclude that the crack-down is in violation of Article 19.

*Havana: industrial/governmental censorship*

Many musicians who left Cuba permanently after the Cuban revolution, whether for political reasons or simply to try to explore a possible career somewhere else in the world, are heavily censored by the government-backed broadcasting centre, the Cuban Institute for Radio and Television (ICRT). Therefore, such artists are normally not heard on national radio stations. Should the destination of such a musician have been the USA, the above form of censorship will certainly occur. In addition, the artist's albums will be unavailable for purchase, save on the black market. Between the 1960s and 1970s, the island performed a cultural genocide the consequences of which are still difficult to calculate today.[8] Important Cuban musicians such as Mario Bauzá, dubbed 'the father of Latin jazz', and Arsenio Rodríguez, one of the important developers of Cuban *son*, have been deemed enemies of the state since they left after the revolution. Other names important to the history of Cuban music who have had issues with state censorship include: Miguelito Valdés, Arturo 'Chico' O'Farrill, Orlando Guerra (Cascarita), Armando Oréfiche, Machito, Mongo Santamaría, Antonio Machín, and even Silvio Rodríguez and Pablo Milanés. The list could continue. The albums of these artists literally served as fuel for the fires set by government and media officials claiming that the burning of their work was an appropriate way to make the artists pay for their treason.

Beginning in the 1990s, the ICRT tried to show that it was being more lenient in its programming by claiming that it would 'analyse' all music before deciding what was appropriate for airplay. Of course, any artist in exile or tied to the USA in any way went into analysis and never reappeared. In essence, if anything censorship was heightened as more musicians' music came under analysis. Examples of this new wave of censorship affected complete orchestras such as Sonora Matancera, composers such as José Antonio Fajardo and Willy Chirino and an uncountable number of musicians. To name just a few of the world-renowned names who have been under analysis for years, the list includes: Cachao, Paquito D'Rivera, Arturo Sandoval, Gloria Estefan, Juan Pablo Torres, Patato Valdés, Orlando Vallejo, Olga Guillot, Blanca Rosa Gil, Orlando Contreras, Ñico Membiela, Bienvenido Granda and René Cabel.

In discussing such a list of new Cuban musical talent enjoyed throughout the entire world except in the artists' own nation, one has to consider the censorship and treatment of La Reina, Celia Cruz. The 'Queen of Salsa' is certainly one of Cuba's most famous artists; indeed, one of the most famous to have originated in the entire Latin American and Caribbean region. But were it not for piracy and the black market, it is quite possible that for post-revolution Cuban generations the voice of Celia Cruz could have been silenced within the island. For some, the first they heard of Celia was through international news coverage of her surgery in December 2002. Michel Suárez comments: 'Will Celia pass, as will eventually happen someday by the law of nature, without the generations of the last 44 years having had the privilege of knowing her better?'[9] There is increasing concern within the international music community that the post-revolution generations are growing up without knowing or hearing any of these censored musicians.[10] With so many important musicians and ground-breaking music prohibited, there could very well be a loss of Cuban identity in future generations.

Also during the 1990s, with the economic and social changes that were implemented with the fall of the USSR and the surge in the Cuban tourist industry, a new form of Cuban dance music evolved. *Timba* and its percussive rhythms began to take the country and tourist industry by storm. Yet lyrically *timba* was to form the basis of an interesting dialogue about the social situation in Cuba at this time. The experience of people having to hustle for money and of prostitutes, or love being replaced by sex for money, were subjects often heard in these lyrics.[11] Not surprisingly, many *timba* songs ended up under analysis by the ICRT. In the case of the band La Charanga Habanera, some songs were completely banned.

Rock music in Cuba has been heavily censored ever since the Beatles arrived on the island. Simply by choosing to play or record rock, a musician is stigmatized for partaking in music of Anglo-Saxon origin. Lyrical content aside, some Cuban rock bands have even been censored just because of their band names. Abbreviations, rather than the real names of some bands, have appeared in the mass media without any consultation with the musicians.[12] A recent case began in April 2003 when the lead singer of a punk rock band was arrested on drug charges after a show. He has been imprisoned at the Kilo Cinco y Medio Prison in Pinar del Rio. Interestingly, this prison is known to contain a number of political dissidents. The singer went on trial in mid-August 2003 but no verdict was pronounced as the judges decided the case needed to be re-examined.

The emergence of Cuban rap appears to have given the ICRT its latest target. In an attempt to control politically driven rap, the state required rappers to join youth organizations throughout the nation. Rappers who refused to do so became 'independent'. This independence granted them freedom in terms of lyrical content, but state censorship soon followed and the musicians were persecuted and not allowed to perform. Carlos Calafell, director of Nueva Gerona radio, found this out the hard way. Calafell was fired in November 2002 for playing a rap song that criticized the social situation in Cuba. Manolo Rivero, of the independent rap group Juglar, says that because of the group's experimental music and aggressive lyrics 'they [the Ministry of Culture] know we'll never join up with the regime'.[13] On 30 April 2003, in response to the crack-down on dissidents, Juglar took to the streets to protest in rhyme. It didn't take long for police to arrive and arrest Rivero and the other members of the group. They were released the following day.

## Miami: recent censorship by the exiles

It is common knowledge that Miami, in particular Dade County, is home to hundreds of thousands of Cuban exiles who fled the aftermath of the revolution and who continue to arrive to the present day. It is also common knowledge that the exiles are anti-Castro, the majority being right-wing conservatives. Because of this, they are granted asylum upon setting foot on US soil. (Nevertheless, it should be noted that there are always exceptions and not all Cuban exiles fit these categories. As we shall see, they allow themselves to be classified as such for fear of what consequences may occur should they speak out against those with power.) Further, it is common knowledge that the Cuban exile community is one of the most powerful lobbying groups not only in the state of Florida but also in Washington, DC. What may not be common knowledge is the exile community's use of music censorship as a political tool against any Cuban artist who does not denounce the Castro government. Because of their political clout, the exiles' policies often go unchecked even if they are unconstitutional. There have been a number of specific cases of music censorship over the past ten years in Dade County, Florida.

After Cuba shot down two exile-piloted planes in 1996, killing four, the Cuban exile community came forward with its 'Cuba Ordinance'. This stated that all groups seeking to book in Miami-Dade County must swear not to 'subcontract with' or 'purchase supplies from' any person or entity conducting business with Cuba. It also bans county vendors (such as concert arenas) from trading in anything related to Cuba, prohibits county contractors from visiting Cuba, and gives local officials unbridled discretion in granting waivers to the policy.[14] The ordinance clearly broke federal law and was deemed unconstitutional by the American Civil Liberties Union (ACLU). Attorney Bruce Rogow commented, 'In effect, Miami-Dade County has adopted its own foreign policy towards Cuba in violation of the Supremacy Clause of the Constitution of the United States.'[15] The ordinance has also been obstructive towards the Miami Light Project and other cultural organizations that try to book artists for live performances. 'The effect of the ordinance has been to impose censorship of a wide range of cultural and artistic expression on the people of Miami-Dade County,'[16] said John de Leon, president of Florida's ACLU.

December 1996 saw Cuban musician Rosita Flores scheduled to play at the Centro Vasco, a popular restaurant in Little Havana (Miami). There had been no record of Flores ever denouncing the Cuban government. Private attorney José Garcia-Pedrosa, who has also held local political positions such as city manager, could not accept such an act of subversion against the Cuban people in Miami. Brett Sokol of the *Miami New Times* commented, 'When it comes to matters of the arts, there's little difference between him and the more obviously Neanderthal types manning the megaphones and AM airwaves of the Cuban-exile community.'[17] Using his political clout within the community,

Garcia-Pedrosa single-handedly cancelled the performance. As if this form of censorship weren't enough, the restaurant was fire-bombed. Three years later Garcia-Pedrosa was using negative rhetoric towards the Afro-Cuban All Stars as they planned their world tour. Should he be elected to other political offices within Miami, other artists may be targeted as well.

In March 1997, Tropical 98.3, a Spanish-language radio station in Miami, broke new ground by playing music by Cuban pop stars. Many recently arrived exiles began to hear the music they were accustomed to in Cuba, by artists such as Los Van Van, Isaac Delgado and Manolín el Médico de Salsa. But station director Zummy Oro found out the hard way that freedom of expression in terms of airing whatever music one wants comes at a cost in Miami. First, irate and profane callers began phoning the station, screaming their disgust at employees. Next, people began gathering outside the station, calling the change in the playlist a plot by Cuban President Fidel Castro to divide the exile community.[18] Finally, four days after the new playlist was aired, the station was evacuated, having received a bomb threat. DJ Elmo Lugo said: 'We had the balls to try something new and we had our balls cut off.'[19] Fearing for the employees' safety, the station reverted to excluding all Cuban music.

The Cuban American Defense League responded by saying the Cuban exiles had acted like the Spanish Inquisition. They added that their behaviour was 'another glaring example of intolerance and censorship in our community'. Lawyer Magda Montil Davis commented: 'Enough is enough. We cannot allow big political muscle to comport themselves in this way. The issue is that in this country you have the right to express yourself freely without death threats and bomb threats.'[20] The organization responded to the exile community's claims that the playing of Cuban music was supporting Castro's repression by explaining that playing such music, even when paying royalties to the artists, did not violate the US embargo, which exempts cultural exchanges. The most powerful exile group, the Cuban American National Foundation, simply commented, 'We are not terrorists.'[21]

Perhaps the most famous examples of Miami's battle against freedom of musical expression were the events related to the Latin Grammy Awards. The awards ceremony was to be held in Miami in September 1999. As Miami can be considered one of the centres, if not *the* centre, of Latin music in the USA, it was an obvious first choice. However, upon hearing of the participation of a number of Cuban artists, Mayor Alex Penalas had other ideas. He refused to make the county-owned American Airlines Arena available for the event should any Cuban artists be included. As a result, the event was moved to Los Angeles.

A case that continues to the present wherein the exile community flexed its music censorship muscles was the scheduled appearance of Cuba's Los Van Van in Miami. South Beach promoter Deborah Ohanian booked the world-famous band at the American Airlines Arena for a show in October 1999. Immediately, the exiles began to take action against 'Havana Debbie', as she was labelled. The exiles would not accept an appearance by what they felt was 'the official band of Fidel Castro'.[22] As the community threatened to take legal action, as it had in the past, Ohanian looked for allies to support her constitutional rights. She received help from the ACLU. In order to prevent violence, the city of Miami increased police security around the arena and charged the $35,000 tab directly to Ohanian. To keep the peace and allow the show to proceed as scheduled, she paid the fee, fearing that otherwise concertgoers would be too scared to attend due to threats of violence from the exiles. Nevertheless, she knew that being charged this sum was unconstitutional, excessive and discriminatory. The concert went ahead as planned, but thousands of demonstrators showed up, throwing rocks, batteries, cans and bottles at those entering the arena. Eleven people were arrested. After the show, both Ohanian and the ACLU were ready to take action and sued the city of Miami. A verdict is yet to be determined.

Returning to the issue of the Cuba Ordinance, in the spring of 2000 the ACLU sued Miami-Dade on the grounds that the ordinance was unconstitutional and an attack on civil liberties and artistic expression. In July 2000, a US district judge was ready with a decision. Judge Federico Moreno said he would prevent the local government from further implementing and enforcing the Cuba Ordinance. The ruling was considered a grand victory by the civil liberties groups that have been in conflict with the Cuban exile community for years. Howard Simon of the ACLU said: 'Judge Moreno has initiated a new day in Miami for tolerance, diversity, and freedom of the arts. We are pleased he will remove Miami-Dade County from the business of foreign policy and end the persistent censorship of the arts in South Florida.'[23] It was certainly a good start, but there is still a great deal of work to be done.

## Latest developments

As this chapter was revised in July 2003, the salsa world lost its queen. Celia Cruz passed on, and she is greatly missed the world over. As final preparations were being made for the Latin Grammy Awards in Miami on 2 September 2003, it was only fitting to include a tribute to the life and music of La Reina. However, what would a Latin Grammy ceremony be without some controversy regarding Cuba? History seemed to be repeating itself. The exile community was not about to let any pro-Castro musicians crash their party. They were

11 The Cuban musician Gorki, sentenced to four years' imprisonment, in front of wall inscription 'We wish to be happy here' (courtesy of Gorki).

quickly granted permits to protest should any such musicians be allowed to participate. Fortunately for the exiles, in August 2003 the US and Cuban governments began feuding over the visa requirements of the nominated Cuban musicians attending the ceremony. The Cuban government believed the USA was deliberately delaying the visas while the USA claimed that the Cuban government was deferring visa requests. In the end, none of the nominated Cuban musicians, such as Chucho Valdés and Los Van Van, was able to attend the ceremony because they did not receive their visas on time.

There have also been tragic developments concerning the trial of musician Gorki Luis Aguila Carrasco, front man of the punk-rock band Porno para Ricardo. Re-examination of his case apparently did not take long. A week after it began, on 15 August 2003, he was informed that he had been sentenced to a four-year prison term on charges of drug trafficking, although no evidence of drug trafficking was presented. Freemuse has called for his immediate release by way of an international campaign. After months of detention at the prison in Pinar del Rio in terrible living conditions, in November 2003 he was moved to a labour correctional institution in Havana. He should be able to receive more visits and be treated with more care in the new location, but the campaign for his freedom continues.

## Conclusions

Because of these examples of infringement of musicians' rights in the different forms presented here, Freemuse calls on both Cuba and the USA to allow musicians their fundamental human rights of freedom of speech and expression. The 'sandwich of censorship' must end. Apart from being in violation of the Universal Declaration of Human Rights, the various forms of censorship inflicted on important musicians who represent the cultural identity of the peoples of both nations could lead to serious problems concerning the collective history and identity of Cubans, wherever they may be.

## Notes

1 'Rising dissent, US pressure led to Cuba repression', Reuters, 16 April 2003.

2 '"Essential Measures?" Human Rights Crackdown in the Name of Security', Amnesty International, 3 June 2003, p. 1.

3 'US envoy caters to needs of island's dissident community', *La Nueva Cuba*, 8 January 2003.

4 'Essential Measures?', p. 14.

5 ibid., p. 74.

6 aka the Cuban Liberty and Democratic Solidarity Act, was US legislation passed by the Clinton administration to strengthen the embargo.

7 'Essential Measures?', p. 16.

8 Michel Suárez, 'Prohibido Escuchar', (my trans.), *Cuba Encuentro*, 23 January 2003.

9 Ibid. Unfortunately as this chapter was being revised, Celia Cruz died.

10 Ibid.

11 Author's source.

12 Author's source.

13 Author's source.

14 'ACLU Challenges Anti-Censor Royalty Oath on Behalf of Censored Arts Groups in Miami', ACLU, 4 April 2003.

15 Ibid.

16 Ibid.

17 Brett Sokol, 'Will the Afro-Cuban All Stars play Miami?', *Miami New Times*, 9 December 1999.

18 'Anti-Castro exiles force Cuban music off airwaves', Reuters, 25 March 1997.

19 Ibid.

20 'Rights group denounces anti-Castro exiles', Reuters, 26 March 1997.

21 'Anti-Castro exiles force Cuban music off airwaves'.

22 Jay Weaver, 'Promoter fights costs of security in court', ACLU, 17 December 2002.

23 'Judge to halt Miami's controversial Cuba policy', Reuters, 11 July 2000.

# 20 | Mexico: drug ballads and censorship today

ELIJAH WALD

First of all, anyone interested in modern Mexican or Spanish-language music in the United States needs to be aware of a singer named Chalino Sánchez. Chalino, as he is always known, completely revolutionized not only Mexican music but also Mexican identity for a lot of young people in the United States by creating a new image of a hip urban gunfighter. He became a legend in 1992 when he gave a concert in Palm Springs, California, and someone attempted to assassinate him. Chalino pulled out his own gun and returned fire from the stage. That put Chalino in the news, and he became a superstar four months later when he gave a concert in Culiacán, Sinaloa, and four men bearing police credentials came up after the concert and took him away. The next morning he was found in a ditch with two bullets in the back of his head. Chalino became the Mexican Tupac Shakur. You now find posters of him all over the south-western USA and Mexico. There are radio stations that play an hour or two of Chalino every week – their *Hora de Chalino* – and his success gave impetus to a whole movement of Los Angeles *corrido* singers.

*Corridos* have been around for over a hundred years, and have functioned as a sort of musical chronicle of Mexican life. There are *corridos* of every major news event, from local murders to national elections. Starting with the era of prohibition in the 1920s, there has also been a long tradition of *corridos* of the illegal cross-border traffic, and it is the modern wave of these smuggling songs, the drug ballads or '*narcocorridos*', which has sparked most of the recent attention, both from record-buyers and from censors.

To understand the contemporary *narcocorrido* scene, it is important to bear in mind that much of it is coming not out of Mexico but out of Los Angeles. Chalino emerged at the same time and in the same place as gangsta rap, and while *corrido* music is completely different – polkas and waltzes, sung to the accompaniment of accordion or brass bands – it appeals to much the same audience, for much the same reasons. At least on the US side of the border, the people who listen to this also listen to gangsta rap, and while it is thought of as a Mexican tradition it is also regarded as the hip street music of LA.

To European or Anglo-American ears, this music sounds old-fashioned, even silly, and it is hard to imagine it as a hard-core gangsta style, but if you wander through a poor Latino neighbourhood anywhere in the south-western

USA, or straight up the West Coast to Seattle, this is what the tough guys have blaring out of their car stereos as they drive down the streets. If you understand the lyrics, it is also quite similar to a lot of rap in its themes: money, girls, drugs, power and gun battles between rival traffickers and with the police. However, because it is all in Spanish it has not attracted the amount of criticism in the USA that has been directed at rap.

In Mexico, there have been attempts to ban *narcocorridos* since the form took off some thirty years ago, and these attempts have grown more forceful in the last decade. In Mexico censorship has always been a rather complicated business, because theoretically there is complete freedom of speech and of the press. This has meant that censorship has often been exercised in complicated ways: for example, for many years newspapers were free to print whatever they wanted, but the government had a monopoly on newsprint. So you could print whatever you wanted if you had paper, but you had paper only if you were printing what the government wanted to read.

In the same way, while there have been outright attempts to ban *narcocorridos* from the radio and television, the more usual censorship is not so clear and direct. Instead of laws against playing the music, you find agreements between state governments and radio and television programmers to the effect that 'voluntarily' they will not play the stuff. I have a wonderful quotation from the president of the Chamber of the Radio and Television Industry of the state of Michoacan, urging local programmers to follow the lead of their peers in the states of Sinaloa and Baja California and agree not to play narco songs. He says this would not be an issue of censorship. 'We are enemies of censorship. This is about getting the media themselves to stop broadcasting this music.'

There have also been calls for more direct bans, and the reason given for these is that the music supposedly not only makes the drug traffickers seem heroic, but actively recruits people into the business. Several of the officials who have proposed legislative bans quote lyrics such as the following: 'I was a poor kid up in the mountains. I had the fields my father left me, but what we grew could not give us enough to eat. We were miserable. Everyone looked down on us. Then a friend came and gave me some seeds to grow marijuana. Now, everybody respects me. The best bands come and play at my parties, and people call me Señor. I am still a farmer, all I have changed is the seeds.' This sort of lyric is frankly fairly rare – most of the songs are about gunfights, with lots of action – but among the thousands of *narcocorridos* one can certainly find dozens on this theme, and hundreds that at least suggest the same idea.

I must point out that the calls to censor these songs come not only from the conservative end of the political spectrum. 'Respectable' people of the left as well as the right are involved. In Tijuana, an agreement to keep *narcocorridos* off the radio was organized by the PRD, which is the main left-wing opposition party. The PRI, which was the old ruling party, has been proposing bans in various areas, and one of the first proposals by officials of the PAN, the conservative Catholic party, after the election of President Fox, was to impose some sort of national ban.

As in the quotation given above, all these officials say they are opposed to censorship – but they are also opposed to this music being played. Senator Yolanda González, who proposed a national ban in March 2001, declared: 'We are convinced of the right of freedom of expression, but also believe that this

12 **Lolita Capilla, 'the Wild Woman of Sonora', one of several child *corrido* stars to emerge in the 1990s.**

freedom has certain limits in the case of attacks on public morals, the rights of third parties, and provocation to crime or distress to the public.'

The argument is that this music is actively functioning as promotion for the drug industry. It is often pointed out that many of the drug lords themselves have hired groups and paid songwriters to compose *corridos* about them. And that is quite true: this was the ancient ballad form, and it makes you feel like a hero, like Pancho Villa, if you have a *corrido* written about you. So if a smuggler makes a successful trip to LA, he uses some of his money to buy a new car, to get a fancy dress for his girlfriend, a fancy cowboy hat and belt, and he hires somebody to record a *corrido* about his deeds. The first three cassettes that Chalino recorded were not sold to the public. He would simply get fifteen clients, write a song for each, record a cassette with the fifteen songs, make one copy for each of them, and that was that. It was only with the third cassette, when he began to get reorders, that it occurred to him that he could also sell the cassettes to other people.

I do not have the space to cover this subject in greater detail, but there is one more point I must make. Many people, including those at Freemuse, argue that even though we oppose censorship there are certain kinds of things which can appropriately be banned. What they forget is that if one allows censorship to take place, it does not really matter what you decide to ban – what matters is who gets to do the banning. You can say that you are only going to accept bans on hate speech, or on songs that specifically incite people to commit criminal acts, but every government will simply declare that the songs they want to ban are hate speech or will cause genuine harm to somebody. When it comes to censorship, the important question is who is in control of the apparatus.

Thus, in Mexico, one finds that an interesting feature of the bans on *narcocorridos* is that it is a class thing more than a matter of crime. This is poor people's music, and not respected, so people who enjoy the Rolling Stones or the Doors singing drug songs can still say this music is bad because it is reaching the sort of poor people likely to get into the drug business. Meanwhile, as with the banning of rap, it does not necessarily hurt the companies who are releasing the music. Many of the *corrido* singers will say, 'OK, they don't play me on the radio – that just means that people have to buy the records.'

At the same time, the principle of banning *corridos* affects not only drug songs. Last year, Los Tigres el Norte, who are the most famous band playing this style of music, wrote a song attacking the Fox government, and it was banned. Not by the government, everyone insists, the government had nothing to do with it, but the major radio stations in Mexico announced in advance that they would not play this single. So the Tigres decided to withdraw it and put out a romantic song instead.

Mario Quintero is the leader of the Tucanes de Tijuana, a group that has been attacked all over the place in the press because they were the first band to have hits celebrating drug use rather than just smuggling. (Traditionally the idea was that Mexican traffickers were just poor guys trying to make a living, and that the depraved drug users were all Yankees.) One of the hardest edged of the drug singers, he was asked during an interview what he thought of the censorship of *corridos* in general, and of the Tigres' *corrido* about the Fox administration in particular. He said, 'You know, the *corridos* have fallen into these vulgar expressions: there are *corridos* that are fictitious, that have no foundation, that are obscene, vulgar and invented, so I think it's a great thing that the government is now stepping in and taking a hand to control this. And as for the Tigres, they prohibited that *corrido* because they were attacking an elected president, and if I was President Fox and they were attacking me and hurting my image, I would shut them down, too.' This is an important point to remember: the gangsta singers, who are the stated targets of the censorship, are completely in favour of the whole thing. And their songs keep selling underground. It is the political songs which are never heard, because they do not have the commercial apparatus to get into all the stores without radio support.

For those who wish to know more about this subject, I have posted a chronology of recent *corrido* censorship on the Web at <www.elijahwald.com/corcensors.html>. I also have a page on recent political *corridos*: <www.elijahwald.com/corridowatch.html>.

# 21 | Responses to censorship in the USA: acquiescence, withdrawal and resistance

IAN INGLIS

I wish to examine three specific case studies which illustrate ways in which popular musicians have chosen to respond to institutional censorship of lyrical content. The case histories themselves will then form the basis for a comparative discussion of the politics of censorship, within the broader context of creativity and control in popular music. In addition to offering significant clues about the artistic integrity and motivations of the performers involved, the events provide useful illustrations of the potential and actual conflict between the entertainment industry and its leading practitioners, especially at a time when it was widely and vocally believed that such restrictions were there to be confronted.

For more than two decades, the most important and influential TV entertainment show in the USA was *The Ed Sullivan Show*. Broadcast nationally on Sunday evenings by CBS, the variety series ran from 20 June 1948 to 6 June 1971; significantly, it coincided with the first two decades of rock 'n' roll's 'unruly history' (Palmer 1995). With its regular weekly audiences of around 40 million (rising to more than 70 million for the Beatles' first appearance in January 1964), an appearance on the show was generally recognized as a critical factor in establishing and maintaining a successful musical presence.

In the 1960s, three of the most celebrated composer/performers of the decade, who were booked to appear on the show on separate occasions, faced objections to the lyrical content of particular songs, to which they responded in different ways. On 12 May 1963, Bob Dylan was instructed to substitute another song for 'Talkin' John Birch Society Blues'; he refused and walked out. On 15 January 1967, the Rolling Stones were told to change the lyrics of 'Let's Spend the Night Together'; they agreed. On 17 September 1967, the Doors were asked to amend the lyrics of 'Light My Fire'; they ignored the request and performed the song unchanged.

The three examples are instructive in a number of ways. They illustrate the perennial concern of the (would-be) censor of popular culture with the themes of sex, drugs and politics. They provide a refutation of the received wisdom that successful challenges to censorship became commonplace through the decade. They present convincing evidence in favour of the assertion that 'the

American tradition that sanctifies abstract principles of free expression is often at war with its cultural biases in favour of repression' (D'Entremont 1998: 34). And their examination may, in a small way, help to counter the oversight noted by Cloonan: 'books on pop usually only fleetingly mention censorship and books on censorship rarely mention pop' (1996: 1).

### Bob Dylan: 'Talkin' John Birch Society Blues'

Dylan had first been asked to audition for *The Ed Sullivan Show* at the time of the release of his first album, *Bob Dylan*, in March 1962; however, no invitation to appear had followed. Since then his reputation as a singer-songwriter of great originality had spread rapidly. Robert Shelton, for example, reported that 'his vulnerability, his identification with his material, suggested a young Sinatra ... [but] ... Dylan broke all past songwriting and performing rules – except those of having something to say and saying it well' (1986: 164–5). By April 1963, conscious of his growing prestige and alerted to the imminent release of his second album, *The Freewheelin' Bob Dylan*, CBS executives contacted him again, and this time he was asked to appear. Dylan's choice for the one song he was to be allowed to perform was 'Talkin' John Birch Society Blues', a track he had written the previous year and recorded during the *Freewheelin'* sessions. The song, which Dylan had frequently performed at appearances in and around New York prior to the show, satirized the extreme right-wing, anti-communist organization, comparing its policies to those of Hitler.

Anthony Scaduto reports that 'when he sang it for Sullivan and Bob Precht, producer of the show, they were delighted' (1972: 138). However, just hours before transmission, Dylan was told by CBS network editor Stowe Phelps that he could not sing it as the lyrics might be considered libellous. Asked to perform another song in its place, Dylan refused and left the studio; he was never to appear on the show. It was later alleged that it was Bob Precht (also Sullivan's son-in-law) who had personally insisted on the song's removal (Hopkins and Sugerman 1980: 139). Sullivan himself claimed no role in the decision, arguing: 'We fought for the song ... I said I couldn't understand why they [the John Birch Society] were being given such protection. But the network turned us down. They told us they understood and sympathized ... but insisted they had previously handled the Birch society on network news programmes, and couldn't take the subject into entertainment' (Scaduto 1972: 140).

Two other developments followed from CBS's decision. Columbia Records insisted that the track be deleted from the *Freewheelin'* album. It and three other songs – 'Rocks and Gravel', 'Rambling Gambling Willie' and 'Let Me Die in My Footsteps' – were subsequently replaced by 'Masters of War', 'Girl from the North Country', 'Talkin' World War III Blues' and 'Bob Dylan's Dream' when the album was released in May 1963.

Second, Dylan's status increased significantly as a result of his refusal to obey CBS's demands: 'Ironically, the uproar about this blatant act of censorship did Dylan considerably more good, by portraying him as a rebel and counter-culture hero, than if he had appeared on the show and performed ... to an uncaring national TV audience' (Heylin 1991: 71).

### The Rolling Stones: 'Let's Spend the Night Together'

The Rolling Stones' performance in January 1967 on *The Ed Sullivan Show* was in fact the fifth time they had featured on the show. Their first appearance, on 25 October 1964, precipitated such a huge outburst of audience hostility that Sullivan, who had appeared initially pleased with their two songs, announced: 'I promise you they'll never be back on the show. It took me seventeen years to build up this show, and I'm not going to have it destroyed in a matter of weeks' (Andersen 1993: 98). However, they did reappear on several occasions – in May 1965, August 1966 and September 1966. By the time of their fifth appearance, on 10 January 1967, the group was clearly one of the world's most popular, if most controversial, groups. They had toured the USA five times, and achieved four number-one singles and two number-one albums in that country.

The group intended to use the TV appearance to promote its new single, 'Let's Spend the Night Together'. Released just a few days before the show, it had already been removed from the playlists of several US radio stations or else played with the offending word 'night' bleeped out. At the afternoon rehearsal, the group was told by Sullivan that he would not permit such a blatantly sexual song to be sung to a family audience: 'Either the song goes ... or you go,' he announced (Sandford 1993: 97).

The group's response was to agree to alter the contentious section of the lyrics, so that 'let's spend the night together' became 'let's spend some time together', and the song was performed accordingly. For some time afterwards, Mick Jagger attempted to deny his actions, claiming, despite the televised evidence, that he had not simply acquiesced to Sullivan's demands: 'I never said "*time*", I said "let's spend some *mmmmm* together, let's spend some *mmmmm* together",' he was still insisting in 1968 (Appleford 1997: 244).

Later, Bill Wyman admitted that 'the value of that programme was too great to jeopardize for the promotion of the single. And it was the only reason we'd flown to New York. So we compromised' (1990: 398). The same commercial rationale was used by Jagger to justify the group's appearance one week later on the UK's leading TV variety show, *Sunday Night at the London Palladium*. On this occasion the media and public outcry was not over the lyrics of the song – which they performed unchanged – but over the group's refusal to appear on the traditional revolving stage at the close of the show! Jagger commented 'the only reason we did the show at the Palladium was because it was a good national plug' (Bonanno 1990: 62). The single reached number one in the US and number two in the UK charts. The Rolling Stones made their sixth and final appearance on *The Ed Sullivan Show* in October 1969.

### The Doors: 'Light My Fire'

Charlie Gillett has pointed out that 'during 1967 the focus of those interested in creative music switched from Britain and New York to San Francisco' (1971: 336). But while several West Coast groups enjoyed considerable album sales, very few had hit singles. One of those that did was the Doors, a Los Angeles group which quickly became noted for its 'psychosexual theatricality and ... aesthetic of direct audience confrontation' (Palmer 1995: 183). The group's first single, 'Break On Through', had been a minor hit in the USA at the start of the year; its second, 'Light My Fire', topped the singles charts for three weeks after its release in April. Both songs were taken from the group's debut album, *The Doors*, released in January 1967. In June of the same year, the group had been excluded from the line-up at the Monterey Pop Festival because, according to drummer John Densmore, 'they were afraid of us. We didn't represent the attitude of the festival: peace and love and flower power. We represented the shadow side ... the demon Doors' (1990: 114–15).

Nevertheless, CBS was very keen to book the group for *The Ed Sullivan Show*, recognizing that its combination of chart success and West Coast creativity might attract a large audience. Joan Didion had written in 1967: 'The Doors are different, the Doors interest me. They have nothing in common with the gentle Beatles. Their music insists that love is sex and sex is death and therein lies salvation. The Doors are the Norman Mailers of the Top 40' (1969: 385).

Before rehearsals, the group was visited in its dressing room by producer Bob Precht, who insisted to them that the line 'girl, we couldn't get much higher' could not be permitted because of its apparent reference to drug-taking. The group promised to substitute alternative words and in fact did so, for the rehearsal. However, during the live transmission of the show itself, they reverted to the original lyrics, singing the offending line with even more emphasis than usual. Precht was reportedly furious, shouting at the television monitor, 'You can't do that! You guys are dead on this show! You'll never do this show again!' (Hopkins and Sugerman 1980: 139–40).

In choosing to distance themselves from the negotiated compromise reached by the Rolling Stones four months earlier, the Doors were able to avoid any accusations of surrender, and instead utilized the incident to confirm the confrontational nature of their music. Jim Morrison explained: 'We're interested in everything about revolt, disorder, and all activity that appears to have no meaning' (Palmer 1977: 254). And John Densmore later commented: 'We agreed that we needed more exposure ... we'd done *Ed Sullivan* because the Beatles, the Stones, and Elvis had been on' (1990: 156).

The Doors never appeared on *The Ed Sullivan Show* again. Numerous concerts by the group were cancelled by promoters or halted by police during 1967, 1968 and 1969 because of actual or feared crowd disorder. Morrison was arrested on several occasions for offences ranging from battery and drunk-driving to lewd and obscene performance. In August 1970 he appeared in Dade County Court, Florida, following a concert at Miami's Dinner Key Auditorium in front of an audience of 13,000: 'Morrison, who had been known for his use of obscenities, went too far ... he made the ultimate *faux pas* by exposing his penis on stage. Six warrants for his arrest were filed. One of the charges was a felony for "lewd and lascivious behaviour in public by exposing his private parts and by simulating masturbation and oral copulation"' (Martin and Segrave 1988: 123). Found guilty, fined $500 for profanity, and sentenced to six months in jail for indecent exposure, Morrison was freed on a $50,000 bond and was awaiting the result of his appeal when he died in Paris on 3 July 1971 from an apparent heart attack.

### Contexts and consequences

The three examples discussed above are by no means the only examples of musical censorship in the 1960s. What makes them significant is that (a) the acts of censorship were quite overt – on national television, in prime-time viewing hours, on the most popular entertainment show in the USA; and (b) their common location (*The Ed Sullivan Show*) allows for direct comparison and evaluation in a way in which many other individual restrictions do not.

It has been noted that throughout its history 'rock'n'roll has ... been described as "dangerous" ... to racists, demagogues and the self-appointed moral guardians of the *status quo*' (Palmer 1995: 11). But such generalized descriptions do not help us to distinguish between 'the twin axes of offence and causality' (Cloonan 1996: 289) employed by the proponents of censorship; nor do they illuminate the specific grounds on which censorship is introduced – sexual content, swearing, blasphemy, drug references, political content, violence; nor do they sit easily with the frankly conservative or sentimental ideology of much of the last five decades' popular music.

Censorship needs to be understood as a process in which two critical factors are related. First, it is imperative to explore the *contexts* in which censorship occurs – the *general* context in which the imposition of restrictions is seen as permissible, and the *particular* context surrounding the individual event. Second, it is equally important to investigate the *consequences* of such censorship – for the censors and for the censored.

Since its development in the early 1950s, the capacity of rock 'n' roll to shock has been well recorded: 'The first blasts of the rock'n'roll era blew away the depression and tedium of the post-Second World War years … it was attacked by priests, journalists and local politicians, who saw the style as both obscene and liable to incite juvenile delinquency … [and] … because it threatened to challenge sexual and racial taboos' (Denselow 1989: 1). Significantly, however, attacks were not confined to sources outside the entertainment industry, but were presented just as vociferously from within. Frank Sinatra's hostility was typical of many within popular music who feared for their own careers: 'Rock'n'roll smells phony and false. It is sung, played and written for the most part by cretinous goons … by means of its almost imbecilic reiteration, and sly, lewd, in plain fact, dirty lyrics … it manages to be the martial music of every sideburned delinquent on the face of the earth' (Hill 1992: 51).

Yet such hostility had to be tempered with a recognition of the music's huge commercial potential. Rather than turn its back on the profits to be made from the emergent teenage market in the USA and elsewhere, the popular music industry's response was to seek to control and restrict its unpredictability. This strategy followed several paths. One was to introduce as replacements for the perceived disorderliness of performers like Chuck Berry, Jerry Lee Lewis, Little Richard, Larry Williams and Gene Vincent a cohort of neat, clean-cut, mainly white 'teen idols' whose music and appearance could be relied on to reinforce the traditional conventions of the pop star – Bobby Vee, Fabian, Bobby Rydell, Rick Nelson, Frankie Avalon.

A second, related tactic was to redefine rock 'n' roll so that it came to exist not as an alternative to but as part of show business. The clearest individual example of this, of course, was the reinvention of Elvis Presley as family entertainer and movie star after his release from the US Army in 1960, when, ironically, the vehicle he chose through which to reintroduce himself to the public was a guest appearance on ABC's *The Frank Sinatra Show* in March 1960. But on a more general level, television began to produce a series of competing shows in which the new 'pop stars' routinely presented a more acceptable face of rock 'n' roll. Among the most important of these were ABC's *American Bandstand*, hosted by Dick Clark, which 'sold America the well dressed, well behaved side of rock music' (Friedlander 1996: 71), and *The Ed Sullivan Show* on CBS and *The Steve Allen Show* on NBC, both of which included rock 'n' roll within their general variety formats.

The shows thus established, the producers were adamant that perform-ances which might interfere with the successful patterns they had evolved should be excluded. In Sullivan's case, his public declaration in May 1956 that he would not have Elvis Presley on his show at any price – 'he is not my cup of tea' (Guralnick 1994: 301) – his insistence when Presley did appear on his show in September 1956 that the cameras should show him only from the waist up because of his pelvic gyrations (Hopkins 1972: 110), and his absolute refusal to book Jerry Lee Lewis in 1957, saying that after Presley he didn't want 'any more of that crap' (Martin and Segrave 1988: 75), provided early indica-tions of the way in which the show was to be organized through into the 1960s. Whether the censorship practised on *The Ed Sullivan Show* took the form of exclusion (Jerry Lee Lewis) or interference (Elvis Presley), it quickly became clear that in order to appear on the show, popular musicians were expected to abide by certain standards and to adapt both the style and content of their performance accordingly.

It is against this general background that the particular circumstances of Bob Dylan, the Rolling Stones and the Doors' appearances need to be situated. Dylan's appearance came at a time when he – and other performers – were becoming increasingly involved in the Civil Rights movement, and in their opposition to racist or fascist organizations such as the John Birch Society and the Ku Klux Klan. In the previous twelve months, the Cuban missile crisis had brought the USA and the USSR to the brink of a nuclear confrontation and hardened many Americans' fears and suspicions of communism, Martin Luther King had been jailed for leading an illegal march in Georgia, the enrol-ment of James Meredith as the first black student at the University of Missis-sippi had led to prolonged rioting and mass arrests in Jackson, more than a thousand marchers (including Martin Luther King) had been arrested during a Civil Rights march in Alabama, and Governor George Wallace had vowed to defy a federal court order to open his state's universities to black students. The early 1960s have been described as 'a time when American protest was becoming a mass movement, no longer some small splinter party of Leftist ideologues meeting in an uncrowded telephone booth' (Shelton 1986: 137) and Dylan was quick to publicly associate himself with that protest through the subjects he explored in his songs: 'I don't have to be anybody like those guys up on Broadway ... there's other things in the world besides love and sex that are important too. People shouldn't turn their backs on them just because they ain't pretty to look at. How is the world ever gonna get any better if we're afraid to look at these things?' (Heylin 1991: 54). Within a few months of making this announcement, Dylan was booked for *The Ed Sullivan Show*, promising friends, 'Well, they won't tell me what to sing' (ibid.: 71).

The Rolling Stones had their first major US hit – 'Time is on My Side' – at the beginning of 1965. Deliberately choreographed by manager Andrew Loog Oldham to be a radical alternative to the Beatles – 'Shock the hell out of everyone, especially the parents' (Scaduto 1973: 96) – the group continued in the USA to pursue the strategy that had brought them public notoriety and generated enormous media attention in the UK one year earlier. Their single 'Satisfaction' had been banned by several US radio stations in 1965 and, in fact, during the group's appearance on Sullivan's show in August 1966, the line 'tryin' to make some girl' had been bleeped over without their knowledge during the live transmission (Norman 1984: 135). In June 1966, fourteen of New York's leading hotels refused to accept the group as they arrived for their fifth US tour. Concerts in Montreal, Ontario and Massachusetts were abandoned because of audience riots. In September 1966 the single 'Have You Seen Your Mother, Baby' was released in the USA in a picture sleeve 'that struck new horror into conservative hearts' (ibid.: 163). Photographed by Jerry Shatzberg on the streets of Manhattan, the members of the group were dressed in drag, depicted as ageing transvestites with new names – Sara (Mick Jagger), Flossie (Brian Jones), Penelope (Bill Wyman), Millicent (Charlie Watts) and Milly (Keith Richards). Another photo session in November featured Brian Jones in Nazi SS uniform and jackboots, crushing a doll under his foot. Bill Wyman has commented that by the time of their engagement to promote 'Let's Spend the Night Together' on *The Ed Sullivan Show*, 'the spring of 1967 found us cast as the world's baddest band ... everywhere we turned and everything we touched became controversial' (1990: 414).

Unlike the Rolling Stones, the Doors were relative newcomers to the structures and cultures of the popular music industry, having released just two singles and one album before their slot on *The Ed Sullivan Show*. Much of the media and audience scrutiny was directed at the group's lead vocalist, Jim Morrison. 'Fronted by former UCLA film student and self-styled poet Jim Morrison, the Doors opposed the "peace, love and flowers" strain of sixties solipsism with darkly droning tales of death and transcendence, murky Freudian freak-outs, and ecstatic derangement of the senses as practised by the late-nineteenth century French poet Rimbaud' (Palmer 1995: 183). The group had been fired from its residency at Los Angeles' Whiskey A Go Go in July 1966 by owner Phil Tanzini after singing the lines 'Father, I want to kill you; Mother, I want to fuck you' in their performance of 'The End' (Hopkins and Sugerman 1980: 94–8). Morrison and the other members of the Doors – Robby Krieger, Ray Manzarek and John Densmore – made no secret of their regular use of marijuana, LSD and alcohol, often appearing on stage at the Whiskey A Go Go and the nearby London Fog under their influence. In order not to discourage radio airplay, their first single, 'Break On Through', had been edited by the group's record label (Elektra) so that the line 'Everybody loves my baby, she gets high, she gets high, she gets high' became, bizarrely, 'Everybody loves my baby, she get, she get, she get' (ibid.: 103).

Often glibly referred to as 'the summer of love', 1967 has been singled out for particular attention by Friedlander in his analysis of the evolution of rock 'n' roll lyrics: '1967 was a watershed year. Lyrics covering the Vietnam War, the search for a new humanistic morality, and the fight for minority rights emerged in the day's rock/pop music ... Music critical of contemporary society became available nationwide' (1996: 285–6). Some of that music was unequivocally about drug use – the Rolling Stones' 'Mother's Little Helper', Canned Heat's 'Amphetamine Annie', Steppenwolf's 'The Pusher', the Velvet Underground's 'Heroin'. But such was the state of confusion that entirely innocuous titles such as 'Puff the Magic Dragon' and 'Up, Up and Away' were accused of being pro-drug compositions, as was almost any contemporary song which included the word 'high' in its lyrics. It was in this climate, in the late summer of 1967, that the Doors were to make their appearance on *The Ed Sullivan Show*, to perform their million-selling, chart-topping single.

These three very public acts of censorship had very public consequences, not the least of which was to remind popular musicians that despite the revolutionary qualities typically attributed to the decade, the 1960s remained a period in which power rested very firmly with the major institutions in the entertainment industry. Gillett records that it was a period in the USA when rock 'n' roll was almost entirely under the control of a handful of major record labels and that 'despite the vaunted political implications of the music, this was a formulated product' (1971: 340); similarly, Dave Harker has pointed out that although there were several thousand radio stations across the USA, the majority were owned by conglomerates such as NBC and CBS (1980: 38).

The impositions visited on those appearing on *The Ed Sullivan Show* need to be seen therefore not as isolated incidents, but as routine examples of the way in which power was broadly, and successfully, articulated within the entertainment industry. For Sullivan in particular, his actions demonstrated and confirmed his ability to undermine the autonomy of popular musicians by threatening to deny them the national exposure they sought. For the performers themselves, such experiences were clear reminders that strategies had to be devised in order to accommodate the demands of those who sat as censors. These strategies included acquiescence, withdrawal or resistance, as discussed above. Increasingly they also included self-censorship, through which many songwriters, anticipating problems, would compromise by amending potentially controversial lyrics in advance; and concealment, where the 'real meaning' of a song could be obscured by 'euphemism and thinly veiled analogy' (Street 1986: 115).

The issue of creativity and control in the lyrics of popular music has a long history. In the 1930s, Silver and Bruce's songwriting manual *How to Write and Sell a Hit Song* warned that: 'Direct allusions to love-making ... must be avoided. Love in popular songs is a beautiful and delicate emotion and marriage is a noble institution. Profanity should never be used in a popular song. Direct references to drinking, and songs that have to do with labor and national and political propaganda are also prohibited on the air' (Harker 1980: 38).

In 1970 – four weeks after Morrison's trial – Vice-President Spiro T. Agnew chose to emphasize the theme of drug lyrics in rock music when he warned against 'the blatant drug-culture propaganda' (Denisoff and Peterson 1972: 308) he saw as inherent in songs such as 'With a Little Help from My Friends', 'White Rabbit', 'The Acid Queen' and 'Eight Miles High', and in movies such as *Easy Rider*. In October of that year, Agnew and President Nixon hosted a drug abuse conference at the White House attended by more than seventy radio broadcasters who were asked to cooperate by screening out rock 'n' roll lyrics that promoted drugs. At the same time, the Federal Communications Commission, under its arch-Republican chairman Dean Burch, launched an initiative against 'obscene or druggy song lyrics' (Chapple and Garofalo 1977: 115), which threatened radio stations with the removal of their licences if they continued to play such songs.

And in the 1980s, the political establishment returned to the ground covered by the Republican administration of the early 1970s. Sponsored by Tipper Gore, wife of the future Democrat Vice-President Al Gore, the Parents Music Resource Center accused the record industry of making records about sex, violence and the glorification of drugs and alcohol freely available to children. Its demands, which included 'a more detailed ratings system, lyrics to be printed on record sleeves, the contracts of those who engaged in violent or explicitly sexual behaviour on stage to be reassessed, [and] broadcasters to be pressured not to air controversial songs or videos' (Denselow 1989: 266) led to the industry adopting a policy of voluntary labelling, whereby any record whose lyrics were deemed to contain explicit references to sex, violence or drugs should contain a warning sticker proclaiming 'Explicit Lyrics – Parental Advisory'.

The experiences of Bob Dylan, the Rolling Stones and the Doors on *The Ed Sullivan Show* are illustrations of tensions that have existed throughout the development of popular music. In this respect there is little difference between the circumstances surrounding the strictures of the 1930s, the television case studies of the 1960s, and the pressure group activity of the 1980s and beyond. In each decade, the contested subjects are identical – sex, politics and drugs/alcohol.

The 1960s are frequently celebrated as an era in which the themes and topics of rock 'n' roll, the activities of its leading practitioners, and the ambitions of its audiences played a central part in fighting for and winning substantial social and cultural liberties: 'They rejected the hypocritical compromises, the puritanical indirection and the exclusiveness of many of the older ballads ... the egocentric monogamous lyrics, the bourgeois orchestrations ... They desired greater sexual freedom ... it was part of a fervent attempt to regenerate man. Youthful energies flowed out toward social reconstruction or into the ... expansion of the individual psyche through hallucinogens' (Mooney 1969: 24). Much of that remains admirable and true. What this discussion suggests, however, is that those victories may not have been so emphatic as we choose to remember; and that then, as now, the popular musician – even if distinguished by the sort of celebrity and success considered here – has much to do in marshalling the regenerative spirit of rock 'n' roll against the institutionalized authority of the censor.

## References

Andersen, Christopher (1993) *Jagger Unauthorised*, London: Simon & Schuster.
Appleford, Steve (1997) *The Rolling Stones: It's Only Rock 'n' Roll*, London: Sevenoaks.
Bonanno, Massimo (1990) *The Rolling Stones Chronicle*, London: Plexus.
Chapple, Steve, and Reebee Garofalo (1977) *Rock 'n' Roll is Here to Pay: The History and Politics of the Music Industry*, Chicago: Nelson Hall.
Cloonan, Martin (1996) *Banned!*, Aldershot: Arena.
Denisoff, R. Serge, and Richard A. Peterson (1972) *The Sounds of Social Change*, New York: Rand McNally.
Denselow, Robin (1989) *When the Music's Over*, London: Faber.
Densmore, John (1990) *Riders on the Storm*, New York: Delacorte.
D'Entremont, Jim (1998) 'The Devil's Disciples', *Index on Censorship*, 27(6): 32–9.
Didion, Joan (1969) 'Waiting for Morrison', in Jonathan Eisen (ed.), *The Age of Rock: Sounds of the American Cultural Revolution*, New York: Vintage.
Friedlander, Paul (1996) *Rock and Roll: A Social History*, Boulder, CO: Westview Press.
Gillett, Charlie (1971) *The Sound of the City*, London: Souvenir Press.

Guralnick, Peter (1994) *Last Train to Memphis: The Rise of Elvis Presley*, London: Little, Brown & Co.

Harker, Dave (1980) *One for the Money: Politics and Popular Song*, London: Hutchinson.

Heylin, Clinton (1991) *Dylan: Behind the Shades*, London: Viking.

Hill, Trent (1992) 'The Enemy Within: Censorship in Rock Music in the 1950s', in Anthony DeCurtis (ed.), *Present Tense: Rock & Roll and Culture*, London: Duke University Press.

Hopkins, Jerry (1972) *Elvis*, London: Open Gate/Macmillan.

Hopkins, Jerry and Danny Sugerman (1980) *No One Here Gets Out Alive*, London: Plexus.

Martin, Linda, and Kerry Segrave (1988) *Anti-Rock: The Opposition to Rock 'n' Roll*, Hamden, CT: Archon.

Mooney, H. F. (1969) 'Popular Music since the 1920s: The Significance of Shifting Taste', in Jonathan Eisen (ed.), *The Age of Rock: Sounds of the American Cultural Revolution*, New York: Vintage.

Norman, Philip (1984) *The Stones*, London: Elm Tree Books/Hamish Hamilton.

Palmer, Robert (1995) *Rock & Roll: An Unruly History*, New York: Harmony.

Palmer, Tony (1977) *All You Need is Love: The Story of Popular Music*, London: Weidenfeld & Nicolson.

Sandford, Christopher (1993) *Mick Jagger*, London: Gollancz.

Scaduto, Anthony (1972) *Bob Dylan*, London: W. H. Allen.

— (1973) *Mick Jagger*, London: W. H. Allen.

Shelton, Robert (1986) *No Direction Home: The Life and Music of Bob Dylan*, New York: Beech Tree.

Silver, A., and R. Bruce (1939) *How to Write and Sell a Hit Song*, New York: Prentice Hall.

Street, John (1986) *Rebel Rock: The Politics of Popular Music*, Oxford: Blackwell.

Wyman, Bill (1990) *Stone Alone*, London: Viking.

SIX | **Europe**

# 22 | Turkey: censorship past and present

ŞANAR YURDATAPAN

*Historical background*
*The religious roots of music censorship* Music censorship in our past finds its roots in Islam. It is believed that these words were uttered by the Prophet Muhammad: 'A woman who lets her melodic voice be heard by a man must be excommunicated.'

This edict has been the reason for forbidding female voices from being heard through the centuries. Even today, choirs singing religious music in ceremonies consist of men only. It is also argued that 'musical instruments' are included in that sentence too. But this interpretation is not widely accepted in Turkey. Both in contemporary Ottoman music – based on the music of Byzantium – and military or folk music, many instruments are used.

*The Ottoman Empire* The Ottoman Empire (1300–1922) was a multinational, multi-cultural union. Every ethnic group could sing its own songs in its own language, in any part of the empire. From time to time songs were banned for political reasons, for example revolutionary Alawia songs, and much more in the time of the 'Red Sultan', Abdulhamid II (1876–1909), as his administration censored almost everything.

Only the ban on female voices was maintained, together with the social ban on female participation in any branch of the arts. Even during the first two decades of the twentieth century, the stage was open only to women of Christian minorities – Greeks, Armenians, etc. Some Turkish women could step on to the stage and act and sing, but only using a pseudonym and by pretending they were non-Muslims.

*After the republic*
*One nation, one music* The Ottoman Empire lost most of its territory in the First World War. Even most of Anatolia was occupied by the Allies, including the capital of the empire, Istanbul. But in 1919 a resistance movement led by General Mustafa Kemal (later Atatürk) started, and after an independence war of three years, Greek armies had to leave Turkey. In July 1923 the new Turkish state was recognized by the Lausanne Treaty. On 23 October 1923 the new Turkish state was declared a republic.

Atatürk's ideal was to build up one 'nation' from the ashes of the empire. The new policies aiming towards a modern society, such as changing the alphabet, the calendar and measures, the acceptance of a new civil law, equal rights for women, improving education – simply 'creating the new citizen' – were formulated in the following years. The basic philosophy was 'One nation, one language, one history, one culture'. (The oppression of Kurds and other minorities, which still continues, is based on this philosophy.)

The first radio stations were established in Istanbul and Ankara in 1925. At this time the first ban was introduced on contemporary Ottoman music and its extension, 'A la Turca' music, which is listened to in Istanbul and other big cities. Although Atatürk himself loved to listen to this 'modal' music, he thought that only Western harmonic music should be transmitted, so that the musical tastes of the people could be changed.

Naturally, another ban was introduced for 'Rebetiko', the music created by Anatolian Greeks. Over 1.5 million of them were 'exchanged' with Turks living in Greece after 1922. Since they were being expelled, their music should go with them. (It is another tragedy that this music was also rejected in Greece, on the grounds that it was 'not pure Hellenic'. It was banned many times, latterly in 1967 in the days of the Colonels' junta.)

*Assimilation of 'others'* Ankara radio station – the principal station – has conducted musical research throughout Anatolia. On the one hand, this has saved many folkloric values from being lost. But on the other it has ruined much else, by trying to amalgamate everything in 'one form'. Turkish lyrics were written for many Kurdish, Armenian and Greek songs and all were performed by a 'one type' orchestra, consisting of *sazes*[1] and choir, called *Yurttan Sesler Korosu*.

Even today, very few people know that 'Sari Gelin' is an Armenian folk song; similarly 'Yaylalar' (one of the favourite songs of Turkish fascists) is also a Kurdish folk song.

Although American, French, German, Italian and Spanish songs were always freely broadcast, we cannot say the same for Russian songs. Starting with the Cold War period, almost everything concerning Russia and the Soviet Union has been taboo. The story is told of a police officer who tried to arrest an intellectual because he saw the Larousse in his library, thinking that it was something from Russia. (In Turkish, 'Russia' is pronounced 'Roussia'.)

Throughout the period of the state monopoly on broadcasts (1925–2000) political censorship and self-censorship always existed, changing only its form or framework. Generally we can say that what came from the West was good and what came from the East was bad. Russian and Greek were almost always dangerous. Kurdish was totally denied – not just the music, but also the Kurdish language, which officially just did not exist.

*The Music Auditing Commission at TRT (Turkish Radio Television)*  Rock 'n' roll music was very popular among the young generation towards the end of the 1950s. Musical groups, trying to imitate American or English models, started to appear in schools. After a short period of 'imitation', these young musicians tried to combine folkloric themes, rhythms and instruments with those coming from the West. This became Turkish pop music.

Young DJs at TRT loved this new music and started transmitting it unadulterated in their programmes. This was too much for the music authorities at TRT. For them, these new sallies into music were very dangerous, because these 'children' had no music education and there was the danger that they would 'harm' listeners. Music auditing commissions were established. All new songs had to be vetted by them, and any song not on the list of 'permitted songs' could not be transmitted by any radio or TV programme.

Later, a single and central commission was set up in Ankara. This commission's decisions were so strict that TRT programme producers and DJs could hardly find enough material to fill their broadcasts. For this reason they collaborated when musicians started a boycott against the TRT in 1972.

The censorship was double edged. While some members of the commission controlled the lyrics, others monitored the music. You could not use phrases reminiscent of Greek themes. You could not use the *saz* and piano together. You could never use bouzouki, balalaika or *cümbüs* (a twelve-stringed, fretless, banjo-type lute). They were totally forbidden.

Between 1975 and 1980, the Supreme Court heard four cases against the TRT's decisions and the artists won each time. Bans on the songs entitled 'Arkadas', 'Bir Gün Gelecek', 'Ninni' and 'Insaniz Biz' were rescinded. But what happened then? The songs were transmitted only once by one of the smallest TRT radio stations and an official letter was sent to the court, giving the transmission date and time. That was all! A verbal – and secret – order was given to department chiefs never to play the songs again.

Then came the days of the 1980 military junta. All the legislation – including the constitution – was changed. My ex-wife Melike Demirag (a famous singer and film actress) and I had to live in exile for twelve years, and our citizenship was cancelled. One day, we saw a photo in a Turkish journal: 'Terrorists captured,' ran the caption. Some young people were shown standing beside a table piled with books; our LPs were also lying on the table. Evidence of crime!

*Today*

*Self-censorship and the media* Some groups and singers, such as Grup Yorum, Kizilirmak, Koma Amed, Koma Denge Jiyane, Koma Asmin, Shivan, Ciwan Xeco, Ferhat Tunç, Suavi and Ahmet Kaya – who died in exile – are automatically *non grata* for private radio and TV stations, for they know that the state does not like them. It is almost the same with the press. Many journals and TV and radio stations belong to just a few bosses. The editors and programmers know what *not* to do, so direct censorship is not necessary at all.

Another factor is RTÜK (Supreme Institution for Radio-TV), which is authorized to ban radio or TV transmissions temporarily – for a few days, a few months, a year – or for ever. The sentences meted out by this institution have spelled the end for many small radio or TV stations in Turkey.

*Auditing commissions of the Ministry of Culture on the phonogram industry* These bodies oversee the open form of censorship of CDs and other audio and video media. The producers are obliged to acquire a general 'producers' licence' and then a 'permission document' for each production from the Ministry of Culture. The 'auditing committee' is established by the ministry and consists of a total of seven members. The ministry appoints the president. Three members are appointed by the State Security Council (military), the Ministry of the Interior (police), and the Ministry of National Education. Two members are sent by organizations representing cinema and musical copyright owners and a musician is appointed by the Minister of Culture. Simply put, five out of the seven members are appointed by the state. The producer may watch the meeting as an observer, but has no right to speak or vote.

In practice, the censorship works only against Kurdish and minority cultures and left-wing protest songs. A signed document is demanded from the producer, declaring that there is nothing in the production contradicting the 'Rules of Audition'; and also accepting complete legal responsibility for the lyrics, if they are in a language other than Turkish.

Reading this, you may think that there is no outright ban on any language. Yes, some music cassettes in Kurdish are produced and you may find them in the market. But you can never be sure that the governor of a particular province or even district will not ban the cassette in his region.

It is the same with concerts. Often groups travel over a thousand kilometres to the south-east of the country and hear that the concert has been forbidden by the governor at the last moment. The reason? In one word: security.

As an example of the auditing commission's activities, in June 2002 KALAN Music producer Hasan Saltık's licence was cancelled by the ministry, owing to a report from the auditing commission about a cassette entitled *Gününü umuda ayarla*, released in 1993. But as a result of strong protests and media coverage, with reminders that Hasan Saltık was also the producer of Prime Minister Ecevit's poetry cassette, his licence was immediately reinstated.

Now KALAN Music and Hasan Saltık are in trouble again for another production. A cassette by the group Yorum entitled *FEDA* was banned and Saltık invited to pay a fine of 2,800,000,000 Turkish lira ($US1,750); otherwise a case would be opened against him. He refused to pay, insisting that he did not accept that a crime had been committed.

*Self-censorship in life as a result of oppression*  Newspapers report daily that the Gendarmerie have taken people into custody during a wedding feast somewhere in the south-east because they were singing songs in Kurdish.

This is still the case even though Parliament has amended the constitution and former laws and officials repeatedly declare that Kurdish is not forbidden. Even if there is no legal or official ban, the practice continues and people have to censor themselves.

*Cases against songs*  A Kurdish group – Koma Aşiti – was sentenced to three years and nine months in prison by the Supreme Court of Appeal. Another case concerns Koma Asmin, a group from the Mesopotamian Cultural Centre, consisting of eleven young women. On 15 August 2002, they were tried at the Istanbul State Security Court for a song they sang at the final concert of the Diyarbakir Cultural Festival on 2 June. The song, entitled '*Herne Pesh*' (Forward), is approximately sixty years old, comes from southern Kurdistan, and has nothing to do with the PKK and Turkey.

Reports consist only of words and statistics. I want to close with the story of their concert and custody as related to me by one member of the group, Ms Serap Sönmez.

### 'Herne Pesh' *(Forward)*

The Diyarbakir Festival of Culture and Arts is the biggest in the region. This year the Mesopotamian Cultural Centre participated at the festival with the music group Koma Asmin of eleven young women. I am one of them.

It was the last day of the festival. Over fifteen thousand people filled the area near the ancient city walls. They had been there since early morning, waiting under the sun. Police were trying to provoke them with insulting words, asking 'Come on, what will you do now?', toying with people's patience.

Everybody was excited. We would be the last and most eagerly awaited group on stage. All went well, and after fifteen songs we came to the last one,

'*Herne Pesh*' (Forward). This is a very old, traditional song. We think that it becomes women: 'You may join me, or you may stay if you like. But I am going forward.'

We started singing. Not just the eleven of us, but fifteen thousand throats and hearts joined in. This was the finale everybody was waiting to hear, such euphoria ...

There seemed to be trouble below the stage. People were refusing to leave, believing that the police would take us away after they had left.

Closing our ears to the insults of the police on both sides, we moved off. But we did not get far. Our minibus was stopped as soon as we left the square. Police ordered those who were not group members to get off. We were being taken to the police station surrounded by insults, no longer whispered but shouted.

After the police station they took us to the hospital. A health report had to be filed in accordance with CMUK (the Criminal Courts' Procedural Law). In the police bus they play Mehter (Ottoman military music) as loud as possible, as if in response to '*Herne Pesh*'.

At the Anti-Terror Centre they laid us down beside a wall. But then something unexpected happened. We heard a voice saying: 'Turn your faces here, children, please relax.'

Who was this? He introduced himself: the chief of the anti-terror department had come to the rescue just in time. The chief said that the treatment we had received was absolutely a mistake. We would not be taken to the custody cells but would be their guests tonight, just to give our statements. He also introduced the police officers to whom we might express our needs and added that we could tell him the next morning if we had any complaints. There was only one policewoman there. He said: 'No! One female policeperson alone cannot take care of all of you.' Two more soon came.

We were kept there until the next morning, sitting on chairs but unable to speak among ourselves, answering their endless questions until eight o'clock in the morning. When the new day began, all the police officers came to their offices after a nice sleep and full of energy. The insults resumed from the point where they had left off the evening before. I couldn't help asking myself: 'What is the reason for this much anger and hatred?'

It was nearly noon when the process of taking our fingerprints and photographs and asking us the very same questions over and over was completed. We should now be taken to court so that we could be remanded in custody or set free by the judge.

But today was the moment everybody had been waiting for for months. The Turkish national football team was playing its first game in the World Cup,

13 The Kurdish group Koma Asmin were taken to a police station after a successful concert and interrogated by the anti-terror department (courtesy of the Mesopotamian Cultural Centre).

against Brazil. The whole country, including police, prosecutor and judge, was glued to the TV screen. We can only hear the reactions of the policemen watching the game. And all of a sudden, GOOOOOOOAL! Turkey 1, Brazil 0.

We were totally forgotten, and we made jokes among ourselves. Who knows? Maybe they will let us go, to honour the goal ... It was only the beginning of the game, but everybody would be so happy if Turkey won. We hoped they didn't lose, otherwise we might have to pay for it.

Then a female police officer asked us: 'Why don't you feel happy? Why don't you sing a song of happiness?' Then came the department chief. After asking us whether everything was OK, he turned to the policewoman and asked her whether or not we were happy about the game. The answer was negative. We had to listen to the chief's long and complicated explanation of how people who have lost their national feeling are almost dead, finished! Then came the surprise: they could bring us a monitor if we wanted to watch the game.

Well, this was a different, strange type of oppression which one could face only once in four years: a Kurdish female music group oppressed by Turkish national football.

'Thanks a lot,' we said, 'but we do not care too much for football.'

But we could not convince them. The chief repeated his offer at least three times but did not succeed in gaining our sympathy for the sport. Then came half-time. And after that Brazil scored two goals and the subject was closed.

One of the policewomen gazed at us constantly with disgusted looks. She was dark and looked like us, and asked us questions all the time: how old were we, where were we from, whose voice was the most beautiful, etc. We were pretending to be asleep, just to avoid her endless interrogation. But she answered her own questions. 'Of course you won't answer. Because you're jealous of each other. You are women too, aren't you?'

Finally she asked the question she had been leading up to: 'Guess where I come from?'

We offered the names of some Kurdish cities, but none of us could guess how deeply she could hurt us. 'I am from Urfa, I am Kurdish too. But I am not like you. I can sing the national hymn.' And she kept on about separatism and betrayal. 'I am a police officer. Nobody hindered me. My father is a colonel. He was not hindered either. Everybody's equal in this country.'

Then she wanted to prove that she could sing in Kurdish as well and started a song, making a lot of mistakes and mixing up the words. She was trying to sing '*Bingol Shewiti*', but no doubt she did not know the meaning of the words: '*wa qomando çı imane!* ... [How cruel is this commander!]'.

She was Kurdish, so were we. She was a woman, so were we. What we felt was a deep sorrow for her.

Then came the prosecutor and the judge, and we were released to be tried later.

But our song did not come to an end. People were waiting for our release at the door.

Yes, the song will continue ...

*Serap Sönmez, musician,*
*Koma Asmin, Mesopotamian Cultural Centre, Istabul*

## Note

1 A stringed instrument made of wood with a long fingerboard. It is a common instrument among Turks and Kurds. The bouzouki is a corrupt version adapted to twelve tones, used by Anatolian Greeks.

# 23 | Rap and censorship in France

DANIEL BROWN

From its beginnings in the seventies the mechanisms of censorship have been flirting with rap music on both sides of the Atlantic. To this day, many albums are deemed too shocking to sell to minors and, in the United States, carry stickers that warn against their lyrical contents ('Parental advisory'). The American multinational Time Warner was at the centre of a controversial censorship issue in the mid-nineties when it distributed 'Cop Killer' (by Bodycount/ Ice-T), as well as the records released by Interscope, a label specializing in gangsta rap.

Given the lyrical contents of rap, it is not surprising that authorities worldwide are uncomfortable with this form of popular musical expression; after all, it nourishes itself on the disenchantment and rebellious nature of today's youth. Like punk music in the seventies, the rap of the past quarter of a century has been a platform for the social and political outpourings of the young disenfranchised in and out of the inner city. To further confuse anyone hoping to attach a pigeon-hole label to this urban art form, the new directions for rap seem to be global, cross-cultural, multi-lingual and mainstream. And, unlike most forms of music, it doesn't hesitate to borrow from classic literature, cinema, dance, video and fine art.

> Social antagonisms are at the heart of all our problems. But in the South, where poorer countries are impoverished by the richer ones, the neo-colonial realities are blindingly obvious, and there is an overlap between colour and the class you belong to. As a cultural crossroad [our rap group] La Rumeur deals with that. Lyricists like me come from Togo, Algeria, Morocco, Guadeloupe. Those who compose our music are from Madagascar, Poland, Brittany.
>
> But these songs have no chance of being played here because they mirror France's responsibility in what it calls the 'dirty war' [in its former colonies]. That's why we are so profoundly subversive. (Hamé, of the Paris rap band La Rumeur, in an interview with the author. All unsourced quotes are from interviews with the author)

## 'Rap is not an expression of music'

One thing that distinguishes French rap from its American counterpart is its métissage.[1] This music is essentially born in the heart of the variegated communities from France's former colonies. The children of immigrants from Africa, the West Indies and the Far East have moulded a musical voice that integrates words from their parents' languages, as well as some of the instruments and rhythms from their grandparents' communities ... worlds many have never known. Such wealth has been lost during the centuries in which African-Americans have lived in the USA and is not expressed in their rap.

The fact that this is a relatively new segment of the population has meant that the youths' quest for a French identity that respects their past is a difficult, often tortured one. This is often reflected in their rap music in ways rarely echoed on the other side of the Atlantic. However, while new French rap groups are hardening their musical discourse, none attains the verbal violence of America's gangsta rap.

'There is a growing disaffection with politics, education and justice [among French youth],' claims sociologist Manuel Boucher (quoted by Reuters, 3 August 2002). 'People no longer believe in French institutions. These institutions have failed young people from working-class immigrant neighbourhoods because they have been instruments of discrimination rather than integration.'

And it is in French rap music that these disenfranchised and ghettoized youths express their rage at a society divided in two. '*La fracture sociale*', a term that Jacques Chirac coined to win his first tenure in office in 1995, was repeatedly described by rappers in the early nineties.

Over the past decade, France has also had its share of controversial judicial and extra-judicial decisions geared to silencing certain hip-hop groups and artists. On 14 November 1996, the two lead singers of its best-known band Suprême NTM (Nique Ta Mère[2]) were condemned to two months in prison and banned from playing their music for six months. The decision followed the singers' violent verbal attack against the French police and the judicial system during a concert in Toulon, a town governed by the extreme right-wing National Front party. It underlines the limits of freedom of expression in France in a way no other music has done.

Meanwhile, NTM's third record '*Paris sous les bombes*', was rarely heard on France's radio airwaves, prompting leading rap author Olivier Cachin to denounce a concerted boycott against it by the national FM radio stations. Despite the blackout, the album sold over 200,000 copies, a phenomenon that reflects an enduring underground system of production, manufacture, publicity and sales.

At the time, the seminal collective Ministère AMER[3] also provoked the wrath of the Interior Ministry with songs like '*Sacrifice de Poulet*'[4] and '*Brigitte Femme de flic*'. Like their American counterparts, French rappers address police abuse at their peril ...

Until 21 April 2002, many believed that controversy over rap had quietened down since these clashes with the French Establishment. Hip-hop has split into two currents: a mainstream and highly commercial form, and a marginalized street or hard-core rap that the authorities hoped would disappear for financial reasons.

Then came the tidal wave of indignation at the performance of France's xenophobic party, the National Front, in the first round of general elections. French rappers, who are essentially second-generation migrants from Africa and the West Indies, felt directly targeted. This is hardly surprising given: a) the obsessive theme of insecurity and youth violence used by *all the major political parties* in the run-up to the vote: the young inhabitants of the city suburbs (the equivalent of poor inner cities or projects which the French call *cités* or *banlieues*) continue to be associated with all France's present woes, while issues of unemployment, the economy, foreign policy and corruption are relegated; b) the hostility of Jean-Marie Le Pen's party to all forms of hip-hop culture. Official NF policy states that 'rap is not an expression of music' and 'obviously, will not be given any public subsidy'. The worst clashes between rappers and authorities in the nineties were in towns like Toulon which, at the time, had a National Front mayor.

The first artist to react publicly to the general election results in April 2002 (which saw National Front leader Jean-Marie Le Pen run Jacques Chirac a close second in the first round) was Akhenaton, founder of one of France's best-known rap bands, IAM. He led a plethora of musicians, performers and writers in a denunciation of Le Pen's politics, and the singer was seen as a symbol of the anti-NF campaign. Rap rhythms and lyrics were often chanted by the tens of thousands of youths who took to the streets in France's major cities. For, as Reuters reporter Joelle Diderich recently noted, French rap has for the past decades 'become the mouthpiece of young people, many of them children of immigrants, growing up in city suburbs plagued with crime and high unemployment' (35 per cent of adults in this situation are unemployed, as opposed to around 10 per cent nationally).

Despite the massive vote against the National Front in the second round, high-profile rappers are convinced the same problems of incomprehension and division still exist between the *banlieues* and the rest of France. And those new, subtler forms of censorship continue to harass rap artists. According to the same Olivier Cachin, author of the excellent *L'Offensive Rap* (Gallimard), a new generation of popular rappers is being prevented from playing on most commercial and public radio or television stations; music companies continue to refuse or censor musicians whose texts are too 'raw', 'streetwise' or 'politically volatile'; the mainstream media are prey to stereotypical portrayals of rappers, accusing them of nurturing (sub)urban violence, growing delinquency and the marginalization of minority communities. And audiovisual media refuse to report on certain groups, notably the most outspoken, Scientific 45, Lunatic and La Rumeur. As of writing this in September 2003, this five-man group from the western outskirts of Paris was facing a similar trial to that of NTM, set to start in January 2004. The Ministry of the Interior, headed by conservative Minister Nicolas Sarkozy, is prosecuting La Rumeur for inciting violence against the police.

Ironically, French rap gorges itself on France's 'literary' tradition of popular and protest songs (George Brassens, Léo Ferré, Serge Gainsbourg, Charles Aznavour – elders they see as worthy of respect). It enriches this popular culture by drawing on rhythmical and instrumental cultures from family roots (North African, West Indian, West African, Cape Verdean, Portuguese, etc.).

Rap has become vital for French youths who feel sidelined by mainstream expressions of culture. They consider it *one of the few forms of free expression they have access to in France.* A growing percentage of eighteen to thirty year olds are highly critical of political and media circles and claim that no one is representing their vision of the world they live in – outside of the rappers who are part of their urban environment.

There is a growing economic and mental divide between the rough *cité* and suburban classes and the middle and upper classes. In this chapter, I hope to dissect the discourse of the rappers in order to better understand the daily realities of these suburbs (through interviews, visits to the suburbs and an analysis of the song lyrics). How much self-censorship and censorship do they have to cope with in bringing their message to other youths and the media? How do they circumvent this (community radio stations, live concerts and direct sales of albums, the use of Creole or Arabic to talk about certain taboo subjects, humour ... )? How does their discourse compare to that of the American and other European rappers (interviews with American/European rappers, music companies, their media)?

I will also go to the 'other side' in order to understand the policies of the media (television and radio) and music companies in accepting or refusing certain songs. For years, Skyrock was the emblematic rap radio station, defying the authorities in broadcasting certain artists. But now they are also refusing to air certain songs. What dictates their choice? Why do they feel that the government media watchdog, CSA,[5] is putting an economic noose around their necks? How does the CSA perceive the Skyrock campaign against its policies?

## The state of rap in France

Rap music is France's fastest-growing musical phenomenon. Worldwide it is just behind the USA as a market. And sale figures continue to rise faster than in any other genre. The almost-national Skyrock radio station – which has officially adopted the slogan *'Premier sur le rap'* (First with rap) and is seen as youth's official mouthpiece – tops the radio audience charts in all the country's major cities, especially in the fifteen-to-twenty-six age group. An example of the music's enduring popularity came on 21 September 2002, when Paris's Stade de France stadium staged Europe's biggest-ever rap concert, called Urban Peace. Over forty thousand people paid an average of fifty dollars for the eight-hour bonanza involving some of France's leading rap artists.

However, despite this relatively healthy state of affairs some rappers have fallen victim to various forms of official and unofficial discrimination. Its roots can be traced back to a schism that developed around 1996. When the music media and major labels realized that rap was not going to go away, they decided to initiate what some have called a process of watering it down. This gave birth to a form of pop rap with more socially acceptable lyrics and a commercial tempo. Its success is seen in the emergence of artists accepted across the board, such as MC Solaar, Doc Gyneco, Yanick and Saian Supa Crew. Pop rap now cuts across France's class divide as the number-one youth music for white and black, rich or poor.

But a growing number of youths no longer identify with these artists. And it has given birth to a new generation of names and groups associated with hard-core, underground or street currents. They are 'bringing rap back into the ghetto', in the words of Olivier Cachin, editor-in-chief of the rap magazine *Radikal*. These groups go by the name of La Rumeur, Indo Gotti and Booba. The latter has set up an independent label, Scientific 45, some of whose albums have gone gold through word of mouth and its own independent advertising campaigns alone. They have one thing in common: a feeling of being censored, besieged and marginalized by mainstream media, music labels and concert producers.

Much of their resentment has focused on Skyrock 96.0 FM. The private radio station refuses to air albums by La Rumeur, Booba and many of those produced by the latter's label, Scientific 45. When challenged on a policy it does nothing to hide, Sky invokes the music's hard-hitting lyrics (see below for an example)

201

which, it claims, could have the station closed down by the CSA. We will return to their position later.

*Corporate censorship*

First, it is important to outline the different levels of censorship in France and how rappers believe they operate against them. While their ire is focused on Skyrock, critics admit that they are the *least* guilty among the national radio and television stations. Indeed, there appears to be a total blackout of street or hard-core French rap in other media outlets.

Second, Skyrock claims to have censorship problems of its own with the government's CSA. They accuse the public organization of 'constant discrimination' in the distribution of frequencies around the country. In the war to expand private networks, claims Sky, it is the three media multinationals, Bertelsmann, Lagardère and NRJ, which take the lion's share of the frequencies. 'It's an administrative execution by economic strangulation,' says the independent station in a full-page advert in *Le Monde*, part of an ongoing media publicity campaign denouncing their lack of success in securing new frequencies. As a result, Sky claims, almost half of France is unable to receive its programmes.

When approached in June, CSA's Jacqueline de Guillenchmidt hotly denied the accusations. De Guillenchmidt is one of the nine board members of the CSA, in charge of 'radio and pluralism'. She was emphatic that the CSA is there to 'ensure the full range of socio-cultural expressions' and the diversification of radio operators. She denied any favouritism in allocating frequencies.

Still, Sky advances figures which show that, between 1992 and 2000, its three chief competitors in Paris, RTL, NRJ and Europe 1, have seen the number of frequencies granted to them multiply by 500, 700 and 400 per cent respectively. Sky has seen its frequencies increase in that time by 20 per cent. Independent observers such as Olivier Cachin believe that the rap station is paying for the fact that it is too closely associated with a controversial musical style ... and that it is not part of any multinational conglomerate.

A third level of censorship is that exercised by concert producers and owners of concert halls. They say they fear that the rap public (the 'posses', mainly from the *cité* suburbs, that follow groups like Assassin, Arsenik, NTM, Booba, La Rumeur, etc.) will be involved in violent exchanges and concerts will degenerate. Big and (especially) small rap groups are finding it increasingly hard to book into venues. These artists and bands are consigned to rural venues, or distant suburbs. Many have simply been forced to disband.

Yet experience indicates the producers and concert hall owners' concerns over violence to be overblown. On 21 September 2002, for example, at the Stade de France's Urban Peace concert, no such tension was in evidence. Over forty thousand people congregated outside Paris for eight hours of music by France's best-known rappers. The thousands of riot police inside and outside the stadium reported no major incidents. Yet few mainstream media reported on the musical and commercial success of Europe's biggest-ever rap concert. After the concert rap artists insisted that this was further proof of institutionalized suspicion and fear of anything coming from the ghettos. Kool Shen, the brains behind France's most successful rap duo, NTM, denounced what he called a generalized phobia. He reminded reporters that hundreds of concerts by the now disbanded NTM had passed off without a hitch.

Kool Shen also warned of another form of censorship: that of producers of such major events as Urban Peace. It is they who have become the judges of what is best for the public, he says. And among the forty artists for this show-case event there was, yet again, no place for the hard-core presence of Booba, La Rumeur and other streetwise rap groups; a place, Kool Shen and others stress, they largely deserve, given their popularity. Some observers suspected it was the high-profile support of Skyrock which dictated the organizers' choice of participants.

In terms of the lyrical content of songs by the hard-core rappers, in a recent interview with me the director of musical programming at Sky, Fred Musay, provided the following reasons for not playing the songs of La Rumeur and Booba:

> We want to show the CSA that we're responsible. But these lyrics are too raw and explicit. Artistically, we love their albums. But we can't broadcast these words to our adolescent public.
>
> We anticipate the CSA suspending and possibly closing down our station if we broadcast these songs. And we need to have more frequencies, more advertisers to continue to live and maintain the freedom we so far enjoy.

I asked what would shock the public in these songs. He replied: 'The tone, the flow, the lack of nuance or humour, even if they denounce certain truths and have positions we share. I have great respect for Booba but he himself said he'd forbid his CD to anyone under eighteen. This exists for the cinema, so why not for CDs?'

While it seems that Skyrock and Booba have been reconciled since the end of 2002 (the rapper's new single is one of the most popular on the station's playlist), La Rumeur continue to be marginalized. 'Sky is not our *bête noire*,' insists the band's most articulate rapper, Hamé, a second-generation French singer of Algerian origin. 'But it's emblematic of the decline of French rap. All the ambitions and hope we had in the nineties have been betrayed by the media, the French music industry, the promoters, and so on.'

'Skyrock is just part of a political programme,' adds Ekoué, the angriest of the group's members, whose parents are Togolese. 'It's like the Socialist Party and SOS Racisme. They're just trying to whitewash our past, and mould us into the classic French model of a new integrated generation of French immigrants. Our songs have no chance of being played because they mirror the responsibility France had in destroying our parents' lives with their colonialist projects and the dirty war they engaged in when in Africa.'

La Rumeur is arguably best known for its withering attacks on the legacy of French colonialism. The group is inspired as much by Victor Hugo as Frantz Fanon, Public Enemy, Malcolm X and Patrice Lumumba. Led by two post-graduates from the University of Paris VIII, they stand out from the rest of the French hip-hop groups because of their finely crafted lyrics and outspoken militancy. It has come as little surprise to music specialists such as Claudy Siar that they have been ostracized by mainstream media. 'The taboos around the French war in Algeria and its brutality in its other former colonies are still deep-rooted,' says the presenter of *Couleur Tropicale*, the daily flagship music programme on Radio France International, RFI.[6] 'It's not exactly what they teach you in history lessons at school. La Rumeur challenges what it believes is a revisionist approach to the 1954–61 period there in Algeria, for example. And the hard-hitting nature of songs on their first album, *L'ombre sur la mesure*,[7] makes music programmers squirm in their seats. It's really putting France on trial for crimes against humanity during the colonial times.'

At the time of writing the band was embroiled in separate judicial battles with the Ministry of Interior and Skyrock over a magazine it published to accompany the release of its first CD, issued by EMI. Under pressure from the radio station, the label was forced to withdraw publication. Sky accuses the band of 'inciting hatred and violence' as a result of an article by Ekoué called 'Don't leave your homes without a bullet-proof vest'. The government is prosecuting the five-man band for inciting anti-police violence. 'This action must have been personally approved by [Interior Minister] Nicolas Sarkozy,' said Cachin in a telephone interview. 'I believe he started the ball rolling. The case has all his trademark language ... '

'They are trying to devitalize our rap to better reign over it,' Ekoué explained in a recent interview. 'They devitalize any form of subversion coming from the street, especially if the street has roots in the immigration to France. It's boiled down our rap scene completely, removed its soul. Killed it, in other words.'

La Rumeur's rappers admit to being obsessed with their parents' stories of war and poverty in West and North Africa, the West Indies and, as migrants, in France. They contrast these dark and troubling tales with soft, jazzy and techno layers of music and *film noir* extracts from black-and-white gangster movies from the fifties. We have transcribed one song into English to give an idea of the articulate venom of their lyrics. It reveals La Rumeur's anger, its dark humour, its paranoia, and the violence and division that so many of France's youth are prey to.

*'To Hear Them Talk'*

(From the album *L'ombre sur la mesure* by La Rumeur, 2002)

*Singer 1*

I've made an inventory of my adventure, I've concluded that here you're supposed to shut up and hide behind the blinds.

I've turned the question over in my mind, but questions still prowl around me.

In the land of nutters, it's been a life of clashes, 10,000 leagues below the sun, steaks and the homeland.

And yet, down here, too many barriers, too little solidarity; and too many of us are killing each other.

My conclusion is obvious and terrifying: young scared bandits, their eyes blind-folded, ready to cry.

To hear them all, you'd think we're all on the wrong side of the law, the wrong kind of specimen, 'persona non grata', only here to sponge from others.

Ungrateful, bitter, all failures, bunch of 'niggers' and rats, immigrants to be deni-grated and smashed under a stick.

A baptism of bruises that draws a picture of bitterness, inner wounds and chrysan-themums.

Two beings, one book, chapter two, 'special homicide', doctorates in literature indoctrinating by the gallon-full.

*Singer 2*

I'm swelling up with frustration, stress and unhealthy impulses at every pulsating moment and situation.

I'm the ideal fall-guy, the usual suspect, in my world repression is never virtual.

They asked me to forget about the fields of coke in Panama but my very soul is wounded and has been kidnapped by the ghetto.

Journalists consider me an apprentice terrorist or a reoffending delinquent. To hear all these bleating

You'd think my scars are permanent and I'd be better off joining them and the cops in praying to the devil.

Guys like me live off cyanide pills and get off on police scumbags guilty of commit-ting 'accidental' killings [*des bavures*].

Stirring up shit in a world where vultures dress in three-piece suits and dumb Barbie dolls can become pop stars.

I'm a nightmare that spreads like a rumour with texts that scare because they talk to the people.

*Singer 3*

Number one, and don't forget it, this is the Arabic telephone[8] and, big number two, I master every one of my syllables.

My perfection is born of a complex, I suppose their gossiping wore me down.

So I thank them even if their dirty French breath drives me away,

A breath nourished with the flesh of sows, one that is carried by the sweet rasping wind that blows from here into enemy territory.

Hear them, or ignore them, but see how they penetrate, their thoughts penetrate all the old fools,

Poor souls who know no torment, far from home, and who I consider no better than one of these dumb *gaolis* [pejorative term in Arabic for the French]

What you call exoticism, I call terrorism because this fucking verse that you drink up like sweet nectar,

Is the biggest piece of boring horseshit I've written, yes, I insist.

*Singer 4*

Either I shave the inside of walls or they kick me on to their charter planes, me and my ugly mug.

They say I don't cry colourless tears when it's all gore and I wave a flag with the cross and skulls.

The heavy artillery is in the car boot and they suspect us of foul play right down to the verses we write.

To hear them talk, our very chromosomes are soaked in hatred, if you don't want us to prove it you better not hang round our neighbourhood.

*Singer 5*

To hear them all, I should throw my pride to the lions, I should be on the stock exchange, beefing up my body frame.

Here where lies reign imperial, the bigwigs are busy on the dream machines.

The sheep go on producing wool, bleating in the courtyard, fattening themselves up before they're thrown into the oven.

Too deaf to notice the axe being sharpened on the grinder, the outcome is plain to see, it's the mass grave or the abattoir.

*Singer 6*

To hear them all, when the African leaves his bush, he is either full of vengeful bitterness, or he doesn't give a shit.

The 'bwanas' are so paranoid they even extract anthrax from this song.

The double sentence[9] sleeps on the corner of my street while a fake passport costs a bloody fortune.

I'm married to this sombre age, my eyes wide open, my wallet full of guarantees on all the war weapons I buy.

To hear them all, we have gravel rumbling round in our stomachs, we're from a dirty race of rats that are bred in a closed laboratory.

We're swarming, we're teeming and we're scavenging all the way into their mothers' guts.

Just give us a cow to milk and we'll bring it down with the plague, a kind of greasy, perverted and perfidious stain!

Our spermatozoa have opened up a path into the very heart of their countryside, into the recesses of their daughters' and partners' vaginas.

(Author's translation, printed with permission from La Rumeur)

## Notes

1  There has yet to be an accurate translation of this word, so commonly used in Latin-based idioms. English dictionaries offer only 'hybrid', 'mongrel' or 'mixed'. Yet *métisser* – from the seventeenth-century Portuguese word *metice* – has *tisser* in it, which means to interweave in French. It denotes the interplay of different elements of culture, language and populations, the intertwining of people and their identities. When will the English language renovate or invent a word to designate this essential twenty-first-century concept? See Daniel Brown, 'Musiques Métisses', *Songlines* magazine, January/February 2003, pp. 56–7.

2  Screw Your Mother.

3  '*Amer*' means 'bitter'. This is also a play on France's Ministry of 'Outremer', which governs affairs in the country's extra-territorial regions (the West Indies, French Guyana, Reunion, etc.).

4  '*Poulet*' is the pejorative term for police, the equivalent of 'pigs' in Great Britain; 'Brigitte, the copper's wife'.

5  The government-financed watchdog was created in 1989 to 'guarantee the exercise of freedom in audiovisual communication in France, according to the conditions defined by the law of September 30, 1986' (modified).

6  RFI is a government-financed public radio station, France's equivalent of the BBC World Service.

7  'Shadow on the tempo'.

8  'Arabic telephone' has the same connotation as Chinese Whispers in English; some Rumeur singers are of Arabic origin.

9  A court sentence unique to France, where a conviction against French citizens of foreign origin is followed up by their expulsion to the country of their parents.

# About the contributors

*John Baily* (UK) is professor of ethnomusicology at Goldsmiths College, University of London, with a special interest in Afghanistan, where he has worked extensively since the 1970s. While continuing work on the Afghan transnational community, he has also made a number of field trips in Pakistan, Iran and California. Author of *Can You Stop the Birds Singing? The Censorship of Music in Afghanistan* (Freemuse), he is also a musician, playing the Afghan *rubab*, and has released several records together with Afghan musicians in exile and his wife Veronica Doubleday, ethnomusicologist and singer. In 2002, Goldsmiths College established a unit for Afghan music, of which John Baily is the director.

*Alenka Barber-Kersovan* (Germany), PhD, studied piano, historical musicology, systematical musicology, psychology and aesthetics at the universities of Ljubljana, Vienna and Hamburg. Currently she is working as a lecturer at the University of Hamburg and as executive secretary of the Arbeitskreis Studium Populärer Musik. She has published some fifty articles on popular music and politics, media/multimedia, gender studies and popular music and pedagogy in German, English and American publications and has (co-)edited a number of books.

*Noam Ben-Zeev* (Israel) is a music critic and journalist at the *Haaretz Daily* newspaper and contributed presentations to both the 1st and 2nd World Conferences on Music and Censorship. He teaches music history and music education at the University of Haifa and at Alon School for the Arts and Sciences, Israel.

*Daniel Brown* (USA/France) is a staff journalist and producer with Radio France in the International English Features Department. He has been covering youth and world music for over a decade. The Paris-based journalist has been producing the weekly programme *World Tracks* for RFI since June 1979, winning three international world music awards. Brown is also correspondent for the British publication *Songlines*. He has been an active member of Freemuse since the 1st World Conference on Music and Censorship in 1998.

*Martin Cloonan* is chairperson of Freemuse and is Head of the Department of Adult and Continuing Education at the University of Glasgow. He is the author of *Banned! Censorship of Popular Music in Britain: 1967–92* (Arena, 1996) and co-editor (with Rebee Garofalo) of *Policing Pop* (Temple University Press, 2003) and has written numerous articles on music and censorship.

*Michael Drewett* (South Africa) is a lecturer in the Department of Sociology at Rhodes University, Grahamstown, South Africa. He is also coordinator of the Cutting Grooves Censorship of South African Music Archive, an NGO based in Grahamstown. In his role as coordinator he organized a successful exhibition of South African music at the National Arts Festival in South Africa in 1999. The exhibition has been transformed into a mobile exhibition for educational purposes. He has also been involved in re-releasing previously censored South African popular music and has co-produced the video *Stopping the Music*, the story of a musician and a security policeman in apartheid South Africa. He has recently completed a PhD on the censorship of popular music in South Africa in the 1980s.

*Rania Elias-Khoury* (Palestine) has been director of Yabous Productions and the Jerusalem Festival since 1998. She is a member of several Palestinian cultural and social organizations and a board member of the Bethlehem Peace Centre and Riwaq – the Centre for Architectural Conservation. She was the acting director of the Jerusalem International Festival and project coordinator of music summer camps organized by the National Conservatory of Music – Palestine.

*Paul Erasmus* (South Africa) is a former Security Branch policeman. He started his career with the South African Police in 1974 and served in the uniform branch and the Security Branch until he became medically unfit (post-traumatic stress disorder) and left the SAP in 1993. He participated in the truth and reconciliation process in South Africa. Since then he has worked as a social counsellor, initiated research and development of ten products for, *inter alia*, psoriasis and HIV/AIDS, and is currently CEO of Capstone 191. He is completing work on a book entitled *Q4: Footsoldier for Apartheid*.

*Banning Eyre* (USA) is one of the most respected American writers covering African music today. He is the author of, among other titles, *In Griot Time: An American Guitarist in Mali* and is currently working on a cultural biography of Thomas Mapfumo and the Blacks United. He is also a widely published journalist, commentator on National Public Radio, co-producer and editor for Afropop Worldwide, and a performing guitarist.

*Keith Howard* (UK) is reader in music, School of Oriental and African Studies,

University of London, and director of the AHRB Research Centre for Cross-Cultural Music and Dance Performance. He is author or editor of *Korean Musical Instruments: A Practical Guide* (Segwang, Seoul, 1988), *Bands, Songs, and Shamanistic Rituals: Folk Music in Korean Society* (Royal Asiatic Society, Seoul, 1989), *The Sounds of Korea* (Korean Overseas Information Service, Seoul, 1990), *True Stories of the Korean Comfort Women* (Cassell, London, 1995), *Korean Musical Instruments* (Oxford University Press, Hong Kong, 1995), *Korea: People, Country and Culture* (SOAS, London, 1996), *Korean Shamanism: Revivals, Survivals and Change* (Royal Asiatic Society, Seoul, 1998), *Korean Music: A Listening Guide* (National Center for Korean Traditional Performing Arts, Seoul, 1999). He is editor of eight further volumes, and author of over 100 articles on Korean music, Korean culture, shamanism and ethnomusicology.

*Ian Inglis* (UK) is a senior lecturer in sociology at the University of Northumbria, Newcastle upon Tyne. His books include *The Beatles, Popular Music and Society: A Thousand Voices* (Macmillan, London, 2000) and *Popular Music and Film* (Wallflower, London, 2003). His doctoral research considered the significance of sociological, social psychological and cultural theory in explanations of the career of the Beatles. He is a member of the editorial board of *Popular Music and Society*, and his articles have been published in numerous journals, including *Popular Music*, *Journal of Popular Culture*, *International Review of the Aesthetics and Sociology of Music*, *Visual Culture in Britain*, *American Music*, *Popular Music and Society* and *Journal of Popular Music Studies*. He is currently preparing *The Performance of Popular Music: Traditions and Transitions* (Ashgate, forthcoming).

*Marcel Khalife* (Lebanon/France) studied the oud at the National Academy of Music in Beirut. From 1970 to 1975 he taught at the National Conservatory of Music and other institutions and performed solo concerts throughout the Middle East, North Africa, Europe and North America. He has also written soundtracks for documentaries and films, and the Arabic musical library has been enriched by more than twenty of his productions. Since 1982 he has been working on a six-part anthology, *Studying the Oud*. Khalife has received many honours and awards throughout his long and highly acclaimed career. In 1999 he was put on trial, accused of blasphemy by a court in Lebanon. <www.marcelkhalife.com>.

*Marie Korpe* is the executive director of Freemuse. She is a trained journalist and has for many years reported on political, social, cultural and current affairs from Asia and Africa for the Swedish Broadcasting Corporation and other Scandinavian media. She has produced several exhibitions, among them *The Street Music of India* at the Swedish Music Museum, and others on India, Pakistan and Africa with Stockholm Culture House and Sida, Sweden. In 1993 she was coordinator of an international seminar, 'To See the Other', with Israeli and Palestinian film directors, authors and intellectuals. She has worked as senior programme officer at the Swedish International Development Cooperation Agency, Culture Department. In 1998 she organized the 1st World Conference on Music and Censorship and is co-editor of *'Smashed Hits'. The Book of Banned Music.*

*Roger Lucey* (South Africa) started writing songs and singing in Durban in the 1970s. He moved to Johannesburg in the late 1970s and made his first album, which was banned. His second album was restricted. During this time security police engaged in covert activity to silence him. He ended up working for an international TV news agency covering the war in South Africa and further afield in Africa and later in Bosnia and Chechnya. He has continued playing and writing and has just completed his latest CD.

*Andy Morgan* (UK) is a writer, journalist, label owner and music manager specializing in the music of France, North Africa, the Sahara and the Arabic world. As well as contributing articles regularly to *Songlines, fRoots*, the Rough Guides and many other publications, Andy helps to manage the Touareg group Tinariwen and organize the Festival in the Desert. His record label, Apartment 22, releases artists such as MoMo and U-cef, when time and cash permit. When he's not gallivanting in some far-off sandy place, Andy lives with his wife Kate in Bristol, England.

*Eric Nuzum* (USA) is the author of *Parental Advisory: Music Censorship in America.* He is widely considered one of the leading experts on the history of music censorship in the United States. He has been featured as a frequent commentator on music censorship for VH-1, the *Village Voice*, the *San Francisco Chronicle*, the *New York Times* and National Public Radio. He is also creator and editor of the largest Internet website on American music censorship: *A Brief History of Banned Music* (<www.ericnuzum.com/banned>). Outside his music censorship work he is a graduate of Kent State University, Ohio, and has been a public radio journalist for the past ten years.

*Jonas Otterbeck* (Sweden) has a PhD in Islamic studies from Lund University, Sweden; his thesis was written on twentieth-century Muslim discourses in Swedish. At present, he works as a lecturer at International Migration and Ethnic Relations (IMER), Malmö University, teaching identity, gender and religion. He is presently applying for research funding for a project on Islam, music and modernity.

*Ole Reitov* (Denmark) is a founding member of Freemuse and co-editor (with Ursula Owen, Marie Korpe) of *'Smashed Hits'. The Book of Banned Music* (Index on Censorship, 1998). He is a culture journalist who for the past thirty years has worked in more than forty countries for the Danish Broadcasting Corporation, and served as an adviser in cultural development projects in Mali and Bhutan. Currently he is a project adviser at the Danish Centre for Culture and Development (DCCD).

*Eric Silva Brenneman* (Brazil/USA) studied International Political Economy at the University of São Paulo, Brazil. He has a Bachelor of Arts in Spanish-Portuguese Studies and Global Studies (International Political Economy) from the University of Minnesota. He has worked as an intern for Minnesota Advocates for Human Rights and as a volunteer for the Madres de la Plaza de Mayo organization in Argentina. Besides being a member of the rock band De-Fi (<www.de-fi.net>), he has been actively involved in theatre productions.

*Kurash Sultan* was born in 1959 in Uighuristan (East Turkistan) in the northwestern province of Xingjian, China. He studied music at the music conservatory of Umruchi and has received several awards for his compositions. In the 1980s he worked for a cultural magazine and in his free time he started to record his own material, mainly freedom songs, on cassettes which he distributed in China. In 1993 his songs became forbidden in Uighuristan and he fled to Kyrgyzstan where he was imprisoned for nine months. As a UN refugee he was granted asylum in Sweden in 1999.

*Elijah Wald* (USA) is a writer and musician based in the United States, and author of several books on music and social issues. His most recent books are *Escaping the Delta* (Amistad/HarperCollins, 2004) and *Narcocorrido: A Journey into the Music of Drugs, Guns, and Guerrillas*, the first thorough exploration of the modern Mexican *corrido*, published in English and Spanish editions by Rayo/HarperCollins. For more infomation: <www.elijahwald.com>.

*Ameneh Youssefzadeh* (Iran/France) has studied musicology and ethnomusicology in France and obtained her PhD on the music of the Bakshishi musicians of Khorassan, Iran. She has also done extensive research on music in Iran since the Islamic revolution of 1979. She is a member of the French Society of Ethnomusicology as well as a member of the Iranian World Group at the French National Scientific Research Centre.

213

*Şanar Yurdatapan* (Turkey) was born in Susurluk, Turkey in 1941. He became famous as a composer and songwriter during the 1970s. In addition to his contribution to popular and traditional music, Şanar has written music for films and plays. He composed the music for the film *Arkadas*, which brought him the Golden Orange Award at the Antalya Film Festival. In 1979, he became general secretary of DEMAR (Democratic Artists Community).

Following the military coup of 1980, he left Turkey with his (ex-) wife Melike Demirag – singer and film actress – and went to Germany, where they had to live in exile for over eleven years. The Turkish military regime stripped them of their citizenship in 1983. They were able to return to Turkey in December 1991, after the elections. In 1992, their citizenship was restored. Yurdatapan is the spokesperson for Initiative for Freedom of Expression – a civil disobedience action group for which 1,080 intellectuals have published a book containing banned articles, forcing the courts to try them.

*Aung Zaw* (Burma/Thailand) is the editor of *The Irrawaddy*, a magazine published in Chiang Mai, Thailand. The *Irrawaddy* covers news and offers in-depth analysis of political and cultural affairs in Burma and Asia generally. The *Irrawaddy* is an independent magazine and receives grants from international donors. Aung Zaw is a former student activist and was arrested in the 1988 democracy uprising. He fled to Thailand shortly after the military took over in September 1988. He is a contributor for the *Nation* and *Bangkok Post* newspapers in Thailand. His articles have also appeared in the *Asia Wall Street Journal*. He has been covering Burma and Thailand affairs for more than ten years. He and his correspondents and the *Irrawaddy* office intend to return to Burma to set up an independent newspaper when the country enjoys press freedom.

# Recommended reading

Comprehensive version at <www.freemuse.org>.

Baily, John (2001) *'Can you stop the birds singing?' The censorship of music in Afghanistan,* Copenhagen: Freemuse.

Bremberger, Bernard (1990) *Musikzensur, Eine Annäherung an die grenzen des eralubten in der Musik,* Berlin: Verlag Schmengler.

Cartwright, Garth (2001) *'A Little Bit Special' – Censorship and the Gypsy Musicians of Romania,* Copenhagen: Freemuse.

Cloonan, Martin (1995) 'Popular Music and Censorship in Britain: An overview', *Popular Music and Society,* 19(3): 75–104.

— (1996) *Banned! Censorship of Popular Music in Britain: 1967–92,* Hampshire: Ashgate.

Cloonan, Martin, and Rebee Garofalo (eds) (2003) *Policing Pop,* Temple University Press.

Eyre, Banning (2001) *Playing with Fire: Fear and Self-Censorship in Zimbabwean Music,* Copenhagen: Freemuse.

Fischer, Paul D. (2003) *What If They Gave A Culture War and Nobody Came? Prospects for Free Musical Expression in the United States,* Copenhagen: Freemuse, <www.freemuse.org>.

Fornäs, Johan (2002) *Limits of Musical Expression,* Copenhagen: Freemuse, <www.freemuse.org>.

Hill, Trent (1992) 'The Enemy Within: Censorship of rock music in the 1950s', in Anthony DeCurtis (ed.), *Present Tense,* Duke University Press.

Kagie, Rudie (2000) *De Verboden Saxofoon. Over Muziek & Censuur,* Amsterdam: De Prom.

Korpe, Marie (ed.) (2001) *1st World Conference on Music and Censorship,* Copenhagen: Freemuse.

Matoub, Lounès (1995) *Rebelle,* France: Editions Stock.

Nuzum, Eric D. (2001) *Parental Advisory: Music Censorship in America,* New York: Perennial.

Owen, Ursula, Marie Korpe and Olep Reitov (eds) (1998) *'Smashed Hits'. The Book of Banned Music,* Index on Censorship, 6, London: Writers and Scholars International Ltd.

Pieper, Werner (ed.) (2001) *1000 Jahre Musik & Zensur in den diversen Deutchlands,* Löhrbach: Der Grüne Zweig 206.

— (ed.) (1999) *Verfemt – Verbannt – Verboten Musik und Zensur. Weltweit,* Löhrbach: Der Grüne Zweig 206.

Schade Poulsen, Marc (1999) *The Social Significance of Raî. Men and Popular Music in Algeria,* Austin: University of Texas Press.

Schwarz, Boris (1972) *Music and Musical Life in Soviet Russia 1917–1970,* London: Barrie & Jenkins.

Servant, Jean-Christophe (2003) *'Which Way Nigeria?' Music under Threat: A Question of Money, Morality, Self-censorship and the Sharia*, Copenhagen: Freemuse.

Winfield, Betty Houchin, and Sandra Davidson (eds) (1999) *Bleep! Censoring Rock and Rap Music*, Westport, CT: Greenwood Press.

# Index

Index

# Notes to CD

The accompanying CD presents some of the artists and cases described in the book. Read more about the artists at freemuse.org

**1   Unknown artist: Taliban chant (6:50)**

local production, about 1998.

Taliban *tarana* or chant (from audio cassette). Unaccompanied singing was the only kind of music permitted by the Taliban and this is an example of a new genre they themselves created. Rooted in Pashtun folk song, the text talks about Taliban readiness for sacrifice for their country, and eulogises several Taliban who have died for the cause. (See Chapter 4, Afghanistan.)

**2   Ale Möller Band, featuring Kurash Sultan: 'Atlan Dok' (5:37)**

written by Kurash Sultan
arranged by Ale Möller
from the album *Bodjal*
© 2004 Amigo Musik AB, copyright control

The Uighurs, an indigenous people in East Turkestan in north-western China, are struggling to keep their language and their culture. The Uighur composer, musician and poet Kurash Sultan has been imprisoned and tortured by the authorities. Many of his songs were banned. He now lives in exile in Sweden and performs with the renowned Ale Möller Band. He wrote 'Atlan Dok' (To Freedom) in his prison cell. (See Chapter 7, Uighuristan.)

**3   Roger Lucey: 'Lungile Tabalaza' (3:23)**

written by Roger Lucey
from the album *The Road Is Much Longer*
published by 3rd Ear Music
© 1979–1983 3rd Ear Music, South Africa / SAMRO–HYMAProject

Lungile Tabalaza was a young man from the township of Kwa Zakhele. He was arrested and within days was found dead in his cell. The song tried to tell the story but was banned for possession and distribution. According to the Directorate of Publications it was apparently 'dangerous to the safety of the State'. (See Chapters 8 and 9; South Africa.) Website: 3rdearmusic.com / rogerlucey.co.za

**4   Thomas Mapfumo & The Blacks Unlimited: 'Disaster' (5:45)**

written by Thomas Mapfumo
from the album *Chimurenga Explosion*
published by Chimurenga Music Co. Ltd
1999, Zimbabwe, © 2000 Anonymous Web Productions

From the album *Chimurenga Explosion* (2000), 'Mamvemve' and 'Disaster' were both named by Robert Mugabe as being banned. *Chimurenga Rebel* (2002) was banned as an entire CD, and *Toi Toi* (2003) was treated as if it didn't exist. (See Chapter 12, Zimbabwe.) Website: anonymousweb.com

**5  Marcel Khalife: 'Oh My Father, I Am Yusif' (6:56)**

written by Marcel Khalife
words by Mahmoud Darwish
from the album *Arabic Coffeepot*
published by Nagam Records, Inc.
© 1995 Marcel Khalife/Nagam Records, Inc.

This song, based on a poem by the Palestinian poet and writer Mahmoud Darwish, resulted in Marcel Khalife being accused of blasphemy. (See Chapter 15, Lebanon.) Website: marcelkhalife.com

**6  Amal Murkus: 'La Ahada Yalam' (3:52)**

written by Nizar Zreik
from the album *Amal*
© 1998 Amal Murkus

'La Ahada Yalam' (No One Knows) was written in 1989, shortly after the outbreak of the first Intifada in occupied Palestine. Amal Murkus, a Palestinian singer living in Israel, recorded the song amidst a feeling of helplessness towards the flood of names and TV pictures of the Intifada victims. Amal Murkus took part as a panellist at the 2nd World Conference on Music and Censorship in 2002, and is a member of the Freemuse Advisory Board. (See Chapter 16, Palestine.)

**7  Porno Para Ricardo: 'Tan Loco' (3:38)**

written by Gorki Águila
from the album *Porno Para Ricardo*
published by Discos Antidoto
© 2003 Gorki Águila (SGAE)

I've been so crazy all these years
I've told off so many wiseasses
that want to make out of me
a puppet like they want

I've lost so much weight smoking cigarettes
and I've gone to work reluctantly and bitterly
they disrespect you so much
that make you hate everything ... like this.

I wished I could believe in them
I'd like to but I can't

I am a bad son
– they all complain
they spent their money
teaching me what they wanted

They did get me to think
and now at least my mind is free

I wished I could believe in them
I'd like to but I can't

No more lies, old man

227

In August 2003 Porno Para Ricardo singer and guitarist Gorki Águila was sentenced to four years imprisonment. 'Tan Loco' (So Crazy) by Cuban rock band Porno Para Ricardo has been played on Cuban radio now and then – not so the associated video-clip on TV, where censorship is much more rigid. Once after a concert, a secret police officer asked Gorki to clarify what he meant with this song, and threatened him that he could get into trouble if he kept singing it. (See Chapter 19, Cuba. For more information on the trial against Gorki Águila, see freemuse.org.) Website: pornopararicardo.com

### 8  Andrés Contreras: 'Corrido de Osama Bin Laden' (5:00)

written by Andrés Contreras
from the album *Intifada*
© 2001 Andrés Contreras

Listen, gringo criminal, the devil has appeared to you
A man in a beard and turban has given you a terrible fright
Even your way of walking Osama has taken from you
And just to hear him talk gives you the shakes.

Andrés Contreras was the balladeer of the Zapatista uprising. A street singer, he travels Mexico, going wherever there is political strife, and has often been arrested and beaten by police. This 'corrido' is his tribute to the man who terrorized Mexico's tra-ditional oppressors (translation © 2002 Elijah Wald; full lyrics in English and Spanish are at elijahwald.com/corridowatch.html). (See Chapter 20, Mexico.)

### 9  Şanar Yurdatapan: 'Sela' (4:27)

written by Itri & Şanar
from the album *Kirmizi Yesil Sesler ve Sözler*
published by Cinar Muzik
© 2003 Şanar Yurdatapan

A religious theme: Saluting Mohammad. Composed by Mustafa Itri (17th century). The music is sung at the end of *Mevlid* ceremonies at mosques, with Arabic words. Hearing the appeals from minarets of burning Baghdad, Şanar Yurdatapan was so impressed that he made this song out of the historical melody. Şanar – composer, songwriter and spokesperson for Initiative for Freedom of Expression – has been imprisoned three times and endlessly harassed. (See Chapter 22, Turkey.)

### 10 Koma Asmin: 'Herne Pesh' (2:52)

arranged by Şanar Yurdatapan
not published

A historical song from 1946, from the days of the Mahabad Kurdish Republic (Northern Iran today) that only survived for 6 months. Koma Asmin, a Kurdish female orchestra, were arrested because they sang it together with the public at Diyarbakir Cultural Festival in 2002. (See Chapter 22, Turkey.)

FREEMUSE
THE WORLD FORUM ON
MUSIC & CENSORSHIP

This compilation © 2004 Freemuse